EAP NOW!

ENGLISH FOR ACADEMIC PURPOSES

2ND EDITION

STUDENTS' BOOK

KATHY COX

DAVID HILL

PEARSON
Longman

Pearson Australia
Unit 4, Level 3
14 Aquatic Drive
Frenchs Forest NSW 2086

www.pearson.com.au

Senior Acquisitions Editor: Andrew Brock
Senior Project Editor: Rebecca Pomponio
Production Controller: Barbara Honor
Copy Editor and Proofreader: Editing Solutions
Senior Copyright and Pictures Editor: Emma Gaulton
Copyright and Pictures Editor: Melissa Read
Indexer: Olive Grove Indexing
Cover and internal design by Peta Nugent
Cover image c/- Getty Images
Typeset by Midland Typesetters, Australia

Printed in Malaysia (CTP - VVP)

4 15 14 13 12 11
National Library of Australia Cataloguing-in-Publication entry

Author: Cox, Kathy, 1945–
Title: Eap now! : English for academic purposes : students' book / Kathy Cox and
                David Hill.
Edition: 2nd ed.
ISBN: 9781442528499 (student bk.)
Notes: Includes bibliographical references and index.
Subjects: English language – Study and teaching – Australia – Foreign speakers.
                English language – Problems, exercises, etc.
Other Authors/Contributors:
                Hill, David, 1969–
Dewey Number: 428.2407094

PEARSON
Longman

CONTENTS

CONTENTS MAP

PREFACE

EAP Now! English for Academic Purposes, 2nd edition has been created for you as a course book in English for Academic Purposes (EAP). It has been written to provide a single book which includes the skills that you will need in English language tertiary education (education after high school; post-secondary education). If you wish to attend college or university, or to study in an English-speaking country where you will need to have Upper Intermediate or Advanced level skills, or if you are a native speaker of English who would like to expand your repertoire of English language skills and prepare for university, this book will assist you to achieve your goals.

As experienced English language teachers ourselves, we have brought to the writing of *EAP Now!* 2nd edition our own understanding of the difficulties and cultural challenges that you will face as you undertake study in a language other than your first language. There are intellectual shifts which may be required of you as you learn new ways to present your ideas and arguments in writing and speaking contexts; you will learn to question texts rather than accept them as absolutely always correct; you will make decisions as to the importance of the World Wide Web for your study; you will increase your ability to become independent learners and you will strive for cross-cultural understanding and critical cultural consciousness as a result of your studies within this course.

Learning the academic skills necessary to succeed in a tertiary environment can be an arduous, difficult and complex process. You, the student, and your teacher will set out together on a journey that this course book provides. You will work together in order to attain these skills. They are the skills and thinking modes that you will need in all the various academic environments (universities and other institutions) into which you are heading.

We believe this course book breaks new ground for EAP and we sincerely hope you enjoy using it.

Kathy Cox
David Hill

AIMS AND FOCUS OF
EAP NOW! 2ND EDITION

EAP Now! English for Academic Purposes, 2nd edition is designed to help any student who wishes to succeed in a further or higher education course which is taught in English, in particular at university or college.

The aims of this Students' Book are to assist you to comprehend, question, evaluate and produce a range of discourses which are relevant to academic contexts. We want you to respect and admire your own academic culture and add to it your knowledge of the one you are learning. You bring to the classroom and your classmates a rich knowledge of your own.

We hope to have anticipated some of the problems you may face and to help you overcome them as you begin your preparation in English.

Each unit follows a similar pattern. The sections in each unit are:

1 Speaking 1
2 Reading & Critical Thinking
3 Language Spotlight 1
4 Writing
5 Listening & Note-taking
6 Language Spotlight 2
7 Speaking 2
8 Further Connections
9 Get Ready For …

Vocabulary practice can appear in any of these sections.

Speaking 1

This introduces the topic of the unit and usually introduces some vocabulary. It also should assist you to think about the topic and theme of the unit and practise, as well as acquire, new speaking skills.

Reading & Critical Thinking

The reading texts are designed to reflect the real world and are placed in real world social contexts. The tasks will help you with a wide range of reading strategies. You will be asked to apply a variety of critical thinking skills to the texts you read in this book.

Language Spotlight 1

Grammar is taught as part of whole texts, that is, within readings, discussions and lectures rather than separate from them. You will be asked to examine the social and cultural situations (or contexts) as well as the texts themselves. In Language Spotlight 1, you will look at grammar points as they are used in a reading from the previous section, and in Language Spotlight 2, later in the unit, you will focus on grammar from a listening.

Writing

In writing, a great deal of work is done around essay construction and the types of essays you will be required to produce. You will learn to see the difference between an explanation and an argument, and between an argument and a discussion. Answering exam questions is covered and there are tasks teaching you how to avoid plagiarism and how to reference your essays properly. Many models of varying text types are included.

Listening & Note-taking

You will listen to a lecture in each unit, and practise a variety of listening skills that are relevant to life at university, including note-taking. The vocabulary, format and content of the recording will give you a realistic experience of academic listening. Tasks will also cover critical thinking about the content of the lectures.

Language Spotlight 2

As mentioned in Language Spotlight 1, above, you will look at grammar in the context of the previous section's listening. You will learn new grammar that is relevant to other work for the unit.

Speaking 2

Speaking 2 assists you with the speaking tasks that you will encounter on campus. You will practise discussion and tutorial participation skills such as participating actively. Units and work in an appendix cover research, preparation and presentation of various oral tasks required at university – these are called oral presentation skills.

Further Connections

Extra activities in this section provide further practice of work from earlier in the unit, and/or discussion and writing practice connected with the unit theme. This section gives you an opportunity to apply some of what you have learned within the unit.

Get Ready For ...

An optional internet reading activity is provided to help prepare for the next unit. This section will encourage you in your individual research as well as provide vocabulary, definitions and critical thinking about issues in the coming unit.

Appendices: Projects

Two appendices cover projects which simulate real assignments of the kind you will have to do in your future tertiary education course. These will give you assistance at every step of preparing a researched essay and an oral presentation. After completing these, you will be well prepared for similar assignments at college or university.

Kathy Cox
David Hill

ABOUT THE AUTHORS

KATHY COX

traces her teaching back through her maternal ancestors. Originally from and educated in the USA, she graduated from the University of Hawaii and taught first in Pago Pago, Samoa, before travelling to New Zealand, Thailand, Malaysia and Singapore, finally settling in Australia. She has taught English for Academic Purposes to many students over the years, including within the University of Wollongong's foundation studies programmes. As Director of Studies at Australian Pacific College for a decade, she further increased her travel (China, Korea), her research and article writing. Her experiences and those of the many students she has taught form the basis for this book.

DAVID HILL

grew up in the north west of England. After studying at the University of Durham, his interest in other cultures took him around the world and eventually inspired him to become a teacher of English to speakers of other languages.

After teaching English to adults in the UK, Turkey and Japan, David settled in Australia where he worked as an EAP Coordinator, Senior Teacher and Director of Studies. He is currently a freelance curriculum writer.

David has also authored *Academic Connections 2* and (with Julia Williams), *Academic Connections 3*, both published by Pearson Longman USA.

ACKNOWLEDGMENTS

Kathy would like to thank all the people who assisted in the development and publication of this new edition. To the teachers who reviewed and suggested changes which we duly implemented; to Jana Hubata for allowing us to record her lecture at ACNT, Sydney; to our senior acquisitions editor, Andrew Brock for his continuing support; our editors Rebecca Pomponio and Jane Tyrrell, for clarifying instructions to students and making the process easy; the layout team who has made the new design interesting, fresh and reflective of the values of the book. Kathy would also like to acknowledge the numerous and memorable students and colleagues from whom she has learned so much over a life time of TESOL education. Thank you to the students whose educational and social experiences formed the basis for my interest in creating this book.

• • •

David would also like to express his appreciation to the students, friends and colleagues with whom he has had the pleasure of working over the years. Thanks are also extended to those who have provided feedback about their use of the first edition; all comments were greatly appreciated and have been taken into account during the development of the second edition. The Pearson team of Andrew Brock and Rebecca Pomponio, as well as the copy editor and proofreader, Jane Tyrrell, and the designer, Peta Nugent, have, as always, worked their magic to coordinate the process and to turn our word processed manuscripts into the book you have in front of you. On the personal front, David extends his special thanks to Chie, whose help, encouragement and support have been immensely valuable throughout this project.

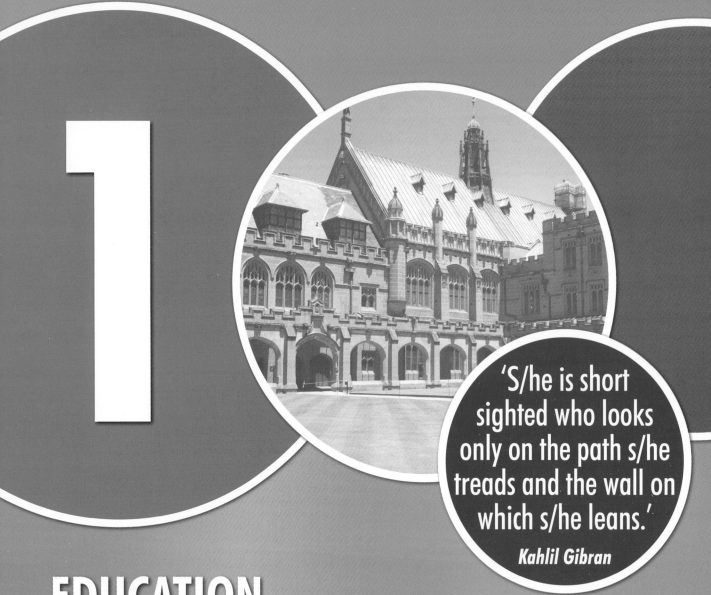

'S/he is short
sighted who looks
only on the path s/he
treads and the wall on
which s/he leans.'

Kahlil Gibran

EDUCATION AND LEARNING

In this unit, you will examine aspects of education and learning and become familiar with some of the situations that exist in tertiary institutions within a Western tradition. Begin by examining your own learning methods, likes and dislikes, increasing your learning strategies and creating a timetable for study. You will look at different ways to create an essay outline, read part of a real student's essay, and find out about register. You will listen to an authentic introduction in a lecture and learn how to recognise key phrases and signals that will help you take notes. Importantly as well, you will begin paragraph writing which will continue in each unit in this book. You also learn about referencing, writing a bibliography and avoiding plagiarism.

BY THE END OF THIS UNIT, YOU SHOULD:

SKILL	TASK	PAGE
know more about life on campus in a Western tertiary setting	Entire unit	4–27
know more about how you learn and increase personal strategies for language learning	**Speaking 1** *Tasks A, B* **Reading & Critical Thinking** Reading 3 *Task A*	4 8–9
be able to locate key words and scan texts for relevant information; find meaning in context	**Reading & Critical Thinking** Reading 1 *Task A* Reading 2 *Task A*	 6–7 8
recognise and write a topic sentence for an academic paragraph	**Reading & Critical Thinking** Reading 3 *Tasks A, B, C*	 8–9
recognise and use discourse markers of time	**Reading & Critical Thinking** Reading 4 *Task B*	 12
write an explanation paragraph	**Language Spotlight 1** *Task A*	13–14
create an essay outline	**Writing** Writing 1 *Tasks A, B*	 16–17
examine schema within explanations	**Writing** Writing 1 *Task C*	 18
understand staging within introductory paragraphs so as to address an essay question	**Writing** Writing 2 *Tasks A, B*	 19
know what register means and apply that meaning to both speaking and writing	**Writing** Writing 2 *Task C*	 20–21
listen for signals and key phrases within an introduction to a tertiary lecture and note-take	**Listening & Note-taking** Listening 1 *Tasks A, B* Listening 2 *Tasks A, B, C*	 21–22 22–23
note-take from whole books and take a global approach to books	**Listening & Note-taking** Note-taking *Tasks A, B*	 23–24
begin to know how to reference and write a bibliography	**Language Spotlight 2** *Tasks A, B, C, D*	 24–26
manage your time for study and learning	**Further Connections** *Task A*	 27

Tasks A and B | Discussion and survey

① Ask your partner the following questions:

[a] Are you studying so you can attend a university where the subjects will be taught in English?

[b] Will this be the first time you have attended a university?

[c] What will you study? What is your field?

[d] What do you want to do in the future?

[e] What do you think are the main skills you will need once you get on a campus?

② With your partner, ask and answer the following questions:

[a] Do you write down new words you are learning in a special notebook?

[b] If you write new words/vocabulary down, do you have a system to organise your book? (eg alphabetically, by grammar, by situation)

[c] Do you read newspapers in the language you are learning? ie English.

[d] Do you read magazines in the language you are learning? ie English.

[e] Do you read books in the language you are learning? ie English.

[f] Do you own an English-to-English dictionary?

[g] Do you look up new words when you come across them and note their definitions in a special notebook?

[h] Do you listen to songs in the language you are learning? ie English.

[i] Do you watch movies in the language you are learning? ie English.

[j] Do you listen for whole phrases that help you understand a conversation?

[k] Do you listen for individual words in a conversation?

[l] Do you try to speak English, even though you might make mistakes?

[m] Are you shy when you speak English, since it is not your first language?

Task C | How you like to learn a language

Take the following survey by circling the letter that is your answer and that is closest to your feeling.

① *In my English class:*

A. I would rather write down most things that I hear.

B. I would rather practise with a partner out loud.

C. I would rather sit quietly until I know the answer.

D. I would rather get the chance to speak than to be quiet.

② *When working in pairs in class:*

A. I like to write what is going on.

B. I like to be the leader.

C. I like to be quiet and let the other person speak.

D. I like to speak.

③ *When speaking in class:*

A. I always want to be corrected.

B. I like the teacher to allow me to finish without corrections in the middle.

C. I feel embarrassed and know I am making mistakes.

D. I want mistakes corrected immediately.

④ *When in class:*

A. I wish I were outside walking or swimming or enjoying myself.

B. I enjoy working and learning English.

C. I don't enjoy it, but I know I must study hard.

D. I like my classmates and know my English will improve if I complete my work.

⑤ *When it comes to grammar:*

A. I like to memorise the rules by heart.

B. I seem to use grammar correctly most of the time without memorising.

C. I like to keep practising until the rule is not in my mind.

D. I don't need rules, because I can hear changes in speech and see them in writing.

⑥ *When it comes to vocabulary:*

A. I like to memorise all vocabulary.

B. I like to try to use new words as soon as I have heard them.

C. I like to write down new words before I use them.

D. I like to practise new words outside of class.

7 *Outside of class:*

    A. I hate making mistakes when talking.
    B. I like to try to talk to people as much as I can.
    C. I always worry and feel embarrassed to speak because I will make mistakes.
    D. I don't care too much about mistakes, I just enjoy talking with someone.

8 *When I'm listening:*

    A. I can't hear well because I'm nearly always nervous.
    B. I don't hear every word, but can usually follow the gist of what's being said.
    C. I want to hear every word so I know I understand the conversation.
    D. I try to follow even when I don't know all the words.

How to calculate your score

As = 2
Bs = 1
Cs = 2
Ds = 1

Add your answers together.

SCORE: _____

Check your score to determine the 'type' of learner you are.
If your score is between 8 and 10 inclusive, look at box X.
If your score is between 11 and 13, look at box Y.
If your score is between 14 and 16, look at box Z.

BOX X

Like many people, you have a combination of learning styles and ways in which you like to learn. You are relaxed and confident in some situations, but like to be accurate and speak correctly in others.

Your task will be to work on study patterns that make the most of both these qualities.

BOX Y

Your learning style is communicative. You like to make friends easily and want to talk to everyone.

Your style is relaxed and you are fairly comfortable in new situations. You will try to talk, even if you make mistakes.

You may need to work harder towards accuracy in your writing when it comes to academic English.

BOX Z

Your learning style is accuracy driven. You like to be sure you are right before speaking and writing. You may be a little shy when it comes to communicating, particularly in unfamiliar situations.

You are probably an analytical person and are neat and tidy with your notes and personal dictionary.

If you take more risks, your English may improve more quickly. Try to communicate in English even when you aren't completely sure whether your grammar and vocabulary are correct.

Discussion

1 Form groups of different learning styles and discuss what you think are the strengths and weaknesses of each learning type.

2 Make a list for yourself of suggestions that you think you might try after discussion with that person. Can you think of ways to add to your learning style? How could you experiment with a new idea after speaking to someone different from yourself?

READING & CRITICAL THINKING ....

The box below explains how to scan for information.

Scanning
Scanning is a reading method where you look over a text and search for certain and specific information. You do not try to read every word. You look (scan) for the words you need.

READING 1

Task A | Scanning and locating key words; comprehension

❶ Scan the reading text (*Science 101*) which follows the questions below and locate the key words. The **key words** you are scanning for are in **bold**.

❷ Write the paragraph *number* from the text above the key words you find.

❸ Next, answer the questions in the spaces provided.

Questions:

A. How do you find out what **subjects** you will be taking?

_____

_____

B. Where do you find your **timetable**?

_____

_____

C. Will the timetable change after the first few weeks of your university course? When?

_____

_____

D. What is a **lecturer**?

_____

_____

E. What is a **tutor**?

_____

_____

F. What is **a tutorial**?

_____

_____

G. With whom do you speak if you have a problem with understanding assignments or difficulty in writing an essay?

_____

_____

H. **Learning portal** refers to what?

_____

_____

I. A **learning development centre** may be found in what part of a campus?

_____

_____

J. An **academic advisor** will assist you with how to write an essay, how to avoid plagiarism, and what other types of things?

_____

_____

K. What is a **module** within a course?

_____

_____

L. Define **prerequisite**.

_____

_____

M. What components make up the **assessment** for the module.

_____

_____

N. What percentage of lectures must **overseas students** attend in order not to be in breach of their visa requirements?

_____

_____

O. What will the **internet-based support website** provide for you?

_____

_____

P. How many hours is the **module duration**?

_____

_____

Q. What **percentage** of the total grade do the 5 class quizzes comprise?

_____

_____

SCIENCE 101

Module code:	SCI 548
Prerequisite:	None (This module does not require you to have studied a previous subject in order to qualify, so there are no prerequisites.)
Module duration:	60 hours
Year:	2010

1. Lecturer: Dr Ian Rujah

2. Session code: 6778

3. **Timetables** are accessed via the **learning portal** at <www. MCLadmin/Science1>. Use your student ID card as the code to enter the portal and download your **timetable** and **subjects**. Your **lecturer's** name will be there and your **tutorial** times. **Timetables** may be adjusted in the third week of the course. The **tutor** is Madeline Everts. She can be contacted via email.

4. **Assessment**
    The following components make up the assessment for this module.

Assessment	Percentage	Required pass
5 Class quizzes	30%	N/A
2 Exams – theory	70%	50%
1 Exam – practical	Competent/Not yet competent	50%
Total	**100%**	**100%**

5. **Students**
    If you need extra assistance with essay writing, you can attend the learning development centre located on the main campus within the library. An **academic advisor** will assist with any course problems. How to avoid plagiarism and how to reference an essay correctly, exam techniques, reading and paraphrasing, as well as improving essay writing, are available.

6. **Attendance**
    Overseas students are required to attend 80% of lectures otherwise they are in breach of their visa requirements. This can lead to termination of their student visa.

7. **Textbooks**
    This **module** requires compulsory textbooks to complete the assessments and course material. Current textbook lists are available from either Bayshore Bookstore on campus or from the **internet/based support website** <http://booklearn.appt.edu.au>.

The box below tells you how to find meaning in context.

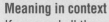

> **Meaning in context**
> If you read all the words around a word you do not understand or know the meaning for, there should be clues that assist you to work out that meaning. Sometimes, a previous sentence or the next sentence will provide clues to an unknown word. Words are also often repeated within a text or substituted by another word. You may understand the other word and then understand the meaning of the word unknown to you. This process of 'guessing' and using the contextual clues from a text is referred to as 'gleaning meaning from context'.

READING 2

Task A | Gleaning the meaning

Read the short text titled *Students protest in Germany – 2009* and fill in the blanks using the words provided.

kingdoms	20th century	change
course	standardisation	protested
ultimately	equivalency	

Students protest in Germany – 2009

Over a thousand students lined the streets in major cities of Germany in December of 2009. They were protesting the lack of recognition of courses between differing universities. The protests were aimed at bringing attention to this lack of [1].......................... between universities within their own country. The education ministers told them that their ultimate aim was to increase standardisation not just within the country of Germany, but throughout Europe as a whole. The aim is [2]........................... for universal accreditation. Students saw this as too distant a prospect and preferred to state their needs concerning [3]................ within the current system. Change needed to be brought about through recognising courses from one university to another. Basically, there is no [4]............................ so it means that if you study Engineering in one city of Germany it may not count in another. It is difficult to accept this lack of equivalency between campuses, student leaders told the press. It means one cannot change from one university to another and have the same [5]...........................

Historically, Germany was divided into separate [6]........................... Since each place was ruled by a separate king during and prior to the 19th century, divisions are traditional. Germany was not united until the [7]...........................

READING 3

There are two reading tasks.

Task A | Skimming a text and finding topic sentences

❶ Skim the text on the next page. This means you do not read every word.

❷ Note each topic sentence at the beginning of the four paragraphs. Topic sentences are bolded for you. You have *two minutes* for this task.

Socrates

Personal learning styles and learning strategies

1 **The 5th century Greek philosopher, reformer and teacher, Socrates, used a method of questioning students as a method of teaching.** Socrates believed that 'no one is wiser than you' (Apololgy 21A). The main idea was that learners should be active participants in their learning and not trust that knowledge is learned by being a passive recipient.

2 **This ties into current theories of language learning and studies of language.** These theories maintain that users construct reality through the use of the language. Language learning is characterised by certain strategies and research has analysed the strategies of good language learners over the years.

3 **Good language learners are known to carry out a number of tasks.** They are supposed to be willing to make guesses, take risks, have a strong desire to communicate, listen to themselves speaking and monitor it, transfer one thing they have learned to new situations, and work cooperatively with teachers and other students in order to develop their language learning.

4 **One researcher, Howard Gardner (1983), suggests that individuals have at least seven different intelligences.**

Task B | Identifying theme from topic sentences

What are the five main themes that the topic sentences tell you about?

(i) _____

(ii) _____

(iii) _____

(iv) _____

(v) _____

Task C | Comprehending what you read

❶ Answer the following questions concerning the text *Personal learning styles and learning strategies.* True or False.

[a] Socrates believed that learners should be active participants in their own learning.

_____

[b] Good language learners do one special thing.

_____

[c] There are more intelligences than one.

_____

[d] One thing that a good language learner does is to make guesses.

_____

❷ Now list all the tasks that good language learners are known to carry out:

[a] _____

[b] _____

[c] _____

[d] _____

[e] _____

[f] _____

READING 4

Every country has some kind of education system. For some, kindergarten begins at 6 years old, and for others 4 or 5 years old. Next, students move on to primary or elementary school. Following that, high school/secondary school/college commences and, finally, tertiary/university studies are completed.

Task A | Reading a lengthy text – Comparisons to known systems

Read the following text about *Western education systems.* It is a lengthy but thorough overview of what the systems are like. While reading, think of comparisons to your own country's education system. What is similar? What is different?

Western education systems

1. Mainstream education systems in most English-speaking countries are broadly similar to each other. Education in general refers to a result and is produced by instruction, training or study. It is also the process involved to obtain this result. This essay will explain some of the common features of typical systems in the United Kingdom, Australia and the United States and give a brief overview of the organisation of education in these countries. However, it should be borne in mind that variations on these systems are not just possible but common, due to the fact that in these countries, the responsibility for organising many aspects of education is at the state (USA and Australia) or county (UK) level. Other English-speaking countries, such as New Zealand, Canada and the Republic of Ireland, have similar systems, but discussion of those is beyond the scope of this essay.

2. Before looking at the organisation of these education systems, it is important to take an overview of what they value and what their overall aims are. These values and aims have changed considerably over the last five decades or so under the influence of the results of educational research and thinking as well as through political influence. As a result, the previous emphasis on memorisation of facts and theoretical knowledge has shifted towards analysis and interpretation. For example, a history essay may include dates and events, but a student would gain higher marks for showing why the events happened, or why they were important.

3. Creativity has also been emphasised, especially in subjects such as English, where for many years such things as grammar and spelling were removed from the school curriculum, and students were expected to write their own stories and other texts, without instruction about how to do it. The result was judged on the impression it made. However, a return is now being made to more traditional areas of learning such as grammar. Learning by doing is also encouraged – in science lessons, instead of being told what happens when one chemical is combined with another, students would first mix the chemicals and observe what happened, then compare the results with what was expected. In most subjects, knowledge is seen as a means to an end, that is, something that can be used in some way, and is usually not learnt for its own sake. In languages, for example, grammar is taught as a way to make communication clear, and communicative ability is tested more often than grammatical knowledge, but a student who can't use grammar well will not achieve high scores on a communicative test. To reflect these aims, exams usually focus on the application of knowledge rather than just repeating it. Therefore, for example, essays that give facts as reasons for an opinion are valued more than essays that simply describe.

4. Methods of instruction fit in with the aims of education. Active learning, that is, learning by doing, is often encouraged over passive learning strategies, such as memorisation (Commonwealth of Australia, 2002). If the teacher simply gives facts which the students then learn, this is seen as a bad teaching strategy and is referred to in a disparaging way as 'spoon-feeding', as when a mother gives food directly to a baby. Instead, good teaching is seen as setting up situations in which students find things out for themselves, preferably in a varied, interesting and motivating way which caters for the wide range of different personalities and learning styles that exist in any class.

5. Exams remain an important part of curricula in Australia, the UK and the USA, although the trend is very much towards forms of continuous assessment, such as essays and other assignments contributing to the overall score for the course, or practical sessions (especially in the sciences) or larger projects that involve research or writing a report based on the students' own reading of the subject. The amount of continuous assessment generally increases at the higher levels – it is rare to find an undergraduate university course which is assessed only by exams and, at the master's level, most courses have no exams.

6. The main source of funds for most schools in each of these countries is the government. The proportion of private schools varies. Education normally culminates in major public exams, whether at private or public schools. Therefore, both public and private schools generally teach, especially in later years, to the same curriculum.

7. As for the way in which education is organised, it usually begins with a period of non-compulsory pre-school or kindergarten education. For example, in Australia, parents are encouraged to send their children to pre-school for two years before compulsory education (DETYA, 2000). Compulsory education begins at different times in different countries: usually just before the 5th birthday in the UK (BBC, 2001), and at age 6 in North America (Fulbright Commission, 2001) and most parts of Australia (DETYA, 2000).

8. Primary or elementary school lasts for around six years, and focuses on basic literacy and numeracy skills, creative skills such as art, as well as socialisation and with a varying element of sport and physical education. Children spend most of their time in the same class with the same teacher, although occasionally subject specialists are brought in, or students are timetabled to spend a lesson or so each week with a teacher who has a strength in a particular area such as science or art. A large part of lessons is spent with children working together in groups and, as a consequence, lessons can be quite noisy. Children sitting in regimented lines of desks, working individually on textbook exercises in silence is regarded as a thing of the past in these countries. Schools are commonly decorated with paintings and posters produced by the children themselves, and considerable efforts are made to ensure that the study environment is bright, cheerful and friendly. In the USA, elementary school is often referred to as grade school: each year is called a 'grade', follows a set syllabus, and students have to pass an exam to move to the next grade the following year.

9. After primary or elementary school, the next phase of students' education (usually at age 11 or 12, depending on the country) is rather different in character. Instead of having the same teacher most of the day, pupils move from classroom to classroom to study different subjects, each taught by a different, subject-specialist teacher. The actual organisation of this period varies between countries and sometimes from area to area (eg, the UK), with sometimes all students from the beginning of this period to 18 years old being at the same school, usually known as a high school (or sometimes secondary school or grammar school in the UK), or this period being divided between two schools, middle school and high school (some parts of the UK), or junior high and high school (most of the USA). Work gets more advanced as the student gets older, culminating in major public exams at age 16 and/or 18. However, it is often just before this point that compulsory schooling comes to an end: students are allowed to stop attending school after their 15th or 16th birthday in each of these countries (BBC, 2001; DETYA, 2000; Fulbright Commission, 2001), though in practice this isn't common. By this time, students have specialised to some extent, in that they choose many of their subjects. In the UK, this is quite extreme – after 16, students are, until quite recently, expected to choose only three subjects, which could be as narrow as 'double maths' and physics, and very soon the content they are studying is at a similar level to the first year

at university in the USA (Fulbright Commission, 2001), where the education system favours breadth of knowledge with, for example, university science students being required to study subjects from the arts or language departments.

10. Most countries have a wide range of options at the next ('tertiary') stage of education, but basically this boils down to two main alternatives. For the more academically inclined, there are universities and junior colleges (USA), while for those wishing for a more practical course, or a trade qualification, colleges of further education (UK) or technical and further education colleges (Australia). After the first (or 'bachelor') degree, it is possible to progress to master's degrees, then to PhD programs, by which time the focus is almost entirely on the student's own original research (except in some North American cases). The first degree is known as 'undergraduate' study, and any course that requires a first degree as condition of entry is a 'postgraduate' degree.

11. Thus, Western education systems have many common features, especially in terms of their aims and methodology, but under the surface there are a significant number of differences, which anyone visiting any of these countries for educational reasons would do well to become informed about.

References

BBC (2001) *Secondary Schools*. BBC News, <http://news.bbc.co.uk/hi/english/education/uk_systems/newsid_115000/115872.stm> (6 May 2002).

Commonwealth of Australia (2002) 'Australian way of studying'. *Study in Australia*, <http://studyinaustralia.gov.au/Contents/WhatToStudy/AustStudy.html>(21 April 2002).

DETYA (2000) *Australia Country Education Profile*, 3rd edition Online. Canberra: DETYA, < http://www.detya.gov.au/noosr/cep/australia/index.htm> (21 April 2002).

Fulbright Commission (2001) 'School Education in the USA', <http://www.fulbright/co.uk/eas/school/school/htm> (12 May 2002).

Structure/Schema

The *structure* of the explanation essay you just completed reading is as follows:

- There is an introductory statement which lets the reader know something general about the subject.
- There is a sequenced explanation. Sequencing can be temporal (time markers are used = time sequence) or participatory (the same participant is used as the theme and constitutes evidence).

Task B | Outlining structure

❶ Underline the introductory general statement

❷ Underline the definition found in the introduction.

❸ Underline the sentence that reveals the purpose of the writer's explanation.

❹ Highlight or underline markers of time, ie temporal sequencers. These are words like **next**, **after that**, **finally**, **before**, **after**.

LANGUAGE SPOTLIGHT 1

Explanation paragraphs

Explanations are a form of writing and speaking that explain something.
Statements are written in sequential order to explain how something works or why something happens.

Grammatical characteristics of an explanation (language features) are:

• Processes (similar to verbs)	Use mostly verbs of being
• Tense	Use present tense and passive voice (is made, is accessed)
• Cohesive words (linking words)	Use sequencing words like after, before, next
• Purpose	Is to explain using factual and detailed information
• Participants (the actors or subjects (nouns) that are commonly found in an explanation text).	Are generalised in explanations. First and second person (I, you) are rarely used.

Schema (layout, structure) of an explanation:

- Topic stated clearly in lead-in sentence
- A number of sequential paragraphs.

The reading *Science 101* on page 7 contains explanation paragraphs and serves as an explanation to students about the Science module within a course of study.

Here is the same paragraph with its structural and grammatical requirements in **bold.**

Model paragraph – Explanation

The human heart

The human heart is a strong, muscular pump a little larger than a fist. It pumps blood continuously around the body. It pumps blood through the circulatory system. Each day the average heart 'beats' (expands and contracts) 100 000 times and pumps about 2000 gallons of blood. In a 70-year lifetime, an average human heart beats more than 2.5 billion times.

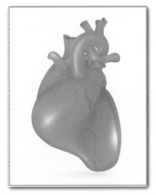

The human heart (ie How does the human heart work?)

First sentence: Use a definition or description	The human heart is a strong, muscular pump a little larger than a fist.
Second sentence: What it does	It pumps blood continuously around the body.
Third, fourth, fifth sentences: How the parts work in conjunction with something else	It pumps blood through the circulatory system. Each day the average heart beats (expands and contracts) 100 000 times and pumps about 2000 gallons of blood. In a 70-year lifetime, an average human heart beats more than 2.5 billion times.

Task A | Writing an explanation paragraph

Read topics 1–4 for explanatory (explanation) paragraphs. Beneath each topic are some words to help you develop an explanation paragraph. Choose words to create sentences within the paragraph. You need to create each topic sentence and then write an explanation paragraph.

Explanation
Remember: How something works or why something happens is an explanation.

❶ Data transfer (eg from a camera, ipod, thumb drive) to a computer.

_____

_____

_____

_____

Definition or description:	Portable media devices, for example an iPod, SD card or camera work by...
Information	_____
Songs, data or photographs	_____
Transfer	_____
Uploading	_____
Downloading from a website	_____
Device	_____

❷ Why it appears that the sun rises each day

Every 24 hours the earth spins on its axis	_____
revolution	_____
different part of the earth	_____
from west to east	_____
day time in the USA	_____
night time in Africa	_____
day time in Europe	_____
night time in Australia	_____

❸ How a tadpole becomes a frog.

_____

_____

_____

_____

_____

_____

_____

_____

_____

A tadpole is

It emerges from an egg laid by a frog. After five weeks, a tadpole begins to change.

Grows

Legs and forelegs

Tail becomes smaller

Then lungs begin to develop

Next, legs

After 11 weeks, a fully developed

The tadpole has become

❹ How does yeast raise bread and pastry?

Rearrange the sentences below in the correct order to create an explanation.

That's how yeast raises bread and pastry.

The process of leavening bread is an organic process. Starch cells in flour get eaten by yeast.

Sugars are metabolised to produce alcohol and carbon dioxide. Carbon dioxide is a gas and forms the bubbles in the particular pastry.

Yeast is a raising agent. It's a living bacteria.

The gluten structure in the flour traps the carbon dioxide and as the yeast keeps feeding the bread keeps rising.

_____

_____

_____

_____

_____

_____

_____

_____

_____

_____

Task B | Explanations and discourse markers of time sequence

> ✳ **What is an explanation? What is an explanation essay?**
> All language is situational. It has a social function. Explanations in writing are usually found in science or social science. They often use the simple present tense and explain things or processes in an order or sequence.

The next reading text is an explanation of a tutorial at a Western tertiary institution. The *explanation* applies to undergraduate students.

The structure for the *explanation* essay *What is a tutorial?* is as follows:

❶ *An introductory statement.* This lets the reader know something general about the subject.

❷ *A description or definition of terms.*

❸ *A sequenced explanation.* Sequencing can be temporal (time markers are used = time sequence) or participatory (the same participant is used as the theme). The steps are linear a   b   c   d, and/or vertical.

A
↓
B
↓
C
↓
D

Task C | Reading and reviewing staging/structure/schema

Read the text below and note the staging.

> # What is a tutorial?
>
> 1. Tutorials occur in all Western university systems. The term *tutorial* derives from *tutor* which means 'instructor'. A tutorial comprises an instructor and a group of students. It used to mean a small group of students, but today there may be as many as 60 or 70 in a group or as few as 8 or 10. So, what is a tutorial and what does it have to do with you, the student?
>
> 2. First, students attend lectures within their chosen fields of study. These lectures take place in large halls with seating for up to 300 or even 1000 students. Students must listen carefully and take notes while the lecturer is speaking. Students do not usually interrupt the lecturer in order to clarify something they do not understand or did not hear.
>
> 3. After the lecture students should review their notes and prepare for their tutorial. The tutorial will be held in the same week as the lecture, but with fewer students. The tutor or instructor is usually not the same person who gave the lecture in the hall.
>
> 4. While students attend their tutorials, the tutor will point out important, relevant issues or points that were made at the lecture. They may also ask for students' input in the form of a discussion or prepared paper.
>
> 5. During the tutorial, a student is allowed to ask questions, to speak and indeed, at times, they are required to speak whether they are prepared or unprepared.
>
> 6. Following the tutorial, students will have time to prepare assignments that may have to be submitted to their lecturer and/or their tutor. You will learn more about this later in this book.

Task D | Outline the stages in the introduction

❶ Underline the *introductory* general statement.

❷ Double underline the *definition* found in the introduction.

❸ Triple underline the sentence which reveals the *purpose* of the writer's explanation.

Task E | Time discourse markers

❶ Name as many time markers as you can think of, such as *secondly* or *next*.

_____   _____

_____   _____

_____   _____

_____   _____

❷ Write each time marker that you find in the text, *What is a tutorial?*

_____, _____, _____

_____, _____, _____

WRITING 1

Task A | Learn different ways to create an essay outline

Look at these types of essay plans/outlines.

1. Map type essay plan

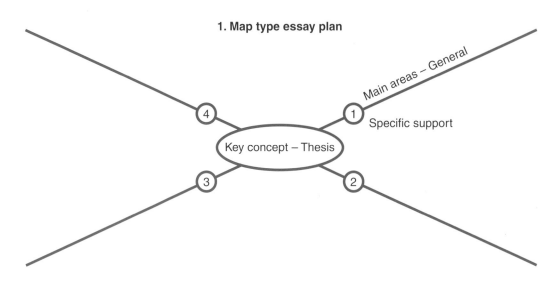

2. Sequenced and numbered outlines

```
I                          Main idea
    A                      1   support
        1                  2   variation
        2                  3   support
        3                          a]  further support
            a]
            b]
II                   or    Next main idea
    B                      1
        1                  2
        2
        3
III                        Next main idea
    C                      1
        1                  2
        2                  3
        3
            a]
            b]
IV
    D
        1
            a]
        2
            b]
V
    E Conclusion:
        1   Summary
        2   Recommendation
```

3. Circles connected with arrows

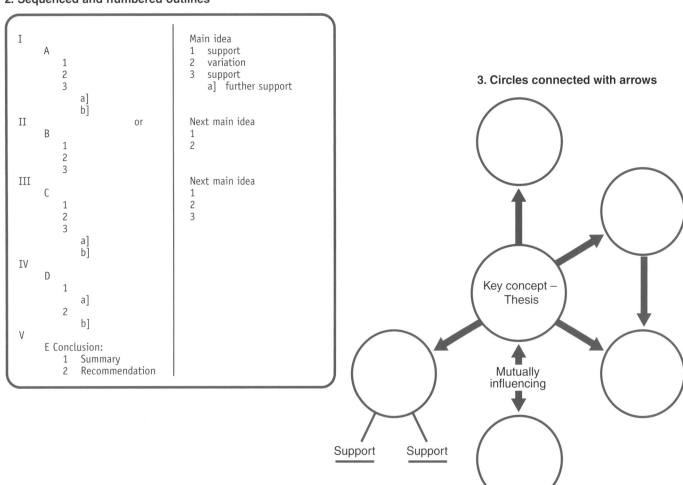

Task B | Create your own outline

❶ Write down the following question and then begin breaking down possible answers to the question by formatting it. Choose the format that you like the best from the models on the adjacent page.

❷ Map your essay in the space provided below.

QUESTION: Many countries have differing political systems. Some countries have better systems than others. Democratic countries believe their system is the best system. Describe at least two, different political systems and answer the question – To what extent do you agree or disagree that democratic forms of government are the best forms?

---

1. Map type essay plan

2. Sequenced numbered outline

3. Circles connected with arrows

Task C | Study introductory paragraphing

Introductory paragraphing in essay writing
A paragraph in English is like a little essay all on its own. It has an introduction, a body and a conclusion.

The introduction is the topic or initial sentence, the body is made up of sentences which provide concrete, supporting evidence of the topic or about the topic, and the conclusion is the last sentence of the paragraph.

Other terminology that may be clearer is **theme** for sentence 1, **support** for other sentences and **rheme** for the last. The theme is all the information up to the first verb, the support is just what it says – support (props up, verifies, holds up, gives meaning to the first sentence), and the rheme is where new information is allowed to be introduced.

❶ Read about introductory paragraphing in the box on the left.

So the structure of an introductory paragraph is:
1. Theme/topic sentence
2. Support sentences
3. Rheme/concluding sentence.

Here's a model paragraph which is at the <u>beginning</u> of an essay (thus it is the *introductory paragraph*) where a student who is studying to become an English teacher has been asked the following essay question:

ESSAY QUESTION: **Consider and evaluate Rubin and Thompson's description of the 'good language learner'.**

In the past ten or fifteen years a great deal of research has been carried out in the field of Linguistics. A significant portion of this research has held as its focus the learner and how learners actually acquire or set about to acquire language. More specifically, much of the research has been concerned with learning strategies and cognitive styles and in particular with the '… identification of learning strategy preferences with a view to isolating those characteristics of the 'good language learner' (Nunan, 1991, p78).

---

❷ Examine the following table:

THEME or TOPIC SENTENCE *Sentence 1* Also: STAGE 1 – A general statement (Linguistics is general)	In the past ten or fifteen years a great deal of research has been carried out in the field of Linguistics.
CONCRETE SUPPORTING EVIDENCE *Sentence 2* Also: STAGE 2 – More information, sometimes a definition	A significant portion of this research has held as its focus the learner and how learners actually acquire or set about to acquire language.
RHEME or CONCLUDING SENTENCE *Sentence 3* Also: STAGE 3 – Scope and focus of the entire essay signalling what will come next	More specifically, much of the research has been concerned with learning strategies and cognitive styles and in particular with the '… identification of learning strategy preferences with a view to isolating those characteristics of the 'good language learner' (Nunan,1991, p78).

REVIEW

The model paragraph you have just examined follows certain other rules because it is the *first or introductory paragraph* of the essay. It has **stages**. All introductions in English have stages. There are at least three stages to an introduction. Look at the stages outlined in the table.

WRITING 2

Task A | Work out the staging

In the following two introductory paragraphs, underline and identify:

❶ The topic sentence – Stage 1

❷ Concrete supporting sentence/s – Stage 2

❸ Concluding sentence – Stage 3

Paragraph 1

> **ESSAY QUESTION: Define survey research and discuss the method.**
>
> Survey sampling is a quantitative method of research which is a 20th century phenomenon with most of its growth since the 1930s. Today, it is a widely accepted method for providing statistical data on an extensive range of subjects. Disciplines such as sociology, social psychology, demography, political science, economics, education and public health all rely on sample surveys.

Paragraph 2

> **ESSAY QUESTION: Refugees seeking safe havens around the world are becoming a global issue. Discuss.**
>
> Some 20 years ago, this writer read that in the new millennium, the biggest problem on earth would be homeless people seeking refuge. These people, it was said, would sail from port to port because their own countries were ruined as a result of pollution, war or famine. Other homeless peoples would be living in their own countries, but would have to live on the streets without shelter or employment. Sadly, it appears that this prophecy has begun to come true as countries that are United Nations members seek solutions to the growing number of refugees from a growing number of countries.

Task B | Write about what you know about

❶ Write a text/essay outlining the education system in your own country.

- You may decide to use sequenced writing since education is chronological. For example, it begins at youth, then, next, after that, following this, and then, finally.

_____

_____

_____

_____

_____

_____

_____

_____

_____

_____

_____

_____

_____

_____

_____

_____

_____

_____

_____

_____

❷ Use the following checklist to examine your paragraphs.

Does my paragraph contain:	Yes	No
• A topic sentence?	❏	❏
• Concrete supporting sentences?	❏	❏
• A concluding sentence or sentences?	❏	❏
• Theme, support, rheme (where new ideas are presented that lead into the topic sentence of the next paragraph)?	❏	❏

Register involves the particular situation of a social activity with its particular participants (where, with whom, about what, how). Register occurs in all discourse (both talking and writing are discourses) and must be appropriate. For example, if you write a letter to a company complaining about a service or product, you will use a different register, say, from writing an essay about a political or environmental issue. And, if you write a letter home to family that is a different register than if you were writing an email to one of your university lecturers.

Register occurs in both writing and speaking and depends upon:

- where you are
- with whom you are speaking or writing and the power you have or don't have, and
- the type of communication: *Writing* – emails/letters/essays/ lists/books; *Speaking* – conversation/presenting an oral presentation/speech making/making a request.

In writing, a lot of nouns and noun groups are used, whereas in speaking a lot of verbs and verb groups are used.

Task C | Analysing register

The two texts on the next page are about veterinary science.

❶ Underline the nouns and noun groups and verbs and verb groups in each text. Complete the table below. They are both about veterinary science.

NOUNS/NOUN GROUPS	VERBS/VERB GROUPS
Text 1	Text 1
Text 2	Text 2

❷ Count the words in each text? _____

❸ Count the words in each sentence? _____

❹ After you count, which text is longer? _____

❺ Which text has more words in its individual sentences? _____

TEXT 1

Veterinary scientists are people who practise all around the world. A veterinarian is a person who is like a doctor for animals. They help animals who are sick and/or injured to recover. They also perform surgery on animals and when people bring them their house pets, they save the pets' lives sometimes. There are veterinarians who look after large animals like the ones from farms and even zoo animals. Veterinarians are specialists and they have to go to school for a long time. They have to study a very long time to be able to work as a veterinarian. In some Western countries they charge a lot of money and are able to become quite wealthy.

TEXT 2

Veterinarian science is a practice around the world. A veterinarian assists animals from house pets to farm, zoo and even wild animals both as doctor and surgeon, and is a life saver at times. Veterinarians become qualified after a lengthy educational process and may acquire a comfortable level of wealth.

6 What are your conclusions about the differences between these two texts?

_____

_____

_____

_____

Nouns vs verbs – Academic register
It is very important that you use this knowledge in your written work. Academic writing is a specialised type of writing (and speaking) and uses more nouns and noun groups and fewer verbs and verb groups than ordinary speaking and writing.

LISTENING & NOTE-TAKING

LISTENING 1

MARKERS WHICH INDICATE MAIN IDEAS

When speakers speak, they 'signal' you as to what may come next. In this listening, try to listen for the order, main ideas, definitions and when the conclusion will occur. Listening for signals will help you understand the content of the 'Talk' because you will learn to predict what you will hear.

Task A | Listen for signals or cues (discourse markers) which signal important ideas and features of a listening

Listen to the *University library orientation talk*.

As you listen to Recording number 3 tick how many times you hear the following using the grid below.

CD 1

LECTURER SIGNALS ORDER/ USING THE FOLLOWING PHRASES		LECTURER SIGNALS IMPORTANCE (MAIN IDEAS)		LECTURER SIGNALS DEFINITIONS		LECTURER SIGNALS CONCLUSION OR END OF PART OR WHOLE	
I'm here to tell you …	❑	The most important thing …	❑	What I mean by that is …	❑	Finally…	❑
First …	❑	You also need to know …	❑	There are several ways to look at …	❑	To sum up …	❑
Next …	❑	It's essential that …	❑	For example …	❑	In conclusion …	❑
		You certainly need to know	❑				
Now …	❑	There is/there are a couple of important …	❑			So …	❑

Task B | Listen for specific information

CD 1

Listen to the *University library orientation talk* again and answer the following questions as you listen.

1 How much does it cost to get an inter-library loan?

_____

2 What does she say is the 'most important thing to remember'?

_____

3 Why is it 'essential' that you bring your student card to the library?

_____

4 How much is a library fine for a day?

_____

5 For how long can you borrow popular books?

_____

6 For how long can you borrow books from the reserve collection?

_____

7 What happens to you at the end of the year if you have library fines which are outstanding?

_____

8 What is one of 'several things' that can help you find information?

_____

9 What are the names of the two libraries discussed in her talk?

_____

10 May anyone request an inter-library book loan?

_____

LISTENING 2

Task A | Listen for signals including tone of voice

CD 1

1 Listen to the lecturer explaining and outlining the lecture *The human senses* that the students will hear. She talks about what they have previously covered first, then tells the students what will be covered in the coming few hours of her talk. She also mentions what will be covered in the future. Listen for these stages within her brief introduction and answer the questions that follow. Study the vocabulary first so when you hear the words they will be familiar.

Pre-listening practice

pheromones (n)
a chemical compound, produced and secreted by an animal, that influences the behaviour and development of other members of the same species.

nervous system (n)
the network of nerve cells and nerve fibres in most animals that conveys sensations to the brain and motor impulses to organs and muscles.

peripheral (n)
the part of the nervous system that lies outside the brain and spinal cord.

spinal cord (n)
a thick whitish cord of nerve tissue extending from the bottom of the brain through the spinal column and giving rise to pairs of spinal nerves that supply the body. The spinal cord and brain together form the central nervous system.

cranial nerves (noun group)
either of a pair of nerves that originate in the brain stem and pass out of the skull to the surface of the body.

receptors (n)
physiology – a nerve ending that is sensitive to stimuli and can convert them into nerve impulses.

molecules (n)
the smallest physical unit of a substance that can exist independently, consisting of one or more atoms held together by chemical forces.

Note: The underlining of syllables in multi-syllable words is to indicate which syllable carries word stress.

2 Listen for each phrase that tells you the speaker is speaking an explanation, giving a definition or telling you they have just concluded an explanation. On first listening, listen for and tick the words and phrases below each time you hear them.

WORD OR PHRASE, VOICE INTONATION	TICKS
Voice up	
Voice down	
Remember…	
so…	
This is because…	
Now…	
Which means they are…	

Task B | Note-taking for definitions and explanations within the introduction to the lecture

Listen to the recording a second time and when you hear the signals you have ticked, write notes after these words. Your notes will have definitions and explanations within them.

CD 1

②

Sentences are provided below which include significant phrases and words as your guide to listening for definitions and explanations. Finish the sentences in note form as you listen. Note how 'so', 'now', 'which means', 'are', 'was', 'is', 'includes', and 'they are called', signal to you, the listener, that an explanation or a definition will be given. Listen carefully when you hear these particular words.

❶ So if you remember the two main parts of the nervous system _____,
_____

❷ The central nervous system *includes*
_____, _____

❸ and the peripheral nervous system *included your*
_____, _____

❹ Now part of the nervous system also (uh) *was*
_____ _____

❺ ...receptors are mechano receptors *so* they are pretty much sensing changes in _____

❻ ...and we have receptors that measure changes in
_____

❼ ...special functions.... *Now*, some of these receptors will be called photo receptors *which means* _____
_____.

❽ ...and we have receptors that monitor the different chemical composition of the blood. *And they are called*
_____ _____

❾ So these receptors are pretty much also part of your
_____ _____.

❿ *But what I want to discuss today*
_____ _____

⓫ *So*... special senses include... _____,
_____, (which is called) _____,
vision, _____ and equilibrium.

⓬ *So*, these are _____ _____.

Task C | Questions

❶ Humans have unique, specialised senses. Some of these senses are... _____

❷ Receptors that measure the chemical composition of the blood are called _____.

❸ Receptors found in the eye are called _____.

❹ How many main parts are there to the nervous system?
_____

❺ The central and the peripheral are what parts of the human system?

❻ What two parts make up the central nervous system?
_____, and the _____.

❼ Which nervous system are the cranial nerves a part of?
_____

❽ What will the remainder of the lecture focus upon?
_____

NOTE-TAKING

NOTE-TAKING FROM WHOLE BOOKS

When you read for assignments, examinations and research for presentations, how will you take notes and organise your study materials? The following tasks will help you to:

* improve your speed
* know what to write down and what to leave out
* improve your ability to organise your notes.

Task A | Getting a global view of a text

Using a text provided by your teacher or yourself:
* examine the whole book.
* tick the following when you are finished.

Did you	Yes	No
❶ Look at the cover?	❏	❏
❷ Open the front pages and note the copyright date?	❏	❏
❸ See who the author/s are?	❏	❏
❹ Note the publisher and the city where the book was published?	❏	❏
❺ Open the book to the back and find the index pages?	❏	❏
❻ Open the book to the back and find the references?	❏	❏
❼ Examine the Table of Contents if there is one?	❏	❏
❽ Examine the chapter headings?	❏	❏
❾ Examine the chapter subheadings?	❏	❏
❿ Read the back cover of the book carefully – more than once?	❏	❏

Task B | Getting around a book – The whole book

Ⓐ Using the same text complete the following:

1. Write the complete title, the author/s names, the publication date, the publishing house and city of publication:

_____

2. Note the pages where you found the index:

_____

3. Note the pages where you found references:

_____

4. Scan the index and search for one topic. Look for all the words that are similar or related to the topic. Write the page numbers here:

_____

_____

_____

Ⓑ Look at the references.

1. Summarise the back cover in your own words. After your summary, write the author's name and year of publication like this example … (Smith, 2008)

_____

_____

_____

_____

2. Quote two sentences from the back cover. After the quote, write the author's name and year of publication like this example … (Smith, 2008)

_____

_____

3. What have you done by quoting the author and date in parenthesis from the book you used?

_____

LANGUAGE SPOTLIGHT 2

REFERENCING AND BIBLIOGRAPHIES

You will cover this subject more than once in this book.

Referencing means to refer back to the sources you used to gather information for an essay. **You must reference!** You must reference within the writing and use the same information to write the bibliography at the end of your essay.

The use of the titles 'Bibliography' and 'References' are equal. Some faculties like you to title your references as 'References', others want you to use the title of 'Bibliography'. Each subject at university has methods for referencing. Without referencing you have committed the crime of 'plagiarism', which means you have used someone else's ideas and thoughts but haven't told the reader. That is stealing. And, in Western institutions, it means an instant FAIL. So, have a brief look now at some references which were taken from the internet and examine how they are included in the reading text and at the end of the reading text.

Task A | Understanding internal referencing from source material within a university essay

❶ Read the introduction from a university Business and Management course student essay below.

❷ Note the university lecturer/marker's comment next to the last line.

(*Ref*) means the student did not provide a proper reference for the information included in the paragraph.

Show me how you will measure me and I will show you how I will perform

Performance measures and metrics are essential for effectively managing the supply chain, particularly in a competitive global economy. The real challenge for managers is to develop suitable performance measures and metrics to make right decisions that would contribute to an improved organisational competitiveness. The old adage 'you can't improve what you can't measure' is particularly true for buyer-supplier alliances, it is essential to measure the right things at the right time in a supply chain so that timely action can be taken.

Studies in recent years indicate that researchers have classified or categorised performance measures according to several different criteria in supply chain systems. These include: (i) balanced score card perspective; (ii) components of performance measures; (iii) location of measures in supply chain links; (iv) decision levels; (v) nature of measures; (vi) measurement base; and (vii) traditional vs modern measures. Each of these performance measures will be briefly discussed as a driver to supply chain improvements. (*Ref*)

3 Read the beginning of the second/next paragraph from the same essay and note how references *are* included.

> The balanced score card (BSC) approach to performance measurement was developed by Kaplan and Norton in 1992, as a way to align an organisation's performance measures with its strategic plan and goals, thus improving managerial decision making (Wisner, 2005).

Task B | How was the essay referenced?

Answer the following questions:

1 Name the reference provided for the BSC approach to performance measurement.

_____

2 What is the date that the BSC approach was written about by the authors?

_____

3 Who said that managerial decision making would improve by using a BSC approach?

_____

4 What year did Wisner write the information referenced?

_____

5 What words introduced the part of the essay that the university marker said/noted needed referencing?

_____

Task C | The Bibliography – References at the end of essay

1 Look at the references in the next column. Underline the references within this list which match to the ones quoted within the student essay.

2 What punctuation do you see used for the names of journals?

_____

3 What punctuation is used for the title of an article found within a journal?

_____

4 Are the titles of books italicised?

_____

5 In what way are the names of the authors organised and presented within this list of references?

_____

6 How should you present the dates of publication?

_____

7 Where are the initials of the authors?

_____

8 How are the volume numbers presented?

_____

9 Why are there no page numbers used for some of the books that are referenced?

_____

10 Write the names of two books from the references.

_____

_____

References

Beamon, BM (1999) 'Measuring Supply Chain Performance'. *International Journal of Operations & Production Management*, Vol 19, No 3, pp 275-292.

Gunasekaran, A, Patel, C & Tirtiroglu, E (2001) 'Performance Measures & Metrics in a Supply Chain Environment'. *International Journal of Operations & Production Management*, Vol 12, No 1/2, pp 71-87.

Kaplan, RS & Norton, PD (1992) 'The balanced score card–measures that drive performance'. *Harvard Business Review*, January-February, pp 71-79.

Maskell, BH (1991) *Performance Measurement for World Class Manufacturing*. Portland, OR. USA: Productivity Press.

Wisner, JD, Keong Leong, G & Tan C (2005) *Principles of Supply Chain Management: A Balanced Approach*. South Western USA: Thompson.

Task D | Referencing from the internet

You may recognise the following references. They are from Reading 4: *Western education systems* on pages 10–11.

References

BBC (2001) *Secondary Schools*. BBC News, <http://news.bbc.co.uk/hi/english/education/uk_systems/newsid_115000/115872.stm> (6 May 2002).

Commonwealth of Australia (2002) 'Australian way of studying'. *Study in Australia*, <http://studyinaustralia.gov.au/Contents/WhatToStudy/AustStudy.html> (21 April 2002).

DETYA (2000) *Australia Country Education Profile*, 3rd edition Online. Canberra: DETYA, <http://www.detya.gov.au/noosr/cep/australia/index.htm> (21 April 2002).

Fulbright Commission (2001) 'School Education in the USA', <http://www.fulbright/co.uk/eas/school/school/htm> (12 May 2002).

You may have noticed that there are several brackets with a name and a date, for example: (Detya, 2001). These correspond to lines ('entries') in the bibliography at the end. These are references.

All academic essays that you produce must be referenced. All the books, articles, information from the internet and newspapers that you have used will be listed as your bibliography. References are the same thing. Examine the references on page 25 and answer the following questions:

❶ Where does **http://** come from?

   a. the internet
   b. an educational journal
   c. a book.

❷ Is the http:// and the information following it a web address?

   a. yes
   b. no.

Now examine the information that comes before the web addresses.

❸ The first reference comes from what news source?

_____

❹ The second reference comes from

_____

❺ Where does the third reference titled DETYA (2000) *Australia Country Education profile*, 3rd edition Online come from?

❻ The last reference is from the Fulbright Commission. What is the title of the article?

_____

❼ In two of the references dates are found in two places. Do you know why?

_____

_____

❽ Write the four dates when the references were actually published.

_____

_____

_____

_____

SPEAKING 2 ··

Task A | Giving a spoken explanation

Prepare a spoken explanation (based on the paragraph writing you did in the writing section of this unit about a subject you know something about). Present this explanation in your groups.

> **Remember:**
> • Introduce your topic with a clear sentence.
> • Provide a definition or description.
> • Sequence your explanation using chronological order, eg *first*, *next*, *after that*, etc.
> • Use spoken register which contains more verbs than its written counterpart.

Task B | Discussing the usefulness of a whole book

In pairs, follow the instructions and discuss answers together as you move through the questions.

❶ Look at the Table of Contents at the front of this book.

   [a] What sections come before Unit 1?

   _____

   _____

   [b] Skim these sections. How do you think they can help you? Many books have similar sections, so it's useful to know their purpose. Choose one each with your partner and summarise what you find by skimming.

   _____

   _____

❷ Look at the Contents Map on pages iv–ix at the front of this book. Where will you look:

   [a] If you're going to write an argument essay, and aren't sure you remember all the features of one?
   Unit ___ page ___

   [b] In which units will you find further practice on paragraph writing?
   Units _____ pages _____.

   [c] In which units will you learn about discourse markers?

   _____

Task C | Using the cross-references

Cross-references are given to help you find where the skill you are working on has previously appeared in the book, or where you can find more practice later in the book.

Other helpful features in this book are:

- margin notes next to essays to explain vocabulary
- paragraph numbers beside texts

- line numbers beside texts
- headings to each task which tell you why you are doing the task
- a summary page at the beginning of each unit which shows what you will study in the unit; and
- an index for quick reference.

FURTHER CONNECTIONS

Task A | Time management at university and in study situations – Examining your own use of time

Students write next to the times a few words explaining everything they did and will do today. Using the five days within the timetable, write your schedule as it exists at the moment.

	MONDAY	TUESDAY	WEDNESDAY	THURSDAY	FRIDAY
6 am					
7 am					
8 am					
9 am					
10 am					
11 am					
12 noon					
1 pm					
2 pm					
3 pm					
4 pm					
5 pm					
6 pm					
7 pm					
8 pm					
9 pm					
10pm					

Task B | Create a personal timetable that includes 30 hours of study

Create a timetable for yourself that includes 30 hours of studying per week.

GET READY FOR UNIT 2: SOCIETY

Read the following article to help you get ready for Unit 2:
- <www.simple.wikipedia.org/wiki/poverty>

While you are reading this article, think about:
- What problems does poverty cause?

Also, make notes of some vocabulary from these readings.

Be prepared to share your answers next time you meet.

2

'A nation's greatness is measured by how it treats its weakest members.'

Mahatma Ghandi

SOCIETY

In this unit, you will look at several aspects of society including families and crime. You will build upon the reading techniques you learned in Unit 1, and will also look at how to use collocations to make your English sound natural and fluent. There is a strong focus on argument essays (essays giving one point of view), and on writing essay body paragraphs with strong supporting evidence. You will look at several techniques for taking notes during lectures and then use your notes to evaluate the strength of a lecturer's evidence. Finally, you will give short talks in which you signpost your ideas clearly, give supporting information and avoid over-generalisations.

BY THE END OF THIS UNIT, YOU SHOULD:

SKILL	TASK	PAGE
have gained confidence in discussing issues around society	**Speaking 1** *Task A*	30
	Reading & Critical Thinking *Tasks B, F*	33, 38
	Listening & Note-taking *Tasks A, F*	44–45, 49
	Further Connections *Task D*	57
be aware of the importance of collocations	**Speaking 1** *Task B*	31
be able to quickly find the main ideas in a text by skimming	**Reading & Critical Thinking** *Tasks A, C*	31–33, 34
have improved your skills at finding meaning from context	**Reading & Critical Thinking** *Task D*	36
be able to differentiate between weak and strong evidence	**Reading & Critical Thinking** *Task E*	36–38
	Further Connections *Task A*	55–56
be able to achieve cohesion in writing through the use of discourse signals of addition and contrast	**Language Spotlight 1** *Task A*	38
understand the structure of an argument essay	**Writing** *Task A*	39–41
be able to provide strong supporting evidence in body paragraphs	**Writing** *Task B*	42
be able to select ideas for, and plan and write an argument essay	**Writing** *Tasks C, D*	43–44
be able to continuously predict the next points while listening to a lecture	**Listening & Note-taking** *Task B*	45–46
be able to use a range of note-taking formats while listening to spoken arguments	**Listening & Note-taking** *Task C*	46–48
have practised using symbols and abbreviations while taking notes	**Listening & Note-taking** *Tasks D, E*	48–49
have gained confidence at listening for supporting information	**Listening & Note-taking** *Task E*	48–49
be able to evaluate the strength of supporting information presented in lectures	**Listening & Note-taking** *Task E*	48–49
be able to avoid over-generalisations by using modality	**Language Spotlight 2** *Task A*	49–51
be able to give short talks with main ideas signposted, strong supporting evidence used	**Speaking 2** *Tasks A, B*	51

Task A | Discussion and vocabulary about social issues

Work in small groups for this task.

1 Discuss these points:

[a] List three or more people who are 'successful'.

[b] What is it about each that makes you say they are 'successful'?

[c] What did they do to achieve their success?

[d] Could anyone achieve the same success? Or does success also depend on other factors, such as the people who you and your family know?

[e] In general, what can give people advantage in society? What can cause social disadvantage?

2 Complete the following with a partner.

[a] What do the following mean? Put them in the correct column of the table.
- fall (v)
- increase (v)
- decrease (v)
- reduce (v)
- rise (v)

GO UP ↗	GO DOWN ↘

[b] Using your shared knowledge and/or a dictionary, decide which of the words in the table:
- have the same form as a noun and as a verb
- can be changed from a verb to a noun by removing the last letter and adding –tion

3 In groups, give your impressions about the points listed under the 'Features of societies' heading below, using the questions in the next column as a guide.

Features of societies

leisure time	immigration	disposable income
the wealth divide	equality	discrimination
crime	poverty	life expectancy
infant mortality	household size	welfare

[a] Which of the points are positive, which are negative and which are neutral? Or does your answer depend on the context? If so, in what way?

[b] Are any of these serious issues in your country? Or are they discussed a lot in the media?

[c] What can governments do to help deal with the negative issues to encourage the positive issues?

[d] For each of the issues, has the trend been upwards or downwards since your grandparents' time? If you're not sure, speculate. Give reasons.

Vocabulary

immigration (n)	moving to another country to live; *migrate* to (v)
diversity (n)	including many different types of people (or things); *diverse* (adj); *diversify* (v)
leisure time (n)	free time
equality (n)	being treated equally; having the same rights and responsibilities as other people
discrimination (n)	being treated differently in an unfair way, usually because of things you can't control, such as skin colour or where your family is from (examples are *sexism* and *racism*); *discriminate* (v)
poverty (n)	being poor
life expectancy (n)	the amount of time a person can expect to live, on average
infant mortality (n)	the number of babies who die in every 1000 that are born
the wealth divide (n)	if a country has a large wealth divide, there is a big difference between the rich and poor in that country.
a household (n)	the people who live in the same house
a trend (n)	the general way in which something is changing with time, eg *In the last century, there has been an upward trend in the amount of leisure time that people have*
welfare (n)	money paid by the government, usually to people who don't have enough money to look after themselves, eg *unemployment benefit*

4 Look at the quotation at the beginning of this unit. Do you agree with it? Why? Discuss with your group.

Task B | Collocations

> ### Collocations
> Notice the words 'life expectancy' in the vocabulary box in Task A. Now, 'lifespan' means 'how long a person lives'. So, why don't we say 'lifespan expectancy'?
>
> The answer is that the words 'life' and 'expectancy' form a *collocation*. A collocation is a combination of words that just fit together. We can say that 'life' collocates with 'expectancy'. There is often no special reason that they fit together; it's just that they are very frequently used together by speakers of English. Using word combinations that don't collocate, such as 'lifespan expectancy', sounds strange.
>
> Using collocations will help your English sound natural. Try to notice collocations and use them – this is one of the best ways to make your English sound natural.
>
> If you're not sure whether words collocate, you can ask your teacher:
> * Is xxx xxx a good collocation?
> * Does xxx xxx sound natural?

❶ Work in small groups. In each of the following, cross out one that doesn't collocate. Using your experience of English and each others' knowledge will help.

[a] have dinner
eat dinner
prepare dinner

[b] members of the family
members of the company
members of the group

[c] high quality
top quality
large quality

[d] have contact with
do contact with
make contact with

[e] considerable advantages
considerable good points
considerable benefits

[f] friend support
government support
family support

[g] do a crime
commit a crime

[h] migrate in Australia
migrate to Australia

❷ As you work through the rest of this unit, make a list of collocations that you come across. You will compare lists at the end of this unit.

READING & CRITICAL THINKING ···

Task A | Skimming

❶ Imagine you have to read a chapter of a book about sociology of the family. Match the techniques to the tasks listed. Discuss the answers with a partner.

Tasks – you want to:
* find the average number of members of a household in the UK in 2010
* understand just the main points made in the chapter
* thoroughly understand each major point

The best reading technique is … :
* read the whole chapter carefully, one sentence after the next
* read sub-headings, topic sentences and captions only, missing out the bits in between
* look quickly through each page, looking only for small numbers

❷ Which of the reading techniques in question 1 did you practise in Unit 1? What is it called?

Reading many pages quickly

You will have a lot of reading to do at university – maybe hundreds of pages every week. It is not possible to read every word. Thus, it's important to think carefully about how you will approach each text.

As well as the technique we looked at in Unit 1, there is also **skimming**. You skim when you are looking at a text quickly to find out only the author's main points. You only spend a few seconds on each page, without reading every word. When you skim, it is useful to pay attention to:

- introductions
- the beginning of a paragraph, where the theme or topic sentence is usually found
- titles and captions of pictures and diagrams, etc
- headings and titles
- words in bold or italics: these are often key words.

Skimming is sometimes called *reading for gist*. If someone asks you to read just for the main ideas, skimming will help you do this.

Some examples of when you might skim include:

- when you first see a text (eg an article or a book chapter on your reading list, or something you have to read in an exam)
- to decide whether a text might contain useful information for your assignment
- when you have a lot of reading to do, skimming can help you find the most important parts of a text to focus on and read in more detail.

3 The table below shows some differences between skimming, scanning and reading in detail.

Work in pairs. Tick the best column(s) for each row. More than one answer is possible for each row.

	READING IN DETAIL ✓ = YES	SKIMMING ✓ = YES	SCANNING ✓ = YES
This technique			
[a] … needs more time than the others			
[b] … is very quick			
[c] … helps you understand a text thoroughly			
[d] … helps you efficiently get just the information you need			
To use the technique, you need to			
[e] … know which word or idea you're looking for before you begin reading			
[f] … read every word of the text			
[g] … look for main ideas only			
[h] … look for specific information, such as numbers, dates or specific facts			
[i] … focus on topic sentences, summary sentences, introductions, abstracts and conclusions			

4 In the following situations, which technique would you use: skimming, scanning or reading in detail? Why? Sometimes, you may be able to justify more than one answer. Discuss with your partner, then write the answers you decide.

[a] Reading the TV guide/TV times pages of a website to find when a particular programme is on.

_____

_____

[b] Reading a film review to decide whether it's generally good, OK or bad.

_____

_____

[c] Reading the blurb on the back cover of a book to find out whether it is useful for beginning students in a particular field.

_____

_____

[d] Reading the contents page of a book to decide whether it covers the area you're looking for.

_____

_____

[e] Reading an article to find the percentage of people who said that they believe TV violence affects children negatively.

_____

_____

_____

[f] Reading an index to find the pages on which something called _the demographic time bomb_ is mentioned.

_____

_____

[g] Reading a chapter of a book to find out whether it mentions Yang Tingzhong (a sociologist).

_____

_____

[h] Reading a journal article to decide whether it might contain information useful to your research project.

_____

_____

Task B | Introducing the topic and vocabulary

1 Imagine your friend has an elderly grandparent who lives many hours away from their children. The grandparent is struggling to look after themselves.
   Which of the decisions below do you think is best? Work with a partner to number them in an approximate order of preference. What factors might affect your decision?

_____ Invite their grandparent to live with them.

_____ Do nothing, because older people prefer to live independently.

_____ Look for government-run retirement homes nearby — these are paid for by the person's government pension, and in some cases government subsidies also help.

_____ Look for a private retirement home nearby — usually these provide more attractive accommodation and may have a better staff–resident ratio, but are much more expensive than a government retirement home.

Vocabulary

a childcare centre (n)	a place where very young children are looked after while their parents work
a retirement home (n)	a place where old people who can't look after themselves are cared for
private (adj)	operated by a company or similar organisation; can be for-profit or non-profit. Also _privately-run_ (adj). The alternative is _government_ (adj) or _government-run_ (adj)
an extended family (n)	a family group that includes more than just the parents and children; may include grandparents, aunts, cousins etc
a pension (n)	money that people receive when they are retired
a profit (n)	money that a company has after paying its expenses
a subsidy (n)	money (usually from the government) to reduce the cost of something; _subsidise_ (v)

2 Work in pairs.

[a] Discuss why people might or might not want to live in extended families. Complete the table over the page with as many ideas as you can. Think about three generations: children, parents and grandparents. Use notes: don't write sentences. Try to use vocabulary from the box in your discussion.

REASONS WHY PEOPLE MIGHT WANT TO LIVE IN EXTENDED FAMILIES	REASONS PEOPLE MIGHT NOT WANT TO LIVE IN EXTENDED FAMILIES

[b] Which reasons can you relate to? Which are more difficult to relate to?

Task C | Skimming, scanning and reading in detail

1 Skimming race. Read the questions below. Then skim the text *Extended families in Western society* opposite which you might find in a sociology textbook.

Who will answer the questions first? Put your hand up when you finish.

[a] Which organisational pattern does the text follow?
- **[i]** Introduction
  Reasons for living in extended families
  More reasons for living in extended families
- **[ii]** Introduction
  Reasons why some people don't live in extended families
  Reasons for living in extended families
- **[iii]** Introduction
  Reasons for living in extended families
  Reasons why some people don't live in extended families

[b] How are paragraphs 2 to 4 organised?
- **[i]** by order of importance
- **[ii]** by generation
- **[iii]** from easiest to most difficult to understand
- **[iv]** no particular order

2 [a] Scanning race. Scan the text for paraphrases of the following statements. Write the paragraph number next to each statement.

Who will be the first? Put your hand up when you finish.

- **[i]** Government retirement homes _____
- **[ii]** Experience in bringing up children _____
- **[iii]** Child care centres _____
- **[iv]** Family size _____
- **[v]** Health problems _____
- **[vi]** Feeling in control _____
- **[vii]** Number of houses _____

[b] Did you skim to help you scan? If so, how did it help you? Discuss with a partner.

3 Look at the statements below. [i] here matches with [i] in question 2, etc. Read in detail around the part of the text where in question 2 you found the ideas discussed. Then mark them either T (true), F (false) or NE (no evidence given) according to the text. Compare your answers with your partner's.

- **[i]** Government retirement homes are very professional _____
- **[ii]** Children gain in extended families because grandparents have lots of experience in bringing up children _____
- **[iii]** Child care centres are definitely good for children _____
- **[iv]** Families in developed countries are getting smaller _____

[v] Older people who look after children might get sick more easily _____

[vi] Living independently helps some older people to feel in control of their lives _____

[vii] If people live in extended families, fewer houses are needed _____

Tip for reading exams

As you noticed in question 3, scanning is a very useful technique for answering exam-type questions. Just scan for the key ideas in the question.

4 Read the whole text quickly for a sense of the main ideas. Then work with a partner and answer these questions.

[a] Which of the ideas you spoke about in Task B are mentioned in the text?

[b] Add to the table any ideas in the text that you didn't speak about before. Keep your notes short – don't quote from the text.

[c] What other arguments are presented?

[d] Which arguments do you agree with? Disagree with? Tell a partner.

Extended families in 'Western' society

1. There is a clear trend in developed countries towards smaller families (eg Salcedo et al, 2009). The typical household nowadays comprises only parents and children, while grandparents tend to live elsewhere. Exceptions to this do exist, of course, including single people, single-parent families and blended families, but it is rare for a married couple to live with either of their parents. So, what are some of the factors causing this phenomenon? In order to examine this, we will look at the effect on each generation in turn.

2. From the grandparents' point of view, extended families can provide enjoyment and stimulation that improves their old age. Most grandparents and great-grandparents enjoy spending time with their grandchildren–it is common to hear them say that having children around them makes them feel younger. Further, the kind of stimulation that children automatically provide, with their energy and eagerness to talk and to find out about the world, has been shown to have positive health benefits for older people.

3. Parents may benefit as well from living in an extended family, possibly more than the other generations. Research in Australia and the USA has made it clear that working hours are increasing in those countries. It is likely that the same is true in other developed countries. This, together with the fact that it is now common for both parents to be working, means that people of working age are becoming increasingly time-poor. Grandparents at home mean that the expense of childcare may not be necessary.

4. Potential benefits for the children are numerous. Many people say that family care is of higher quality, on average, than in childcare centres. It will be better tuned in to the children's needs because the family members know their children better and because there are fewer children to look after than in a childcare centre. In addition, families generally have greater emotional involvement in a child's development than people who are looking after the child as a job. More time spent together can also strengthen family bonds. More practically, grandparents are likely to bring a great deal of experience of child-rearing, from the years spent raising their own children. This isn't to say that childcare centres don't have some role to play, though – their staff are professionally trained and may have knowledge and skills that parents don't have. Furthermore, external child care, in many cases, provides greater opportunities for social interaction with other children than home-based child care.

5. There are also some valid reasons why extended families benefit society as a whole. As countries develop and their health care systems improve, people live longer and the proportion of older people increases. The result is that public services for looking after the elderly, such as retirement homes, are under increasing strain. Where older people live with their children, they are less likely to need to use such facilities, thus saving money for the government and helping to keep tax under control.

6. Extended families also help to reduce the use of resources. When more people live in the same house, not only does it mean that fewer houses are necessary, but also the amount of energy used for such things as heating and air conditioning is reduced.

7. Looking at the points above, it would appear that the advantages of extended families are overwhelming. So, why aren't they much more popular then they are? There are several factors that may help to explain this.

8. Often it is the elderly themselves who are reluctant to live with their children. One reason is that many want to keep their independence. They want to be able to come and go as they please, and to be able to live their lives in their own way and not have to fit in with other people, even if they are family. When living with their family, they often feel that they have lost some control over their own lives, even if the alternative is to rely on support services such as visits from nurses or Meals on Wheels services. Secondly, many elderly people are proud of being able to look after themselves and would feel shame to be looked after by anyone else, even close family members. They don't want to be a burden on other people.

9. Also, some parents are reluctant for their parents to look after their children, because doing so reduces their leisure time at a time in their life when they have earned the right to enjoy themselves. Parents also worry that having the grandparents look after children might affect the grandparents' health. However, Mary Hughes, Linda Waite and colleagues (Hughes et al, 2007) have found that looking after grandchildren does not lead to health problems in older people.

10. In other cases, the middle generation may have had to move to a distant city for work or other reasons. Their parents might not want to leave the house and the place they have lived all their lives, leaving behind all their friends and neighbours, to join their children in a city or town that is strange to them.

11. It is quite possible that greater wealth has made it easier for families to live apart, but it is unlikely that money alone was the deciding factor. Social factors are also likely to have a strong role to play. Culture may be a powerful factor – it will be interesting to see what will happen in those countries where it was traditional for grandparents to move in with their children as personal wealth increases. There is some evidence that the same trend is happening in at least three Mediterranean countries, and it is thought that it is the growing middle class that is driving this trend in those countries (Addato et al, 2007).

References

Addato, AVD, Vignoli D & Yavuz S (2007) 'Towards smaller family size in Egypt, Morocco and Turkey: Overall change over time or socio-economic compositional effect?' *MPIDR Working Paper WP2007-012*. Rostock: Max Planck Institute for Demographic Research.

Hughes, ME, Waite, LJ, LaPierre, TA & Luo, Y (2007) 'All in the family: The impact of caring for grandchildren on grandparents' health'. *Journal of Gerontology: Social Science* Vol 62B, No 2, pp S108-119.

Salcedo, A, Schoellman, T & Tertilt, M (2009) *Families as roommates: Changes in U.S. Household Size from 1850 to 2000. SIEPR Discussion Paper No 09-01*. Stanford: Stanford University Press.

Task D | Finding meaning from context

❶ Scan and mark in the previous text the words in the boxes below.

external	tuned in (to)	exception
factor	potential	a burden
reluctant (to)	involvement	resource
tax	facility	potential
stimulation	phenomenon	comprise
strain	bond	rear
social interaction	overwhelming	valid

❷ Mark the words that you already know the meanings of. Explain their meanings to a partner if he or she doesn't already know them.

❸ Using context, match the words with the closest meanings below, writing them in the gaps.

[a] ____resource____ things that people use

[b] _____ possible in the future

[c] _____ reasonable and sensible

[d] _____ very, very strong; having a strong effect; much stronger than the alternatives

[e] _____ something different from the previous statement, idea, or something different from the usual rule

[f] _____ aware of other people's thoughts and feelings; aware of what is happening in a particular situation

[g] _____ something that encourages you to do things or think in new ways; something that keeps you or your mind active

[h] _____ talking with other people

[i] _____ taking part in something; being part of something

[j] _____ outside

[k] _____ something that happens or exists in society, science etc, especially something that is studied academically

[l] _____ something that causes something else to happen; reason that something happens

[m] _____ something difficult or worrying that you are responsible for

[n] _____ not really wanting to do something; doing something only if you have to, not because you want to

[o] _____ something that makes people feel close to each other

[p] _____ rooms, equipment or services for a particular purpose

[q] _____ possible in the future

[r] _____ difficulty, pressure

[s] _____ be made of; consist of

[t] _____ helping children develop into adults

[u] _____ money that the government collects from people

❹ Explain your answers to a partner and discuss any differences. Also, discuss how you found the meanings. For example, which words could you find just from the sentences before and after the word? For which words did you have to read large parts of the text to find their meaning?

Task E | Critical thinking – Differentiating between weak and strong evidence

❶ Look at the following points. Which opinions do you find easier to believe? Which ones are you more sceptical about? Why? Discuss with a partner. Use the 'useful expressions' in the box and the vocabulary where you can.

[a] Take AcheGone! Headaches will never again slow you down! **[advertisement]**

[b] Statistics clearly show that people in most Western countries are spending longer in retirement than the previous generation (Anderson, 2010). **[academic paper]**

[c] Childhood is the best time of life. **[conversation]**

[d] People are clearly living more healthily and for longer. My grandmother is still alive at age 85, but my great-grandmother died when she was 64. **[conversation]**

[e] I believe that the best time of life is after retirement. **[conversation]**

[f] The early years of retirement are, for many people, a very enjoyable time. Responsibilities such as work and looking after children have gone. And most people of this age are still healthy enough to do what they enjoy. **[textbook]**

[g] *Nurse:* I think it's a good idea for your mother to go into a retirement home. If she stays living by herself, she might have a serious accident. **[conversation]**

[h] My grandmother likes living alone. I've never actually asked her about it, but she's never complained about it. **[conversation]**

Supporting ideas

One of the most important things to think about when reading (and when listening to lectures) is the support for each point.

You have to ask yourself all the time:
- What support is given?
- How strong is the support?

Also, every time you think about something in your studies, try to also remember what evidence there is for the point – even if it's something your university lecturer said or something you've read in a well-known book. This is more important than memorising the facts.

Vocabulary

evidence (n)	information that helps to show that something is true
sceptical (adj)	not being confident that something is true; *scepticism* (n); *sceptic* (n-person)
a claim (v)	to say something as if it's true; *a claim* (n)
credible (adj)	able to be believed; *credibility* (n)
justify (v)	to give a good reason (or good evidence) for something; *justification* (n)
biased (n)	having a reason to hold a particular opinion, eg because of a job or money; *bias* (adj)
a logical argument (n)	thinking in a step-by-step way, like a police detective or a scientist; also *logical reasoning*
assume (v)	to make a guess that something is correct, usually without thinking about it much or without collecting evidence; *assumption* (n)

❷ With a partner, put the types of supporting ideas onto the scale below.

[a] references to other people's ideas and research

[b] no explanation

[c] logical reasoning (explanation)

[d] only personal opinion

[e] one person's experiences

[f] explanation of other people's research without references

[g] assumptions

←—————————————————————————————————————→

**signs of
stronger support**

**signs of
weaker support**

3 For each of the points from the reading (given below), how strong is the evidence provided in the text? Discuss with your partner. Give reasons for your answers.

[a] 'extended families can provide enjoyment and stimulation that improves their old age'
[b] 'parents may benefit as well from living in an extended family'
[c] 'potential benefits for the children are numerous'
[d] 'extended families benefit society as a whole'
[e] 'extended families … help to reduce the use of resources'
[f] 'often it is the elderly themselves who are reluctant to live with their children'
[g] 'some parents are reluctant for their parents to look after their children'.

4 Follow these instructions with a partner.

[a] Find two medium-length newspaper articles (your teacher will tell you more about this).
[b] Find the main points made in each.
[c] Decide how strongly the main points are supported.
[d] Meet with another pair. Explain your article and the strength of support. Do your new partners agree with you?

Task F | Discussion

1 Discuss these questions in small groups.

[a] Could some of the benefits of extended families be obtained simply from grandparents living separately but visiting?
[b] Which of the points presented in the textbook extract (*Extended families in 'Western' society*) can you relate to the most easily? Which (if any) feel uncomfortable?
[c] Thinking about your own situation, who will look after your parents when they grow old? How?

LANGUAGE SPOTLIGHT 1

Task A | Cohesion through discourse signals

1 Look at the extract from the reading section, reproduced below, and answer the questions.

[a] Are the ideas in this paragraph similar or opposing?
[b] Which word in the paragraph helps you with your answer to question [a]?

---

2.   … Most grandparents and great-grandparents enjoy spending time with their grandchildren – it is common to hear them say that having children around them makes them feel younger. Further, the kind of stimulation that children automatically provide, with their energy and eagerness to talk and to find out about the world, has been shown to have positive health benefits for older people.

✱ Indicating whether ideas are similar or opposing

In writing and speaking, discourse signals often link ideas. Discourse signals also show the relationships (types of connection) between ideas.

There are many types of discourse signals. In Unit 1, you looked at discourse signals of time sequence and you will look at more discourse signals in later units. Here, you'll look at discourse signals of *addition* (which connect similar ideas) and discourse signals of *contrast* (which connect different or opposite ideas).

2 With a partner:

[a] Write the discourse signal you found in question 1 under the correct heading.
[b] Add discourse signals from the text on page 35 to the table. Include signals that connect paragraphs as well as those that link ideas within paragraphs.
[c] Add as many other words that you think may function as discourse signals (your teacher will confirm later whether they are correct). Which pair can add the most?

SIGNALS INDICATING SIMILAR IDEAS (ADDING IDEAS)	SIGNALS INDICATING DIFFERENT, OPPOSING OR CONTRASTING IDEAS
_____	_____
_____	_____
_____	_____
_____	_____
_____	_____
_____	_____
_____	_____
_____	_____
_____	_____
_____	_____
_____	_____

Task A | Structure of an argument essay

1 Read Essay 1 *Family responsibility: A dangerous policy* below. Answer the questions with a partner.

> An argument essay gives an opinion and supports it with evidence. Its purpose is to persuade the reader to agree with the opinion or to show reasons for a particular opinion.

[a] Which of the following do you think this essay is most likely to be? Give a reason for your answers.
> **[i]** A university assignment written by a student
> **[ii]** An exam paper written by a student
> **[iii]** An extract from a textbook

[b] Essay 1 is an argument text. By looking at the essay again, deduce which of the boxes to the right is correct. Cross out the incorrect box.

> An argument essay looks at two sides of an opinion, giving evidence for both sides. Its purpose is to evaluate the strength of an idea by looking at it from different angles.

Essay 1

Question: *Some people believe that the government should use tax revenue to provide services to assist families. Others believe that this is not the role of government. Which opinion do you agree with? Give reasons for your answer.*

Family responsibility: A dangerous policy

1. Certain politicians often say they want 'small government' and 'individual responsibility' – in other words, they feel that people should be responsible for themselves and not rely on the government to solve their problems. Applying this idea to family policies can have significant negative consequences. It will lead to a variety of social problems, not only for the elderly themselves, but also for their families who would have to look after them.

2. The elderly themselves have a lot to lose through small-government policies. If no support services are provided, they may have to move in with their adult children. Not only will this make them feel uncomfortable about being a burden to their families, but they may also have to move away from their homes, friends and communities. In many cases, adult children have had to move to another area for work reasons, thus the grandparents may have to move a considerable distance. Relationships that may have developed over a lifetime would then be lost.

Such circumstances can lead to serious problems such as depression, as well as a loss of a sense of independence.

3. Families with children would also be disadvantaged by a reduction in government services for the elderly. Spending time to look after elderly family members will have an adverse effect on the family's free time, their lifestyle and possibly even their work. Further, families with children will face even greater difficulties if governments withdraw subsidised child care in the name of 'small government'. Firstly, without affordable child care, at least one parent would find it hard to go to work. In some cases, the grandparent may be able to help look after the children, but if the grandparent has moved in because he or she is finding it difficult to look after themselves, this may not be possible. Secondly, the resultant loss of income will lead to loss of opportunities for the whole family, including the children.

4. In conclusion, government support is clearly essential to ensure that families have opportunities and maintain an appropriate standard of living. It would be an unfortunate situation if having young children or elderly relatives caused a financial burden. That situation is clearly best avoided. Thus, government subsidies for social services that benefit the young, elderly and others not able to look after themselves, should be preserved.

2 Essay 2 *Big government: Too much tax* on the next page is also an argument essay and was written in response to the same question as Essay 1.

[a] Read Essay 2 and the table below. While you read, notice how the purpose of each stage (explained in the table) is fulfilled in the essay.

[b] With a partner, go back and mark the stages on Essay 1.

STAGES OF ARGUMENT ESSAYS	SUB-STAGE	PURPOSE OF STAGE
Introduction Gives an overall view of the essay	General statement	To introduce the reader to the subject of the essay.
	Definition(s) (optional)	To explain any important technical words to the reader.
	Thesis	To give the opinion of the writer.
	Preview/Scope or Essay map	To tell the reader what parts of the topic will be included in the essay.
Body The main part of the essay, where evidence is presented, with support.	Arguments (in order; the most important ideas usually come first)	To explain to the reader the evidence which supports the thesis.
Conclusion To relate the argument to real-world action (No new evidence is given in the conclusion)	Summary	• To briefly remind the reader of the thesis now that the arguments have been read • To give a sense of wrapping up the essay.
	Recommendation	To tell the reader what the writer believes is the best action to take, considering the evidence in the essay.

Vocabulary

equitable (adj)	treating all people in a fair and equal way
extent (n)	how much, big, serious or important something is
incentive (n)	something that makes you want to do something or work hard
investment (n)	the use of money (such as buying houses or shares in a company) to make more money; *invest in something* (v)

Question: *Some people believe that the government should use tax revenue to provide services to assist families. Others believe that this is not the role of government. Which opinion do you agree with? Give reasons for your answer.*

Big government: Too much tax

General statement ——→

1 For the last hundred years or more, there has been a trend in many countries towards governments spending more money in ways designed not just to run the country, but to improve the lives of particular groups of people. These kinds of policies cause a

Thesis statement ——→ number of problems that are detrimental to society as a whole.

Preview/Scope ——→ This essay will demonstrate some of these problems: it will show firstly that such 'big government' policies cause an unfair tax burden on all people, not just those who benefit, and secondly that it removes incentives to work hard.

introduction

Argument 1's topic ——→

2 It is important that the taxation system is fair and equitable. This means not only that people should all pay the same amount of tax, but also that they should benefit to the same extent from

Supporting evidence for Argument 1 ——→ what the government's tax revenue is spent on. For some items of government expenditure, such as defence of the country, this isn't difficult: everyone benefits to the same extent. However, other areas are far more problematic. If child care is subsidised, for example, that means that people without children are paying for something that only benefits those who choose to have children. Similarly, subsidised services to assist the elderly would be paid for by people who don't use them. This is clearly unfair, and

Optional paragraph conclusion ——→ also means that tax becomes higher than it would be without the subsidies.

body

Argument 2's topic ——→

3 It is very important for the economy that people have a strong incentive to work hard. If life is too easy and people can be comfortable without hard work, then the economy will suffer.

One item of supporting evidence for Argument 2 ——→ For example, if people are able to send their children to child care at little or no cost, why would they work hard to earn extra money?

Optional demonstration that an opposing viewpoint has also been considered ——→ It's true that child care can free up a parent's time so that they can work and thereby contribute to the economy, but for fairness, these services should be provided by private organisations. Similarly, if

A further item of supporting evidence for Argument 2 ——→ people know that the government will look after them in their old age, they would have no incentive to work hard during their lives to ensure that they have adequate savings and investments to last them through the later years of their lives.

Summary ——→

4 To sum up, a fair approach to providing incentives to work hard will benefit society. Government subsidies to particular groups of people are unfair to people who are not members of those groups, and will also damage the incentives to work hard, leading to problems with the country's economy. It is important, therefore,

Recommendation ——→ that governments avoid such subsidies wherever possible.

conclusion

Task B | Paragraph development – Providing supporting evidence in body paragraphs

> **Structure of body paragraphs**
> You have seen from Task A that a body paragraph of an argument essay may have several stages:
> * Topic sentence (which you looked at in Unit 1)
> * Supporting evidence (there may be more than one item of supporting evidence in each paragraph)
> * Paragraph conclusion (optional).
>
> As we saw in the writing section of this unit, there are several kinds of supporting evidence, including:
> * mention of other people's ideas and research
> * logical reasoning (explanation), and
> * examples.
>
> There may also be definitions. Often writers will use a combination of these.
>
> As we saw in the Language Spotlight 1 section of this unit, items of evidence are often linked using discourse signals of *addition* and *contrast*.

❶ With a partner, decide what kind of support is used in the body paragraphs of Essay 1 and Essay 2 (pages 39 and 41).

❷ Look at these beginnings of body paragraphs, which are related to the topics of Essay 1 and Essay 2. With a partner, think of ideas that could be used to develop the paragraph.

[a] Subsidised services are essential for families with disabled members.

[b] While most old people have children who can look after them when they get old, this is not the case for everyone.

[c] Education is another area in which government support is necessary for fairness and for a country's success.

❸ Write supporting evidence to each paragraph in question 2. Remember to use discourse signals.

> **Paragraph conclusions**
> Paragraph conclusions are usually used:
>
> * where there is a sense that the paragraph needs a 'wrap-up' to make it feel complete
> * to tie together the points made in the paragraph
> * to draw a conclusion from the supporting evidence.
>
> It is is a matter of style and personal choice whether you use them; they are not essential. But, sometimes, using them can help people to follow your essays more easily.

❹ Read these two example paragraphs, which don't have summaries at the end. Could they be from the same argument essay? Why?/Why not?

Paragraph a

Governments and societies are spending more money on health care for older people than ever before. There are two main reasons for this. One is a trend that is happening across all sectors of society, not just the elderly – as medical research develops, treatments and medicines are becoming more and more expensive. The other reason is that older people are living longer. Thus, on average they fall victim to more illnesses than the previous generations, who often lived only a few years past retirement. _____

_____

_____

_____

_____

Paragraph b

Unemployment benefits are a problematic form of social welfare. They provide an income to people who are not working, thus providing a disincentive for those people to get a new job. If people have the essentials of life – enough food to eat and a roof over their head – provided for them, there is no incentive to go out and work for more money, or even to look for a job. Further, such benefits need to come from somewhere; they are paid for by higher taxes that everyone has to pay. Thus, the majority (those who work) subsidise a minority (those who are unemployed). This is clearly highly inequitable and, therefore, undesirable. _____

_____

_____

_____

_____

❺ Complete the paragraphs in question 4 by adding a summary at the end in the space provided.

❻ Add paragraph summaries to the paragraphs you wrote in questions 2 and 3.

Task C | Brainstorming ideas and planning essays

You are going to plan and write an essay on one of the topics below:

[a] Which is a better living arrangement, nuclear or extended families?

[b] It is the duty of the eldest child to look after parents.

[c] Men are just as good at looking after children as women.

[d] Divorce is always bad for children.

[e] Increasing ease of divorce threatens to destroy the traditional family unit.

[f] Family is more important than friends.

❶ For each of the topics listed above, tell a partner whether you agree or disagree with it.

❷ Choose three of these questions. With the same partner, think of as many arguments and supporting ideas for them as you can.

❸ Find a different partner. Compare and discuss your ideas. Feel free to agree with, disagree with, and question your partner.

❹ **[a]** Look at this essay plan format (below), which is just one way to write an essay plan. Have you seen this kind of plan before? Tell a partner.

[b] The essay plan on the right is for Essay 1 in Task A on page 39. It follows the same format as below. Complete it by placing the notes from the box below it in the gaps.

Essay plan format

There are many ways to write an essay plan, but this format is one that many people find useful. It is sometimes called an *outline*, especially in the US.

* Thesis
  * 1st main idea
    - 1st item of supporting evidence for 1st main idea
    - 2nd item of supporting evidence for 1st main idea
      * item of supporting evidence for 2nd supporting evidence
    - 3rd item of supporting evidence for 1st main idea
  * 2nd main idea
    - 1st item of supporting evidence for 2nd main idea
  *
  * … etc …
  *
* Recommendation in the conclusion

Brainstorming ideas with other people

Discussing the issues in an essay before you start writing can help in a few ways. It can:

* help you think of arguments and supporting ideas;
* help to make ideas clearer in your mind; and
* help in making sure that the support for your ideas is strong and logical.

Essay plan for Essay 1

Note: advs = advantages. gvt = government. 'cos = because. ⇒ = *therefore* or *leads to*

* small government, individual responsibility ⇒ social problems for elderly, families
  * problems for elderly
    - no gvt support ⇒ move in with children
      * burden on family
      * _____
      ⇒ depression, loss of sense of independence
  * problems for families with children
    - _____
    - _____
      * _____
      * _____
      ⇒ _____
* _____

Notes to go in essay plan for Essay 1

* keep government subsidies
* looking after parents: burden
* maybe 1 parent can't work
* away from friends/community
* no subsidised child care: burden
* maybe grandparent can look after children – but can't if moved in 'cos too old
* loss of opportunities for whole family

⑤ How useful were the discourse signals in the essay, in helping you with question 4? Discuss with your partner.

⑥ Write a similar plan for Essay 2 of Task A, page 41.

⑦ Plan the essay you brainstormed in questions 2 and 3.

> ✳ **Essay plans**
> An essay plan shows how the ideas in the essay are organised. Making an essay plan before you start to write will help you to:
> - organise your thoughts and thus organise your essay;
> - check that the flow of ideas is logical; and
> - write your essay quickly.

Task D | Writing an argument essay

① Write the essay that you planned in Task C question 7. Remember to:

- use the argument essay structure on page 40
- use discourse signals such as those on page 38.

Task A | Discussing the topic

① Work with a partner and answer these questions:

[a] Have you ever been the victim of crime? What happened?

[b] What are the most common crimes in the area you're from?

[c] Why do you think people commit crimes? Give as many reasons as you can.

② Look at these quotations and the vocabulary box. Which of the quotations do you agree with? Do you agree with them completely or just to some extent? Why? Explain your reasons to your partner. Try to use the words in the vocabulary box in your responses.

> *The most effective way to reduce the crime rate is to first deal with the social issues, such as poverty and income inequality, that encourage crime*

> *The only way to prevent crime is to give out harsh penalties as a deterrent*

② When you have finished, swap with a partner. Read your partner's essay and use the checklist below.

> **Argument essay checklist**
>
> ❏ Does the introduction include a clear General Statement, Thesis and Preview/Scope?
> ❏ Do the body paragraphs have clear topic sentences?
> ❏ Do the supporting ideas flow logically, with discourse signals showing the relationships between them?
> ❏ Does the conclusion have a clear Summary and Recommendation stage?

③ Discuss with your partner what you noticed about each others' essays.

④ Write a second draft of the essay, based on feedback from your partner.

> *The main causes of crime are simple: drugs and alcohol. Stop people from taking these, and crime levels will fall dramatically.*

> *We need more resources in order to reduce crime: police, TV cameras and surveillance of people*

Vocabulary

prevent (v)	stop something from happening; *prevention* (n)
harsh (adj)	very uncomfortable, cruel and unkind; *harshness* (adj)
a penalty (n)	punishment for breaking the law or for breaking a rule; *penalise* (v)
a deterrent (n)	something that makes a person not want to do something, because if they do it, problems will happen; *deter* (v)
surveillance (n)	watching people very carefully
effective (adj)	successful; working in the way that is wanted
income inequality (n)	a large gap between rich people and poor people; eg large income inequality
a rate (n)	the number of times something happens, or how fast something changes

❸ With a partner, match the words in the two columns to make likely noun-noun collocations related to the topics you talked about in questions 1 and 2.

crime	rate
prison	rate
income	penalty
crime	reduction
violent	prevention
commit	population
death	inequality
unemployment	a crime
crime	crime

Task B | Predicting during the lecture

Lecture introductions

Lectures are structured in a similar way to essays. The introduction often has three stages: General statement, Thesis and Preview/Scope.

Listening carefully to the introduction can help you understand the rest of the lecture, because you will often hear:
- some background information, which may help you understand some of the concepts
- the main opinion or points to be expressed or examined during the lecture
- the supporting points to be made during the lecture, and the way the lecture will be structured.

❶ Listen to the introduction of the lecture *The causes of crime* and complete the table by writing notes about what was said at each stage. Then compare with a partner.

CD 1
4

❷ With the same partner, speculate about what the lecturer might talk about next.

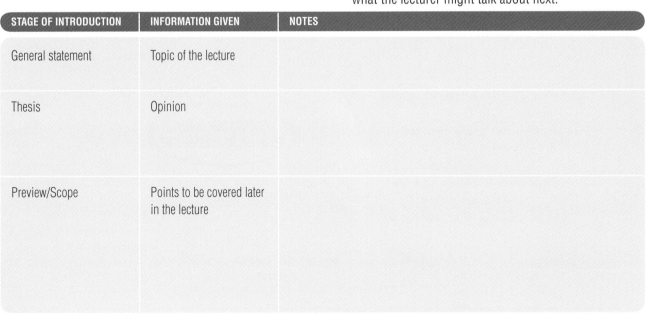

STAGE OF INTRODUCTION	INFORMATION GIVEN	NOTES
General statement	Topic of the lecture	
Thesis	Opinion	
Preview/Scope	Points to be covered later in the lecture	

Task C | Techniques for listening and note-taking

❶ You may already use some techniques for taking notes from talks and lectures in your own language. With a partner, answer these questions:

[a] Why is taking notes useful? Think of as many reasons as you can.
[b] Show each other some of the techniques you use in your own language to take notes

A. Spider diagram/mind map

[c] What techniques does your partner use that you don't?
[d] Would you like to try these techniques? Why (not)? Compare your answers with others in the class.

❷ Look at the following notes, which were taken from a lecture about the death penalty. Then, answer the questions in pairs.

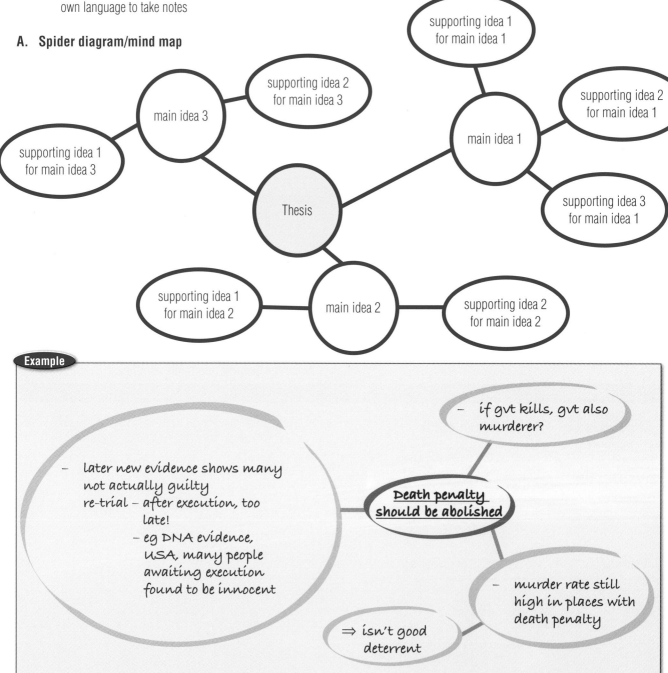

B. Linear

Thesis

- *main idea 1*
  - supporting idea 1 for main idea 1
  - supporting idea 2 for main idea 1
  - etc
- *main idea 2*
  - supporting idea 1 for main idea 2
  - supporting idea 2 for main idea 2

etc.

14th March

'Dr Bernhard'

<u>Death penalty should be abolished</u>

- later new evidence shows many not actually guilty
  re-trial – after execution, too late!
  - eg DNA evidence, USA, many people awaiting execution found to be innocent
- if gvt kills, gvt also murderer?
- murder rate still high in places with death penalty
⇒ isn't good deterrent

C. Table

	THESIS
main idea 1	supporting idea 1 of main idea 1
	supporting idea 2 of main idea 1
main idea 2	supporting idea 1 of main idea 2
	supporting idea 2 of main idea 2
etc	etc

Death penalty should be abolished

later new evidence re-trial	shows many not actually guilty – after execution, too late! – eg DNA evidence, USA, many people awaiting execution found to be innocent
gvt crime?	if gvt kills, gvt also murderer?
deterrence	murder rate still high in places with death penalty ⇒ isn't good deterrent

[a] Which of these note-taking formats have you:
- used before?
- seen before and not used?
- never seen before?

[b] Which do you think will be:
- easiest to use?
- most difficult?

[c] If the lecture is an explanation rather than an argument, which note-taking format would still be useful? Would it depend on the type of organisation within the explanation (eg chronological order)?

[d] How useful and practical do you think the ideas on the next page are? Rank them in order of usefulness and practicality by writing 1st, 2nd etc in the empty columns.

Using abbreviations and symbols such as *gvt* for *government* and *eg* for for *example*.

Marking the important points by circling them, underlining, using highlighter pens or using symbols (such as stars).

Marking points you're not sure about, or think you should read more about, on your notes during the lecture.

Looking at your notes after the lecture to make sure you understand them.

Adding information to your notes straight after the lecture, eg information you didn't get chance to write down.

Writing a short summary of your notes a short time after the lecture, eg the next day.

Task D | Using symbols and abbreviations

Below are some common abbreviations and symbols that you may see in text books or that lecturers might write on the board. You may have seen some of them before.

❶ With a partner, match the symbols and abbreviations with their meanings. Your teacher will help you with any you haven't seen before.

Common symbols

____ greater than
____ less than
____ equals, is the same as, means
____ and
____ and
____ or
____ add extra information here
____ previous idea influences or leads to the next one
____ ideas that affect each other
____ thus, therefore, so
____ therefore
____ very important point
____ is not equal, is not the same as

Common Latin abbreviations

____ for example
____ that is ..., used to explain what the previous idea means (not for examples)
____ compared with
____ important note
____ someone or something just referred to – a previous reference, namely, ...
____ and others, or all of us
____ same reference as the previous one
____ and so on, and so on

SYMBOLS			ABBREVIATIONS		
>	<	=	eg	ie	cf
+	&	/	NB	viz	et al
∧	→	↔	Ibid	etc	
∴	⇒	*			
≠					

Task E | Listening for supporting information

CD 1

❶ Listen to the whole lecture and take notes, using one of the formats in Task C above (you can choose which one). In your notes, make sure it is clear which points are main ideas and which are supporting information.

❷ Compare your notes with a partner's.

❸ Which main idea wasn't mentioned in the Preview/Scope?

❹ **Critical thinking about supporting ideas.** Work with a partner and use your notes to answer these questions.

[a] What kind of supporting evidence is used for each point i to iv below? More than one kind may have been used with each point. Choose from:
- other people's ideas and research (with references)
- other people's ideas and research (without references)
- logical reasoning (explanation)
- examples.

i. effectiveness of harsher punishment
ii. effectiveness of more police
iii. effectiveness of social programs
iv. effectiveness of dealing with the wealth divide.

[b] Does the lecturer agree or disagree about the effectiveness of each point i to iv? What reasons does the lecturer give for his opinions?

[c] The lecturer says:
- *'the British Inspectorate of Policing reported ... in 1998 and 2000, as did the National Research Council in the United States in 2004. After spending a lot of money on their research, all found little evidence that increasing the number of police on the streets had any effect.'*
- *'Well, several studies have shown that social policies are more effective at reducing crime than simply having more police.'*

Which point has stronger evidence?

[d] Comment on the strength of the evidence in the lecture for each point i to iv in [a] above.

[e] Which statement is most accurate, according to the lecturer:

   x. Harsher punishments and more police probably lead to a decease in crime.

   y. Harsher punishments and more police definitely don't lead to a decrease in crime.

   z. Harsher punishments and more police probably don't lead to a decrease in crime.

❺ Listen again and refine your answers to question 4.

CD 1

❻ Use your notes and your answers to the previous questions to write a short summary of the lecture (50 to 100 words). Include all of the points i to iii in question 3, and show clearly whether or not the lecturer agrees with them.

Task F | Discussion and personal reaction

❶ Discuss these questions in small groups.

   [a] Which of the lecturer's points do you agree with? Disagree with? Why?

   [b] Which of the ideas in the lecture had you heard about before?

   [c] Which of the ideas in the lecture get talked about in your country (for example, by your friends and family, in newspapers or on television)

   [d] Which do you think would work best in your country? Why?

   [e] After listening to the lecture, have you changed your mind about any of the points you talked about in Task A?

LANGUAGE SPOTLIGHT 2

Task A | Modality, critical thinking and the strength of evidence

❶ Look at these claims:

   • The death penalty deters people from committing serious crimes.

   • The death penalty can deter people from committing serious crimes.

   [a] Which one sounds like a stronger statement?

   [b] Which is easier to prove wrong?

   [c] Which one is more likely to be said by an academic? Why?

   [d] Which one is more likely to be said by a politician? Why?

Modality and avoiding over-generalisations

Look at this statement:

   Reducing the gap between rich and poor will lead to less crime.

It is unlikely that this statement is always true. There is always likely to be someone who doesn't follow the rule expressed by this statement.

We call statements like this *over-generalisations* – they are too general to be true. In academic English, it's important to avoid over-generalisations because they could weaken your arguments. Here are two examples showing how over-generalisation can be avoided:

   Reducing the gap between rich and poor may lead to less crime.

   Reducing the gap between rich and poor is likely to lead to less crime.

Expressions such as *may* and *is likely to* are examples of modality. Modality includes any expressions that show how certain someone is – not just modal verbs. Using modality in this way is sometimes called *hedging*. Hedging is quite common in academic English, because in academia, people have to be very careful not to make something sound like a fact when it isn't.

Apart from modal verbs, useful grammatical forms include:

• Adverbs of certainty and of frequency. For example:

   Employing more police <u>is unlikely to</u> have a large effect on crime rates.

   Often an increasing wealth gap <u>is associated with</u> a rising crime rate.

   Researchers <u>sometimes</u> find that increasing the number of police does not reduce crime.

• <u>Verbs indicating lack of certainty</u>. For example:

   Large gaps between rich and poor <u>appear</u> to be related to many social problems.

   Research <u>suggests</u> that simply employing more police doesn't work.

• <u>Expressions with 'it' + passive, adjective or adverb</u>. For example:

   <u>It is believed</u> that the death penalty is not an effective deterrent

   <u>It is rare</u> to find low crime rates and large gaps between rich and poor in the same area.

• <u>'There is' + noun phrase + 'that'</u>. For example:

   <u>There is a possibility that</u> the death penalty will be a deterrent in some cases.

• <u>Expressions of quantity</u>. For example:

   <u>Many</u> politicians say that crime levels will go down if they employ more police.

Be careful not to accidentally state that something is true unless you have very strong evidence that it really is true. Be especially careful with statements about people!

❷ [a] Complete this table with expressions of modality from the text on page 35 of this unit.

[b] Listen to the lecture again and add expressions of modality used within it.

[c] Discuss your answers with a partner, and add any other expressions that you and your partner can think of.

CD 1

EXPRESSIONS OF MODALITY			
'IT' & 'THERE IS' CONSTRUCTIONS	VERBS	ADVERBS (not in 'it' & 'there is' constructions)	QUANTITY (not in 'it' & 'there is' constructions)
'it' constructions	modal verbs	… of certainty	
	verbs for lack of certainty		
		… of frequency	
'there is' constructions			

3 With a partner, make the following bad example of academic writing better by adding modality. Use a variety of different types of modality. You may have to remove some words.

Japanese police station

Education and training solves crime. Crime is committed by younger people – those in their late teens and early twenties. Training makes people feel good about themselves and makes them feel part of society, because with training, it is easier to get a job. Areas with higher rates of unemployment have higher crime rates, so if more people get jobs, crime will fall. People with jobs have more money than the unemployed, and therefore have no incentive to obtain money from crime. Also, people who are working have less free time to become involved in crime.

4 **[a]** For two of the following discussion points, using modality where appropriate:
  • Write a statement giving an opinion.
  • Write a few supporting statements.
[b] Find a partner who has chosen one of the same discussion points. Discuss your opinion with him or her, using the statements you wrote.
[c] Cover the statements you wrote in part [a] and find another partner. Discuss the second discussion point you chose without looking at your statements.

DISCUSSION POINTS

• Should the death penalty be used? Why (not)? If so, for which crimes?
• Should it be a crime to download music and films from the internet without paying? Why (not)? If so, what would be an appropriate punishment?
• Should the police be allowed to freely check personal information on the internet, such as postings on social networking sites?
• Should the primary purpose of prisons be to punish criminals, to deter people from committing crime, or to turn prisoners into good citizens? Give support for your opinion.

5 Look again at the essay you wrote in the writing section of this unit. Check whether modality needs to be added and add it where necessary.

SPEAKING 2 ••

Task A | Signposting in talks

Signalling transitions between ideas

Lecturers often signal the stages of their lectures by using signposting expressions. These are similar to the topic sentences that are used in writing (see Unit 1), but in spoken English these transitions are often longer and more conversational in style. Often, they are whole sentences.

For example, the following expressions show that the speaker is moving to the next point:

- *Now, let's move on to …*
- *Next, we're going to look at …*

Sometimes, questions are used. The speaker will ask a question, and then answer it. The audience is not expected to answer. Questions like this are called *rhetorical questions*.

Discourse signals such as those showing contrast between ideas that we saw in this unit (page 38) can also have a similar function. For example, the following indicate that the speaker is about to talk about the opposite point to the previous one:

- *However, …*
- *Conversely …*

❶ Work with a partner. Write the signposting expressions against the function you think they best represent.

Function

Signposting expression

To indicate:
… a new main idea

_____

_____

_____

… an additional idea (similar to previous idea)

_____

… opposing idea (opposite to previous idea)

_____

_____

… an example

_____

_____

SIGNPOSTING EXPRESSIONS

As for …   *Let's look first at …*
For instance, …   *But, …*
On the contrary, …   *Similarly, …*
So, what evidence is there that … *…, such as …*

2 Work with a partner. Prepare and give very short talks to each other on any of the following topics. Use signposting expressions to signal your main ideas. Your partner will count how many times you use each function by marking in the table.

- *My family*
- *Why I want to study [name of subject you want to study]*
- *Why I want to study in/at [name of country, city or university]*
- *Why tourists should visit my home town*

SIGNPOSTING FUNCTION	TALK 1	TALK 2
… a new main idea		
… an additional idea (similar to previous idea)		
… opposing idea (opposite to previous idea)		
… an example		

Task B | Short presentations with strong supporting evidence

You are going to prepare, give and refine short talks incorporating strong supporting evidence. Follow these steps:

1 In small groups, think of as many supporting ideas as you can for each of these topics.

- *Is it better to live in an extended family or a nuclear family?* Give reasons for your opinion.
- *Should the government provide social services such as support for the elderly?* Justify your opinion.
- *Consider crime in an area you know (such as your home city or country). What, in your opinion, can be done to control it?* Argue for your position.

2 Choose one of the topics. Prepare a talk on the topic, in which you state a point of view and justify it with evidence. Remember to include these features that you looked at earlier in this unit:

- discourse signals to show addition and contrast of ideas (see page 38)
- argument genre staging (see page 40)
- strong evidence, such as examples and logical reasoning (see page 49)
- modality/avoidance of over-generalisations (see page 49)

3 Deliver your talk to another group. While listening, the other students should complete this checklist and write comments.

POINT	INCLUDED? ✓ = YES	COMMENTS
General statement introduces the topic		
Thesis is clear		
Preview/Scope clearly indicates what is coming in the body		
Each main idea is clearly signposted		
Discourse signals clearly show relationships between ideas		
Main ideas have strong, logical support		
Over-generalisations are avoided		
Conclusion includes a summary and a recommendation		

4 After all members of the group have made their presentations, discuss each. What worked well? How could you improve them? Focus on the areas in the table in question 3.

5 Refine your presentation in the light of your discussion

6 Change groups. Give your presentation to another group. While listening, take notes using one of the formats you looked at in the listening section.

7 When finished, compare notes. Which ideas were easiest for the audience to catch? Which appeared to be more difficult?

> **Presentations at university**
> When you prepare presentations at university, it's often a good idea to brainstorm and practise your presentation with other students. The feedback they give you can help you to make your presentation better.

FURTHER CONNECTIONS

Task A | Another look at supporting evidence

1 Look at the following extracts from texts and then:

[a] Underline the evidence in each.
[b] Decide which evidence is strong and which is weak. Think about your reasons.
[c] With other students, compare your answers and discuss your reasons.

[i] Another reason that women are better than men at raising children is that they are kinder. My mother was a good example. She did many kind things not only for me but also for many other people she met, including strangers.

[ii] Living costs are also increasing in the area of housing affordability. In a recent survey, 68% of people said that they found it more difficult to pay their rent or housing loan than last year.

[iii] The decline in the fertility rate is a further reason that immigration will become more and more important. According to Weston (2001), the fertility rate in this country has fallen from 3.5 live births per woman in 1961 to its lowest level ever, 1.8 babies per woman, in 1999 and 2000. This trend looks set to continue into the future. Weston (2001) also states that the minimum fertility rate necessary to sustain a population at a constant level is 2.1 births per female. Therefore, unless this trend reverses, immigration is necessary to sustain the population.

[iv] No evidence has yet been found of a direct link between this particular product and heart disease or other illnesses. Therefore, we would conclude that it is perfectly safe for people of all ages to take it.

[v] It appears for the moment that there is unlikely to be a connection between eating this product and ability to concentrate, despite the claims made by the manufacturer. Despite extensive research focused on investigating this link, such as Crumlin (1996), Detford (2000) and Gandiger-Hertzog (2002), no evidence has yet been found.

[vi] People from Govirmda can no longer be trusted. This conclusion stems from the fact that two tourists from that country were recently convicted of murder while visiting this country. Also, the Prime Minister of Govirmda has declared that he will search any fishing boats from our country if his police suspect them of carrying illegal drugs, which is obviously a ridiculous accusation. Any country that does that clearly does not respect our national sovereignty.

[vii] Despite popular myths, chocolate contains little that is bad for the skin. The Confederation of Chocolate Product Manufacturers report of 2002 states that 'Our research demonstrates there is no direct link between chocolate consumption and teenage acne' (page 35).

[d] What traps should you avoid? Add to this list.

- *over-generalisation* _____
- _____

- _____
- _____

Task B | Using two-stage correction codes

❶ With a partner, discuss this point:

- Do you remember something better if:
  [a] someone tells you something
  [b] you discover something for yourself?

❷ A teacher has added the two-stage correction symbols to the piece of student writing below. Using the codes to guide you, make the corrections. Then, compare your answers with a partner.

How two-stage correction works

When marking your written work, your teacher may use correction codes for mistakes that he/she thinks you can correct yourself. This is because people usually learn better when they work out something for themselves, rather than just being told the answer. A set of codes is shown in Appendix A of this book, or your teacher may use other codes.

Your teacher might put the codes where the mistakes are, or in the margin on the same line as the mistake – or a combination of these.

The codes are designed to help you learn. After making the corrections using the codes, you can check your corrections with your teacher.

	A common crime-reduction technique is to use CCTV (Closed-circuit
	television) in public places to watch people. In some cases, such as
T	shops, the CCTV images might have been watched by security guards. In
O, T	other case, such as CCTV in the street, the pictures might have been
	recorded. Then, if a crime takes place, police can look at the recording
s	later. CCTV is very controversial, because people are conserned about
↑	their privacy. Example, some people might be worried that their boss
p, c	or their wife might see where they go this concern is especially strong
#	in the UK, where there is said to be more CCTV cameras per person than
ref, #	anywhere else in the world. However, there is usually strong laws to
ps, //	prevention the recordings from getting into the wrong hands. One reason
	against using CCTV cameras is that they do not actually seem to make
reg	much difference to crime. In fact, there is loads of evidence that CCTV
ps	does not deterrence criminals from committing crime, and in Glasgow,
[ ]	Scotland, the amount of the crime actually increased after cameras were
ref, /	installed. And in 2008, a report by policeforces in the UK found that
↑	very few crimes were solved using CCTV, and that the number cameras
ref	made little difference to the number of crimes solved.

Task C | Collocations

❶ At the beginning of this unit, you were asked to make a list of the collocations you noticed as you worked through these units.

[a] Compare and discuss your lists with another student

[b] Add to your list any collocations on your partner's list that aren't on your list

[c] Repeat [a] and [b] with another partner.

Task D | Business connections

❶ Discuss and/or write about one or more of the following topics:

- Can large companies benefit from looking after the welfare of their workers?
- Some companies have family-friendly policies, such as maternity/paternity leave, to encourage the best workers to stay with the company. Others say that such services are expensive and do not help the company. What is your opinion on this matter? Give reasons for your answer.
- More and more services provided by the government, such as entrances to buildings and stations, are being re-designed to make them more accessible to the disabled. Do you believe the money spent on this is money well spent? Justify your point of view.

GET READY FOR UNIT 3: SCIENCE, TECHNOLOGY AND MEDICINE

Read the following articles to help you get ready for Unit 3:

- <http://en.wikipedia.org/wiki/Fundamental_science>
- <http://en.wikipedia.org/wiki/Applied_science>

While you are reading these articles, think about:

- What is the difference between pure science and applied science?
- Which do you think is more useful to society?

You may want to make notes of some vocabulary from these readings.

Be prepared to share your answers next time you meet in class.

3

SCIENCE, TECHNOLOGY AND MEDICINE

'Say not, "I have found the truth," but rather, "I have found a truth".'

Kahlil Gibran

In this unit, you will look at several aspects of science, technology and medicine, including issues such as childhood obesity. You will have a further look at the style and purpose of written texts, and further practise the reading skills learned earlier in this book. You will have the opportunity to extend the range of discourse signals that you use. Discussion essays (essays giving more than one point of view) are introduced, and there is a focus on writing conclusion paragraphs. Note-taking in this unit focuses on the transitions between ideas, and after that you will practise tutorial discussions in which you suggest ideas, accept and reject others' ideas. You will also learn a technique to help you remember anything more effectively.

BY THE END OF THIS UNIT, YOU SHOULD:

SKILL	TASK	PAGE
have gained confidence in discussing issues around science, technology and medicine	**Speaking 1** *Task A*	60–61
	Listening & Note-taking	
	Task A	73–74
	Task E	78–79
be able to follow the stages of a written text	**Reading & Critical Thinking** Reading 1 *Task A*	61–63
have developed awareness of the relationship between style and purpose in academic and semi-academic written texts	**Reading & Critical Thinking** Reading 1 *Task B*	63–64
have practised identifying main ideas	**Reading & Critical Thinking** Reading 2 *Task A*	64–66
be able to use a range of discourse signals for deduction, example and summation	**Language Spotlight 1** *Task A*	66–68
understand the structure of a discussion essay	**Writing** *Task A*	68–69
have developed awareness of lexical cohesion and how to achieve it through the use of synonyms	**Writing** *Task B*	69–71
be able to write clear, well-staged conclusion paragraphs	**Writing** *Task C*	71–72
be able to write a discussion essay	**Writing** *Task D*	72–73
be able to understand and express orally some common mathematics	**Listening & Note-taking** *Task B*	75
have practised recognising transitions between ideas in lectures	**Listening & Note-taking** *Task C*	75–76
have practised note-taking from discussions and choosing appropriate templates for this	**Listening & Note-taking** *Task D*	77–78
have gained confidence in using definite articles	**Language Spotlight 2** *Tasks A, B*	79–80
have developed skills at interrupting as well as suggesting, accepting and rejecting ideas in tutorial-style discussions	**Speaking 2** *Tasks A, B*	80–81
be able to choose whether to answer an essay question with explanation, argument or discussion genre	**Further Connections** *Task A*	81–82
have learned how to plan your own revision for optimum learning	**Further Connections** *Task B*	82

Task A | Discussing science, technology and medicine

❶ Work with a partner. Choose an item of technology that has had a big impact on your life. Answer these questions:

- What would your life be like without it?
- How has it improved your life? What positive effect has it had on society? On companies?
- What disadvantages or negative effects has it had for you? What negative impacts has it had on society?

❷ With a partner:

[a] Write the examples next to the appropriate category in the bubbles (some examples may match more than one category).

[b] Add other examples for each concept. Which pair can think of the most examples?

Vocabulary

pure (adj)	focused on increasing knowledge, rather than using knowledge for practical purposes
applied (adj)	used for practical purposes; *application* (n)
an invention (n)	making an new thing for the first time; *invent* (v); *inventor* (n-person)
a discovery (n)	finding or understand something for the first time; *discover* (v)
astronomy (n)	research into the stars, etc; *astronomer* (n-person)
gravity (n)	the force that makes things fall to the ground; *gravitational* (adj)
nanotechnology (n)	the development of very small machines, up to about 100 nanometres in size; there are a million nanometres in a millimetre
a planet (n)	a large, natural object, such as Earth, which goes around a star
genetics (adj)	the study of the parts of a living thing's cells, containing DNA, that control what the living thing looks like, does, etc; *gene* (n); *genetic* (adj)

science   vs   technology

pure science   vs   applied science

invention   vs   discovery

EXAMPLES

- astronomy
- electric cars
- genetics
- gravity
- heart transplants
- mobile phones

- nanotechnology
- research into curing genetic disorders
- space travel
- planets that go around other stars

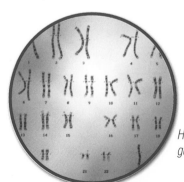

Human chromosomes: genetic material

3 Look at the statements below and decide what your opinions are about them. Take three minutes to prepare your thoughts. Then, explain your opinions to your partner, giving your reasons. Feel free to agree, disagree and/or question your partner.

> We should be grateful to scientists – the technology provided by their insights and discoveries is the reason for the high standard of living that we have now.

> We don't need to worry too much about things like environmental problems … if the need to solve a problem is great enough, scientists will manage to solve it.

> New developments in science often cause more problems than they solve

> There are some areas that should be off-limits to scientific research, such as research involving human embryos or weapons of mass destruction.

> It's better to spend money on solving major problems like shortage of food than on useless things like space travel.

READING & CRITICAL THINKING

READING 1

Task A | Following the stages of a written text

'Moves' within a text

Texts generally consist of 'moves', which are sections of text which have a particular purpose. Together, the sequence of moves achieves the overall purpose of the text, such as explaining a natural process or arguing for a particular opinion.

For example, the moves in the argument essays you looked at in Unit 2 are:

- Introduction, including thesis
- Arguments for the thesis
- Conclusion

Each move might be one paragraph, or several paragraphs.

When reading a text for the first time, it can help to think about the moves. This is like skimming; you do not need to read every word, and focusing on headings and topic sentences can help.

Exam tip

When you first see a text, try to quickly get a 'map' of the text in your mind – that is, a map of where the moves are. Then, when you look at the questions, you will be able to quickly go to the part of the text that most likely has the answer.

1 **Introduction to the topic.** Discuss these questions with a partner:

[a] List as many fields of science as you can. Use a dictionary to check meanings if necessary.

[b] For each, list one of the benefits that it provides to society.

[c] Do you think that some scientific fields are more useful to society than others? Which ones have the greatest benefit? Justify your answers.

2 The text you will read on the next page is a section of the introduction to an undergraduate textbook about physics. Read the text *Pure scientific research is inspiring!* and write 1, 2, 3 etc next to the moves to show the correct order.

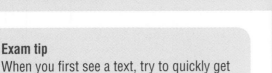

Pure scientific research is inspiring!

Modern technology is an essential part of the lives of most of us. Imagine trying to live in the modern world without mobile phones, computers that allow access to social networking sites on the internet, and GPS satellite technology. But what is behind all of this? What science are these products based on? In answer to these questions, we will see that research in the pure sciences, including physics, was essential to all of this technology. It is clear that without research in the pure sciences, none of this technology would have been possible. We will also see that natural human curiosity, not commercial gain or the provision of a solution to an immediate problem, was most likely the main incentive.

Before we look in detail at that, though, we need to look at what pure scientific research is, and how it is different from applied science. Pure science is sometimes known as *fundamental science* or *basic science*. It concerns research about the basic principles of science, and aims to contribute to our knowledge of how the universe works and how the natural world around us functions. When scientists conduct fundamental research, they are not thinking of a use for the research; they are doing it purely to increase human knowledge. Fundamental research is usually carried out in universities; as we shall see, private companies are usually not interested in paying for it, though they do use the results. Most of the research carried out or funded by companies is applied research.

Applied science, on the other hand, has a practical aim. While it may increase human knowledge, this is not the applied researchers' main aim. Companies often fund applied research, because it can lead to new products that they can sell; companies can gain a competitive advantage through research. Many governments are also happier to pay for applied research than fundamental research. Usually the results come quite quickly. They are usually quite concrete and it is easy to see the benefit of them. For these reasons, it is easier to communicate to the taxpayers that there was a useful result from the tax money that was spent.

Thus, except for some major projects, pure research is often poorly funded in comparison with applied research. Also, when you read about science in the newspapers or hear about it on television, it is often applied research that you hear about. It is simply easier to explain applied research, and members of the public often relate to it better because it often solves everyday problems, such as curing illnesses or enabling smaller, more powerful and more efficient machines.

But, there are several reasons why fundamental research, such as pure physics research, is essential to society. One is that without pure science, there can be no applied science. All of applied science is built upon principles found through pure science. Let's look at one example to illustrate this. For this, we will need to go back to the beginning of the twentieth century. At that time, an unknown office worker in Switzerland, who had failed to get a university teaching job, started to write academic papers in his free time and get them published. This culminated in 1905 with the publication of four startling papers that were,

eventually, to turn the world of physics upside-down. This person was, of course, Albert Einstein. His work, together with that of several other theoretical physicists including Max Planck, Niels Bohr, Erwin Schrödinger, Max Born and Werner Heisenberg, led to the development of what became known as quantum mechanics. All of these people were working on science only for the sake of science; they were not trying to build a better machine or to make money for a company. However, just one of the many consequences of this research was an understanding of how semiconductors work, and that knowledge is at the centre of transistors and microchips, which are at the heart of every electronic device. Without quantum mechanics, there would be no internet, no mobile phones and no computers.

Thus, pure scientific research is clearly of great importance to society. Without it, other areas of science would be uninformed and unable to progress quickly. There is, however, often a very long lead-in time between discoveries in pure science and their application. In the above example, it was not until many years later that researchers could begin to verify quantum mechanics experimentally, and twenty years until it because widely accepted in the scientific community. Further, the application that we mentioned above, the transistor, was not put into commercial production until 1954. Just as the benefits of quantum mechanics to our everyday lives would not have been predicted in the early days, the benefits of current basic research cannot be predicted, but they may well lead to enormous benefits.

Investment in pure scientific research can also have further benefits. It can be important for a country's prestige and for national pride, in the same way as sporting and artistic achievements.

But there is also a much stronger reason for pure scientific research. This is simply to satisfy natural human curiosity. It is impossible to be sure of Einstein's motivation for undertaking research in his own time, but it is highly likely that pure curiosity was a very powerful reason. And it is often curiosity which drives other scientists to pursue their careers. Many people find it far more motivating to discover the fundamental truths of the universe than to have the commercial gain of an employer as their incentive.

Thus, we see that despite the lack of commercial incentives, pure science does not only lead to a very satisfying career but may also provide an extremely important contribution to society. Even if the full effects of that contribution are not felt for a long time, they can be highly significant.

MOVES

____ rebuttal of the problem or issue

____ problem or issue

____ introduction

____ definitions

____ summary of the section

____ conclusion

❸ Read the text in more detail, answering the questions. Then, discuss your answers with another student.
According to the author:

[a] What are some differences between *pure* and *applied* science? Consider:
- what the aims and purpose are
- where it is undertaken
- who pays for it
- how easy it is to explain to the public
- whether it is mentioned a lot in the media
- how long it takes for it to affect everyday life.

[b] What is the connection between Einstein's research and modern electronic devices?

[c] What are three incentives for doing fundamental research?

[d] Which of these reasons is the least powerful?

[e] What incentives are there to do applied research?

[f] Why do you think this text appears in the introduction to a textbook for physics students?

[g] Do you agree with the author's opinion regarding pure vs applied research?

[h] If you were considering a career in science, would you be more interested in pure science or applied science?

Task B | Style and purpose in the texts you read

Written style
It's important to be aware that even within academia, written style can change quite significantly from one situation to another. The example on the previous page is from a modern-style academic text book. Such books are becoming more informal in style than older books, partly to sound more fun, friendly and interesting so that people like reading them. Noticing the differences in style can provide a link from your reading to your writing. It's best not to copy the informal style of modern textbooks in your own essay writing.

❶ Work with another student.

[a] Complete the table to help you notice some of the stylistic differences between the text here and the two essays in the writing section of Unit 2, see pages 39 and 41. Tally the number of times each language point occurs in each text.

[b] Compare the introductions of the essays and the text book, above. Which one do you think tries harder to make the reader interested to read further?

LANGUAGE POINT	ESSAYS IN UNIT 2'S WRITING SECTION	PURE SCIENTIFIC RESEARCH ESSAY
Use of personal pronouns, such as *we* and *us*		
Use of coordinating conjunctions (*and*, *but*, *so*) at the beginning of sentences		
Emotional adjectives such as *startling*		
Asking questions of the reader		

The purpose of introductions in academic texts
In non-academic writing, one purpose of the introduction is often to encourage the reader to read further. To achieve this, the author will try to make the introduction interesting, lively and relevant to the reader's life.

Some textbooks that you may read in an undergraduate course may also try to achieve the same purpose. However, this is not the case in every text and every academic discipline; some disciplines give more importance to an interesting style of writing than others.

Introductions also let the reader know the main ideas of the text, as we saw in Units 1 and 2.

Carina nebula

❷ Write an argument essay to argue for or against one of the following points:

- *Pure scientific research should receive greater funding.*
- *Business is the best source of funding for scientific research; profit provides a powerful incentive to ensure that the money is well spent.*
- *Applied scientific research should receive more funding than pure scientific research.*

You may use ideas from the reading, but you should use your own words. Do not quote directly from it. It is suggested that you follow this process:

- Choose a thesis and plan your essay, referring freely to the *Pure scientific research is inspiring!* text on page 62.
- Close your book so that you cannot see the text, and write the essay following your plan.
- Swap your first draft with another student and discuss it. Does it have all the features of an argument essay listed in the checklist on page 40, Unit 2? Look back at the text at this stage if you like.
- Prepare a second draft in light of your discussion.

READING 2

Task A | Identifying main ideas

❶ With a partner, discuss these questions:

[a] What kinds of food (crops) are grown in your country?
[b] How are they planted? Harvested?
[c] Has planting and harvesting always been done this way?
[d] If there has been a change, what advantages of the change can you think of? What disadvantages? If there hasn't been a change, what changes might occur in the future? What advantages and disadvantages would this change bring?

❷ Read the student essay *The mechanisation of agriculture and its effect on quality of life.*

[a] What is the main issue?
[b] Does it look at one side or two sides of the issue?

❸ With another student:

[a] Put these moves in the order they occur in the essay by writing 1, 2, 3 or 4 before each.

.... advantages

.... disadvantages

.... conclusion

.... introduction

Mechanised agriculture

Vocabulary

mechanisation (n)	changing to make use of machines, instead of doing things by hand; *mechanise* (v)
extensive (adj)	used a lot
output (n)	the things that are made; *output* (v)
phenomenal (adj)	surprisingly more than expected, impressive
contribute (v)	assist or help; *contribution* (n)
a proponent	person who supports the idea mentioned (n-people)
inevitably (adv)	certain to happen; *inevitable* (adj)
a habitat (n)	the trees, plants, rivers etc where a particular animal usually lives
facing (adj)	if you are facing something, it will happen to you soon in the future; *face* (v)
extinction (n)	when a particular type of plant or animal dies out completely and there are none left; *extinct* (adj); *become extinct* (collocation)
unsound (adj)	bad or negative

The mechanisation of agriculture and its effect on quality of life

1. Major developments have taken place in agriculture during the last century, one of the most important of which has been the introduction and extensive use of machinery. This has had great effects on the environment and on the lives of millions of people around the world. For the purposes of this essay, we will take the mechanisation of agriculture to mean the use of any device that is powered by anything other than humans or animals, on a farm. Careful consideration of some of the effects of agricultural mechanisation, both positive and negative, is essential for any country currently experiencing an increase in the use of such machines.

2. The vast increase in agricultural output that has been made possible by more use of mechanisation is probably the most important positive effect of this process. The speed of planting crops, spreading fertilisers and pesticides, and harvesting, is phenomenal. All three of these processes contribute to equally enormous increases in food production. Mechanisation has improved production and has helped to feed the increasing world population.

3. Increased use of farm machinery has also generally led to a decrease in costs. This may seem surprising when the high price of initial purchase of equipment is considered (this may be tens of thousands of dollars for a tractor, or hundreds of thousands of dollars for a large piece of equipment like a combine harvester). However, a tractor enables one person to perform so much more work that the extra profit, made from having more crop to sell, more than covers the purchase and running costs of the machine. Through similar savings using other pieces of equipment, costs per hectare of food production have fallen significantly.

4. Despite these highly positive results of mechanisation, there are also several negative factors that aren't always considered by the proponents of this process. One of the most important of these is employment. As in all other fields of life, the increasing use of machines inevitably results in the same work being done by fewer people. It can be argued that some positions are created in designing and maintaining the machines, but almost always more jobs are lost than created, and in addition the people whose jobs are lost often do not have the skills to undertake the newly created jobs. Therefore many jobs have to go, leading to a variety of social problems in rural communities.

5. One of these problems is that the unemployed of the countryside have to go elsewhere to find work – the obvious places to look are the larger cities, where further problems occur. Thus the increasing use of machinery leads to an explosion in the urban population. In many countries, the people moving to the cities are often poor. This causes problems of sub-standard housing, transport problems and urban poverty, as there are not necessarily more jobs available in the city than there were in the countryside. Also, the movement of people to the cities often means that families are split up, and villages which were once strong communities become too small to support essential services such as post offices and public transport. This leads to the irreversible break-up of these communities as people move to the cities.

6. In addition, the use of machinery on farms contributes to environmental destruction. Machines allow larger areas to be cultivated, thus leading to loss of the habitat in which wildlife lives. For example, in England, the increasing use of machines has made it easy for farmers to remove the hedges that used to separate fields. Thus many species of butterfly are now facing extinction because they have nowhere to live and breed. In Australia, over-use of the land by machines has resulted in many farms becoming like deserts.

7. Furthermore, the energy that agricultural machines use is mostly produced from the burning of diesel, which causes pollution as well as adding to global warming. Electricity that is sometimes used to power farm machinery is also usually produced in environmentally unsound ways.

8. In summary, there are many disadvantages to the mechanisation of agriculture as well as advantages. With the increasing population of the world, most governments consider that expanding mechanisation is the only way to feed the additional hungry mouths. However, it would be sensible for governments to take steps to minimise the disadvantages of this process. Developed countries experienced these disadvantages some time ago, and while many of them have been overcome, a significant number of mistakes were made. It would be wise for countries currently undergoing mechanisation to study these mistakes carefully and to avoid making the same ones themselves.

[b] Summarise the main ideas of the essay by completing the table. Then, compare and discuss your answer with another student.

ADVANTAGES	DISADVANTAGES

4 Discuss with another student:

[a] What was the most surprising point from this essay?

[b] Which are stronger, the advantages or disadvantage?

[c] What is more important, the number or the strength of the items of supporting evidence?

LANGUAGE SPOTLIGHT 1

Task A | Cohesion through discourse signals of deduction, example and summation

> **Cohesion**
>
> Cohesion within a text means that the text makes sense. A text with good cohesion is sensible, not nonsense. Cohesion comes about in a text through choice of vocabulary or grammar. One way of providing cohesion is to refer to the same idea using different words (see previous section). Another way is to use discourse markers. We looked at time sequence discourse markers in Unit 1, page 15 and discourse markers of addition and contrast in Unit 2, page 38. You'll look at cause and effect discourse markers on page 111 and at another way of providing cohesion, using pronouns, in Unit 4, page 115.

1 Function. In the table below, place the words (discourse signals) under their correct function. The first line has been done for you.

Discourse signals

in summary	whereas	~~therefore~~
on the other hand	however	on the contrary
thus	in addition	additionally
such as	…not only…but also	in conclusion
though	~~to summarise~~	moreover
~~and~~	~~but~~	~~for example~~

ADD INFORMATION	CONTRAST	SUMMARISE/CONCLUDE	REASON/RESULT/ CAUSE/EFFECT	GIVE EXAMPLES
and	but	to summarise	therefore	for example

❷ [a] Return to the texts *The mechanisation of agriculture and its effect on the quality of life* at page 65 and *Pure scientific research is inspiring!* in the reading section at page 62. Mark every discourse signal you can find. Add them to the table in question 1.

[b] Look also at other texts that you have read. Add discourse signals from those to the table.

❸ [a] Look at the following two examples. What is the difference between them?

- Mechanisation can help to feed additional hungry mouths. However, it would be sensible to minimise the disadvantages in this process.

- Mechanisation can help to feed additional hungry mouths, but it would be sensible to minimise the disadvantages in this process.

[b] Complete the table below to show how these discourse signals are used in the texts in which you found them in question 2. The same word can go in more than one column.

Sentence starter words and sentence joiner words
'However' contrasts ideas in different sentences, compared with 'but' which contrasts ideas in the same sentence. In formal, written English, the following are considered incorrect (though they are OK in informal situations).

- Mechanisation can help to feed additional hungry mouths, however, it would be sensible to minimise the disadvantages in this process.
- Mechanisation can help to feed additional hungry mouths. But it would be sensible to minimise the disadvantages in this process.

In other words, if you use 'however', you need a new sentence.

This rule also applies to other discourse signals. In addition, some discourse markers can only be used with noun groups.

CONNECT IDEAS IN DIFFERENT SENTENCES (FOLLOWED BY A CLAUSE)	CONNECT IDEAS IN THE SAME SENTENCE (FOLLOWED BY A CLAUSE)	CONNECT IDEAS IN THE SAME SENTENCE (FOLLOWED BY A NOUN GROUP)
addition In addition, ...	... and ...	..., as well as ...
contrast		
summary		
reason/result/cause/effect		
example		

Please turn the page for a practice activity

❹ Put appropriate discourse signals in the gaps below. Use the punctuation around the gaps and the table on the previous page to help you. Then, compare your answers with a partner's.

[a] There are two reasons for supporting pure scientific research. Firstly, it satisfies humans' natural curiosity about the universe in which they live. … Secondly, technological advances that followed on from pure scientific research have led to improvements in our lives. _____, the non-stick coating on saucepans has made washing the dishes so much easier. _____, improved aeroplane materials have made flying faster, quieter and cheaper. _____, we should be grateful for pure scientific research.

[b] Exploration of space has resulted in improved understanding about weather systems on other planets and moons in our solar system. _____, we have an improved understanding of the Earth's weather systems _____ the consequences of future changes such as global warming.

[c] Scientific advances can easily cause problems. _____, nuclear energy sounded wonderful when it was first developed, _____ of its expected low cost _____ lack of pollution. Safety was a concern and was taken seriously _____ careful precautions were usually taken, and in most cases these did actually result in a low chance of an accident. _____, nothing is perfect, including safety systems, and when problems do happen, the consequences are extremely serious. _____, although actual operation of a nuclear reactor produces little visible pollution, disposal of the radioactive materials that are produced is extremely difficult and expensive, _____ consequently nuclear power is now considered too expensive in many countries. _____, many governments have stopped planning to build more nuclear reactors. This example clearly shows that the miracle of yesterday may become the disaster of tomorrow. Not every scientific advance has the expected result.

WRITING ••

Task A | Stages in a discussion essay

❶ Look at the stages and purposes of each stage of a discussion essay. What are the differences between discussion essays and argument essays (introduced in Unit 2)? Discuss with a partner.

STAGES OF DISCUSSION ESSAYS		PURPOSE OF STAGE
Introduction Gives an overall view of the essay	General statement	To introduce the reader to the subject of the essay.
	Definition(s) (optional)	To explain any important technical words to the reader.
	Issue	To give the opinion that will be discussed in the essay.
	Preview/Scope or Essay map	To tell the reader what parts of the topic will be included in the essay.
Body The main part of the essay, where evidence is presented, with support.	Arguments for	To explain to the reader the evidence for the positive side of the issue, with support. The most important ideas usually come first.
	Arguments against	To explain to the reader the evidence for the negative side of the issue, with support. The most important ideas usually come first.
Conclusion To relate the issue to real-world action (No new evidence is given in the conclusion)	Summary	To briefly remind the reader of the main ideas, while restating the issue. Sometimes also says which side the writer believes has the strongest evidence.
	Recommendation	To tell the reader what the writer believes is the best action to take, considering the evidence in the essay.

Note: Sometimes there may be more than two points of view to an issue. In that case, the body paragraphs will describe as many points of view as necessary.

② Read the example of a discussion essay on the next page. It has been divided into the stages as an example. Notice how each marked stage achieves its purpose.

 It is a good idea to keep this model of a discussion. Every time you write a discussion essay, either here, at college or at university, use it to make sure you have included all stages.

Wheat seeds

③ With a partner, draw a box around (or colour) the stages of the introduction, body and conclusion within the *Mechanisation of Agriculture* essay on page 65. Use the marked up essay titled *Genetically modified foods* to help you.

 Discussion essays
Discussion essays consider different points of view around an opinion. For example, they could look at:
• the advantages and disadvantages of a choice of action; or
• the evidence for and against a particular opinion.

Task B | Lexical cohesion and avoiding repetition

Lexical cohesion
We have seen in Language Spotlight 1 how cohesion can be achieved through the use of discourse signals. We noted there that choice of words can also help cohesion. This involves using synonyms (words that have the same meaning as each other). For example:

Agricultural production is extremely important to human survival. … Farming has developed very quickly in line with the rate of population increase.

Agricultural production and *Farming* both have the same meaning. By using different words and expressions with the same meaning, the writer can make the ideas feel as though they are joined together. This is called ***lexical cohesion***.
Furthermore, repeated words in essays can make an essay boring to read. Using synonyms can also help to avoid this problem.
You can use a thesaurus to find synonyms.

❶ Look at the essay *The mechanisation of agriculture* on page 65. Use the paragraph numbers given in the table below to find in the essay the synonyms of the words given. The first one has been done for you. Each answer may consist of more than one word.

WORD OR EXPRESSION	PARAGRAPH NUMBER	SYNONYM
agricultural output	2	*food production*
costs	3	
tractor	3	
work	4	

Genetically modified foods

General statement → 1 Whether or not to allow genetically modified food is a very controversial issue. A considerable amount of money has been spent on research into altering the genes of cereals, fruit and vegetables in such a way that larger harvests can be obtained.

Issue → If this research continues, the whole field of food production will change radically.

Definition → Foods that contain genetically altered ingredients are commonly called GM food, short for genetically modified food. This means that genes from plants or animals are taken and joined with other genes from a different plant in order to change or alter the original plant.

Preview/Scope → This essay explores some of the issues surrounding GM food and considers arguments from both the food companies and groups opposed to those companies.

2 On one side of the discussion are the food companies who say that using GM crops will mean that the food in supermarkets will be of a higher quality and cheaper. On the other side of the discussion are various groups who oppose the food companies because they are very worried about the dangers of introducing manufactured crops into the environment before there has been adequate time for full-scale testing. They are also worried about the livelihoods of farmers who are becoming more closely controlled by these multinational organisations.

'For' statement 1 → 3 The aim of modifying the genetic structure of food crops is to enable more food to be collected from the same area of land. This can be achieved by making the plants more resistant to pests and disease, and

Supporting evidence for 'For' statement 1 → by increasing their yields. The first point means that fewer plants are damaged, thus increasing the quality of the produce. Also, increases in yields mean that there is more produce from which to select, resulting in higher quality food being available to the consumer.

'For' statement 2 → 4 The food companies claim that the increases mentioned above will lead to food prices falling. This applies not only to produce that is sold unprocessed, but also to the ingredients in a wide variety of food on sale

Supporting evidence for 'For' statement 2 → in the supermarket. If the ingredients can be produced more cheaply, this will result in a fall in the price of the foods that contain them.

5

Transition sentence, linking 'for' to 'against' ideas →

However, these claims are questioned by environmental and consumer groups. These groups are concerned about the long-term effects of GM food, which are only slightly understood. Experience over the last century has shown that changes in agriculture sometimes lead to dramatic effects on the environment.

'Against' statement 1 →

Supporting evidence for 'against' statement 1 →

For example, introducing a new crop has often caused one kind of insect, which feeds on that crop, to become much more common than before. If this insect is one that carries a dangerous disease, the effect could be horrific. The environment is such a complicated system that it is very difficult to determine the effect of any changes that are made. The food companies assert that all foods have been thoroughly tested to find out the effects on the environment of growing them, before they are allowed into shops, whereas environmental groups claim that the testing has not been thorough enough.

Another relevant fact →

Consumer groups are concerned about the fact that there is often no way for the ordinary person to know whether the food they are buying contains GM foods. There are moves to introduce labelling of GM foods so that in the future consumers will know.

'Against' statement 2 →

6

Farmers are also affected by GM foods.

Supporting evidence for 'against' statement 2 →

Seeds produced by GM plants are often non-fertile – that is, they will not grow. Therefore, farmers cannot simply take seeds from last year's crops to plant for the next year. Instead, they have to buy the seeds every year from the company. Because the company has the patent on the seeds, the farmer can buy from only one company. Therefore, the company can charge any price they want. This means that the farmer has to pay a high price for something that before GM foods, he or she did not pay for. Farmers need to be able to make a living from farming; if they can't do this, they may have to stop growing food.

body

Summary within the conclusion →

To conclude, the use of GM food could lead to many benefits for the consumer, but it could equally well lead to major environmental disaster.

Recommendations within the conclusion →

Therefore, governments have to consider carefully all sides of the discussion, and to quickly introduce appropriate legislation to ensure the safest course of action is followed. It is to be hoped that governments will consider the long-term future of humanity as well as pressure from the food industry who may only wish to make a quick profit.

conclusion

Task C | Paragraph development – Conclusion paragraphs

Essay conclusions

As we saw in Unit 2, many essay conclusions have a summary and a conclusion stage. Also, they are often introduced with discourse markers such as *in conclusion*.

The language used in the summary stage will vary a lot, depending on the content of the essay body. However, the recommendation stage is more regular in the language used, as the language of recommendations is quite specific.

There should be no new supporting evidence in the conclusion.

In some academic disciplines, it is expected that conclusions have a strong impact. A good way to do this is to:

- show in the summary how serious the issue is; and
- make the recommendation as relevant as possible to the readers' lives.

1 Work with a partner.

[a] Write in the table some ways of beginning conclusions, and ways of expressing recommendations, that you already know.

[b] Look at the essays in the reading and writing sections of this unit and of Unit 2. Add to the table the discourse signals which introduce the conclusion, and the language used to express recommendations (there is sometimes more than one in each conclusion).

USEFUL EXPRESSIONS: BEGINNING CONCLUSIONS	USEFUL EXPRESSIONS: GIVING RECOMMENDATIONS IN WRITTEN CONCLUSIONS
_____	_____
_____	_____
_____	_____
_____	_____
_____	_____
_____	_____
_____	_____

2 Look at these essay outlines. Then, write conclusions for each.

[a] **Issue/thesis:** more attention should be given to science teaching in schools
- **Points for:** economy will benefit from well-trained technical experts science helps keep people's minds sharp
- **Points against:** training teachers will be expensive school curriculum already has many demands on it; not much time left in most schools' timetables

[b] **Issue/thesis:** governments should invest in technology and use it more
- **Points for:** technology will make them more efficient may save money in the long term because won't need so many staff
- **Points against:** costs money to start with; new technology often has big problems; people who use government services but who aren't confident with using technology might have problems

Task D | Writing a discussion essay

1 Below is a table that lists advantages and disadvantages of various forms of technology. In small groups, choose three or four of these developments and discuss them, adding to the ideas given.

ADVANTAGES	DEVELOPMENT	DISADVANTAGES
• Increases in production • • Decreased costs of production	Agricultural mechanisation	• Reduced employment in agriculture • Shift of population from countryside to cities • Loss of habitat for wild animals and other environmental problems
• • • Tourism	Airborne transport	• • • War
• Higher agricultural yields • Lower prices	Genetically modified food	• Unknown effect on environment • Farmers tied more tightly to food companies
• • • •	Information technology	• • • Access to advantages of technology depends on wealth
• • • •	Mass production	• Workers have lower range of skills • Lower personal involvement of workers leads to less pride in the work done. •

ADVANTAGES	DEVELOPMENT	DISADVANTAGES
• • •	Motor vehicles	• • •
• • •	Nuclear power	• • •
• • •	Television	• • •

❷ Follow these steps:

[a] Choose one of the developments from question 1 to write about.

[b] Plan a discussion essay on this topic.

[c] Write a discussion essay. Remember to:
- Follow the format on page 68
- Use a wide range of discourse signals
- Use lexical cohesion.

[d] When you have finished your first draft, swap with a partner. Read and your partner's essay and use the checklist.

[e] Discuss with your partner what you noticed about each others' essays.

[f] Write a second draft of your essay in light of your discussion at Step [d].

Discussion essay checklist

☐ Does the introduction include a clear General statement, Issue and Preview/Scope?

☐ Do the body paragraphs have clear topic sentences?

☐ Do the supporting ideas flow logically, with discourse signals showing the relationships between them?

☐ Is repetition avoided and lexical cohesion achieved?

☐ Does the conclusion have a clear summary and recommendation stage?

LISTENING & NOTE-TAKING

Task A | Introduction to the lecture topic – Teenage obesity and surgery

❶ Discuss these questions in small groups

[a] Do you consider yourself to be a healthy person? Why (not)?

[b] What do you do to stay healthy?

[c] What more could you do to be more healthy?

[d] Why do people develop unhealthy habits?

[e] Think about advertisements you've seen lately. Is advertising more likely to encourage or discourage?

[f] What can governments do to encourage healthy behaviours?

❷ With another student, look at the vocabulary lists. Put the words from the list marked with an asterisk (*) in the correct category in the table. You may want to use an adjective with at least one of the words. Then, add as many other words as you can.

INTERNAL ORGAN	HEALTH RISKS	HEALTH PROBLEMS	TREATMENT
_____	_____	_____	_____
_____	_____	_____	_____
_____	_____	_____	_____
_____	_____	_____	_____
_____	_____	_____	_____
_____	_____	_____	_____
_____	_____	_____	_____
_____	_____	_____	_____

Vocabulary

inactivity* (n)	not moving; *inactive* (adj)
junk food* (n)	food, such as hamburgers, that has very few ingredients that are good for you
lifestyle* (n)	the way that someone lives, including what they regularly do and eat
medication* (n)	medicine
obesity* (n)	being very fat and therefore unhealthy; *obese* (adj)
an operation* (n)	cutting into parts of the body to repair them; *operate* (v)
an organ (n)	a body part, usually inside you, such as your heart or brain
a risk (n)	being in a situation that increases the chances of a problem; *take a risk*; *risky* (adj); *risk* (v)
surgery* (n)	cutting into parts of the body to repair them; *surgeon* (n-person)

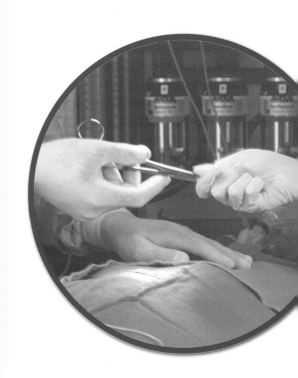

❸ In the same groups as question 1, discuss the following. Try to use the different word forms from the vocabulary box as much as possible.

[a] Rank the treatments in the table in order of your preference. Do you agree with the rest of the group?

[b] Have you ever had surgery? Or has someone you know well? What happened and why? Describe and explain it to the group in as much detail as you feel comfortable with.

[c] Do you think that people in your country have a healthy lifestyle, nowadays? Did people have a healthier lifestyle in the past? What has changed?

[d] In many parts of the world, the number of obese people is rising rapidly. What factors do you think play a role in this?

[e] Children seem to be especially affected by obesity. How can childhood obesity be prevented?

[f] What do you think might be the pros and cons of using surgery to treat obesity?

[g] Do you think surgery might be a suitable treatment for obesity in children and teenagers?

Task B | Vocabulary of mathematics

There is some maths in the lecture you will hear in this section. This task looks as some of the basic mathematical vocabulary that you might hear in almost any discipline at university.

❶ Work with a partner. Share your current knowledge by placing words and/or expressions in the gaps. Your teacher will help you with any you don't know.

[a] $3 + 7\frac{1}{2}$ = three _____ seven and _____ equals …

if you _____ three and seven and _____, you get …

[b] $3 - 7\frac{1}{3}$ = three _____ seven and _____ is …

if you _____ seven and _____ from three, the result is …

seven and _____ _____ from three is …

[c] $3 \times 7\frac{1}{4}$ = three _____ seven and _____ equals …

three _____ seven and _____ is …

[d] $12 \div .012$ = twelve _____ point oh one two equals …

twelve _____ point oh one two equals …

[e] 3^2 = three _____ is …

the _____ of three is …

[f] $\sqrt{9}$ = the _____ nine is …

[g] xy^3 = xy _____ is …

xy _____ three equals …

[h] $3\frac{1}{8}$ = three and _____

[i] $2\frac{3}{4}$ = two and _____

an eighth	a half	a quarter
a third	add	cubed
divided by	minus	multiplied by
over	plus	square
square root of	squared	subtracted from
take	three quarters	times
	to the power of	

❷ How would you say the following?

[a] $E = mc^2$ **[d]** 0.008

[b] $y = \dfrac{4a}{b}$ **[e]** $\dfrac{x}{8}$

[c] 2.68   **[f]** $f = \sqrt{2aw}$

❸ Work in pairs. Student A: turn to page 258. Student B: turn to page 261. Don't look at your partner's page. Take it in turns to read the expression on your page. The other student will write it down.

Task C | Recognising transitions between ideas in lectures

CD 1

❶ Listen to the introduction to the *Treating teenage obesity* lecture. Take notes of the stages of the lecture listed in the Preview/Scope.

❷ Compare your notes with a partner's.

Moving from one idea to the next

As we saw in Unit 2 (page 52), lecturers often use discourse signals and signalling expressions to show where each new idea starts. These often also show the relationship between ideas.

Another way to transition to the next idea is to ask a question. The next idea is the answer to the question. For example, the lecturer may say:

Hmm, OK, so what is the definition of obesity?

This question tells the audience that the next idea will be a definition of obesity. Questions such as this – questions that the lecturer asks and answers instead – are called *rhetorical questions*. The lecturer does not expect the audience to answer rhetorical questions.

Also, there is often a pause before a new idea is introduced, for the lecturer to catch his/her breath.

So, while listening, watch out for:
- signalling expressions
- discourse signals
- rhetorical questions
- relatively long pauses.

CD 1

❸ Listen to the rest of the lecture and complete the table.

TRANSITION SIGNAL	NEXT IDEA (IDEA BEING INTRODUCED)
Let's define obesity	definition of obesity

❹ With a partner, discuss this question:

[a] How well did the main ideas in the body of the lecture match those 'mapped out' in the Preview/Scope?

[b] This lecture combines two genres. Which are they?

_____

_____

_____

_____

_____

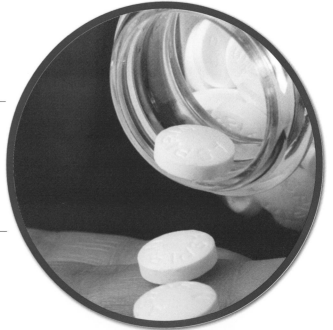

Task D | Note-taking from discussions

❶ With a partner, decide which of the following note-taking templates would be suitable for a discussion.

A. T-chart

Issue	

main idea 1 for the issue
   - supporting idea 1 for main
     idea 1 for the issue
   - supporting idea 2 for main
     idea 1 for the issue
main idea 2 for the issue
   - supporting idea 1 for main
     idea 2 for the issue
   - supporting idea 2 for main
     idea 2 for the issue
etc
	main idea 1 against the issue
	   - supporting idea 1 for main
	     idea 1 for the issue
	   - supporting idea 2 for main
	     idea 1 for the issue
	main idea 2 against the issue
	   - supporting idea 1 for main
	     idea 2 for the issue
	   - supporting idea 2 for main
	     idea 2 for the issue
	etc

B. Table

Issue	
main idea 1 for the issue	supporting idea 1 of main idea 1 for the issue supporting idea 2 of main idea 1 for the issue
main idea 2 for the issue	supporting idea 1 of main idea 2 for the issue supporting idea 2 of main idea 2 for the issue
main idea 1 against the issue	supporting idea 1 of main idea 2 against the issue supporting idea 2 of main idea 2 against the issue
main idea 2 against the issue	supporting idea 1 of main idea 2 against the issue supporting idea 2 of main idea 2 against the issue
etc	etc

C. Linear/Outline

Issue

main idea 1 for the issue
   - supporting idea 1 for main idea 1 for the issue
   - supporting idea 2 for main idea 1 for the issue
   - etc

main idea 2 for the issue
   - supporting idea 1 for main idea 2 for the issue
   - supporting idea 2 for main idea 2 for the issue

main idea 1 against the issue
   - supporting idea 1 against main idea 1 for the issue
   - supporting idea 2 against main idea 1 for the issue
   - etc

main idea 2 for the issue
   - supporting idea 1 against main idea 2 for the issue
   - supporting idea 2 against main idea 2 for the issue

etc.

Templates continued on next page

D. Spider diagram/mind map

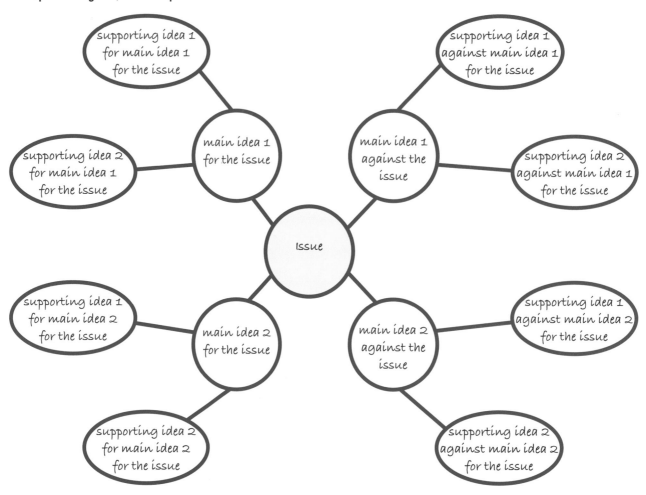

② Work with a partner. Using your answers from Task C question 4, modify the note-taking templates to fit this unit's lecture.

③ Choose one of the templates to use when you listen to the whole lecture. Then, listen to the whole lecture and take notes.

CD 1

④ Discuss your notes with a partner. Refine your notes.

⑤ Using your notes, work with a partner to answer these questions

    [a] If life expectancy is 80 years for an average female non-smoker in the 'normal' weight range, how much would it be for a female non-smoker suffering from obesity?

    [b] What is the BMI of someone 2.0 metres tall and who weighs 100 kg?

    [c] Why are lifestyle changes not the perfect treatment?

    [d] Why is the use of medication not the perfect treatment?

    [e] What is the treatment that is recommended first?

    [f] What are the three main reasons against surgery for treatment of teenage obesity?

    [g] What positive consequences of the surgery are mentioned for adults?

    [h] What positive consequences of the surgery are mentioned for teenagers?

[i] In the study involving Australian teenagers:

    i. What proportion of those who had surgery lost half or more of their excess weight?

    ii. What proportion of the lifestyle group lost half or more of their excess weight?

    iii. How much weight, on average, did the surgery group lose?

    iv. How much weight, on average, did the lifestyle group lose?

    v. What, according to the lecturer, was the most significant result of this research?

Task E | Reaction, discussion and critical thinking

① Discuss these questions in small groups.

    [a] What do you think is the most shocking point made by the lecturer? Most interesting point?

    [b] Which side of the argument, as expressed by the lecturer, do you think has the strongest arguments?

    [c] Has this lecture changed the opinions you expressed in Task A?

    [d] If you knew the parents of an obese child, what would you want them to do to help the child? Why? What would you actually say to them?

② Read this:

Another Australian researcher criticised the findings of the study. He pointed out that a third of the people who had surgery during the study had to have further surgery within the two years following their first operation. He also noted that the study was only for two years and there is, as yet, no certainly what happens five or ten years after the operation.

(Extract from interview with Associate Professor Jeff Walkley, RMIT University, Melbourne, Australia (*ABC Science Show*, 12 June)).

Does this change or reinforce your opinions in question 1?

LANGUAGE
SPOTLIGHT 2

③ Brainstorm ideas, then write a short essay, in response to the following question:

It has been said that the results of the Monash University study send the wrong message to parents and teenagers, in that they might feel that obesity has a simple solution: surgery. To what extent do you agree with this point? Give reasons for your response.

Task A | Definite articles – What does 'the' actually mean?

Articles: Testing an hypothesis
Let's develop a hypothesis by looking at some examples of what someone might say to start a new topic in a conversation.

For example, if someone starts a new topic in a conversation by saying:

*You remember **the** lecture about obesity? Well, I read something interesting about that …*

'the' is chosen before 'lecture' because both speaker and listener know which lecture is being talked about. However, if the same person says:

*I heard something really interesting yesterday. I went to **a** lecture …*

In this situation, 'a' is chosen before 'lecture' because the listener doesn't know which lecture (yet!).

From this it appears that:

• **'the' is used when both speaker and listener know which item they're talking about**

• **'the …X…' shows that we know which …X…**

Let's test this hypothesis. We'll look at some sentences from the lecture, and see if they match this hypothesis.

① For the underlined noun groups in [a] to [h], choose from the list of possible reasons why speaker and listener, or reader and writer, might know which one.

[a] The most commonly accepted definition of obesity comes from …

[b] something called the body mass index.

[c] just take your weight in kilograms and divide it by the square of your height in metres.

[d] If you're 70 kilos, then your BMI is 70 divided by 3.24, which comes to 21.6, well within the 'normal' range.

[e] So, what are the causes of obesity?

[f] While many can lose weight temporarily, only a minority of people are able keep the weight off in the long term.

[g] … surgery – something that is especially controversial for the treatment of teenagers.

[h] all sides of the discussion agree on one thing: that the first line of treatment should always be to encourage the patient to adjust their lifestyle – that is, their diet, and the amount of exercise they do.

Possible reasons why we both know which item is being referred to:

• Only one exists in the context.
• A superlative automatically specifies which one(s) you mean.
• It is referring to all that exist in the context.
• The idea was mentioned before in the text/conversation.
• The noun is defined or made more specific by the phrase that follows it.

② With a partner, discuss these questions:

[a] Does the use of 'the' in this unit's lecture fit the hypothesis?

[b] Does your answer to [a] mean that:
• the hypothesis is true;
• the hypothesis is likely to be true; or
• the hypothesis isn't true.

③ Look at the quotation by Kahlil Gibran at the beginning of this unit, which uses articles in an interesting way. With a partner:

[a] Explain what it means

[b] Discuss whether you agree with it. Do you think it holds true in some situations but not others?

Task B | Using definite articles

1 With a partner, filling in the gaps in the passage with either 'the' or Ø to indicate no article. Note that this is a whole text.

> ¹_____ modern surgery is only possible because of ²_____ relatively recent developments. ³_____ first of these was pain control – that is, anaesthesia. ⁴_____ anaesthesia was developed in ⁵_____ 1840s and led to an enormous increase in ⁶_____ type and complexity of operations that could be performed.
>
> ⁷_____ second of these developments was infection control. ⁸_____ mortality rate from operations was very high until ⁹_____ causes of infection were found. One of ¹⁰_____ first to understand how ¹¹_____ infections could be passed from ¹²_____ person to person by ¹³_____ dirty hands and equipment was ¹⁴_____ Hungarian doctor Ignaz Semmelweiss in ¹⁵_____ 1840s. However, it wasn't until ¹⁶_____ 1870s that ¹⁷_____ medical profession took ¹⁸_____ infection control seriously.
>
> ¹⁹_____ last of these three developments was ²⁰_____ control of bleeding. ²¹_____ development of blood transfusion techniques in the early 20th century enabled operations that would otherwise lead to death from loss of ²²_____ blood.

2 Form groups of three or more.

- In each group, one person should monitor and the others should discuss the questions below.
- The monitor should take note of as many things said as possible that use the definite article.
- After each discussion, discuss as a group whether the uses of the definite article were correct.
- Rotate the monitor role to another person and move on to the next discussion topic.

‹ DISCUSSION TOPICS ›

- *If you lived in the early 19th century, in what circumstances would you agree to undergo surgery? Give reasons for your response.*
- *If you had a choice between surgery and medication to deal with a medical problem, which would you choose? Why? What circumstances might influence your answer?*
- *In the future, medical treatments might be possible that will enable us to live for much longer. Is this a good thing? What would the advantages and disadvantages be?*

 SPEAKING 2 •••

Task A | Expressions for interrupting, suggesting, accepting and rejecting ideas

> **Tutorial discussions**
> At university or college, you are likely to take part in discussions. As we saw in Unit 1, these may happen during tutorials; they may even happen in lectures if the class is small. You may be given a mark for your participation in such discussions, so it is important to make a contribution.
> In these discussions, you will have to put forward your own ideas, with support. You will also have to comment on other people's ideas, with reasons. In this section, you will practise some expressions for doing this politely.

1 With a partner, write the phrases into the correct column of the table on the next page.

2 Add any others you or your partner know or can think of.

Useful expressions

Yes, but on the other hand …	*Could I just say …*
I'm afraid I disagree with that idea …	*What about the fact that …?*
I agree with you to some extent, but …	*No, I don't agree …*
Well yes, however …	*Hang on …*
My view is that …	*That may be so, but …*
Well, I think …	*How about …*
Well, you may have a point there, but …	

INTERRUPTING TO MAKE A RELEVANT POINT	SUGGESTING AN IDEA	REJECTING AN IDEA	ACCEPTING AN IDEA, BUT PUTTING YOUR OWN VIEW FORWARD
_____	_____	_____	_____
_____	_____	_____	_____
_____	_____	_____	_____
_____	_____	_____	_____
_____	_____	_____	_____
_____	_____	_____	_____
_____	_____	_____	_____

Task B | Discussion

❶ In a small group, make a list of scientific, technological or medical issues that have recently been in the news, or that you can think of for any other reason.

❷ Individually, write down your opinion about each issue, and some supporting ideas.

❸ In the same groups as for question 1, discuss these issues, trying to use as many of these expressions as possible. To encourage you to use the new expressions, do this as a game. In this, one person should be a monitor, counting how many times each person uses one of the expressions. Whoever uses the largest number is the winner. Change monitor every time you move to a new issue.

Medical issues in the South Pacific

FURTHER CONNECTIONS

Task A | Analysing questions – Which genre?

❶ Look at the essay questions in the box below. Which can be answered with an argument essay? Which can be answered with a discussion essay? Which can be answered with either? Next to each, write 'explanation', 'argument', 'discussion' or 'argument or discussion'.

[a] *It is too early to know the long-term effects of growing genetically modified (GM) food. Therefore, GM food should not be grown outside well protected laboratories. To what extent do you agree with this point of view?*

[b] *Mobile phones have brought new rules of etiquette to society. What are the rules about the use of mobile phones in your society? For example, should you switch off mobile phones before going into a cinema? What is the rationale behind these rules?*

[c] *Explain your opinion about the following statement: 'The use of animals in scientific research should be restricted to the areas of medical research which could potentially result in human life being saved.'*

[d] *Money spent on sending people into space should be diverted to other more worthwhile causes such as reducing world hunger. Discuss.*

[e] *Scientific research is an expression of humanity's natural curiosity about the universe around us. Give your reasons for your point of view about this statement.*

Vocabulary

potentially (adv)	if something could potentially happen, it's possible that it will happen. *potential* (adj, n)
worthwhile (adj)	useful, not a waste

② Choose one of the essay titles above. Follow these steps:

- Brainstorm ideas
- Plan your essay
- Write your first draft
- Review your first draft when it's finished, perhaps with a friend
- Write your second draft.

Task B | How to remember for longer

① Work through these questions and instructions with another student.

[a] When you learn something new, either on your EAP course or any other course, how much do you remember later? Draw a curved line on this graph to show how much you <u>think</u> you remember:

[b] Next, compare with the other people in the class. Are other people's graphs similar or different?

[c] Now, look at page 258 in Appendix B. This graph (Graph I) shows how most people's memory works. It is adapted from psychologist Tony Buzan's book *Use Your Head* (BBC, 1995), which is a very useful book for anyone wanting to learn how to study more effectively, and is easy to read. Discuss with your partner:

- Is there anything that surprises you about this graph?
- How similar is it to the one that you drew?

② How important is review? Discuss these points with another student.

[a] How do you think that reviewing what you have read changes the graph? Draw a new line on the graph to show what you think will happen if you review at the intervals given on the bottom axis (10 minutes, 24 hours, 1 week and 1 month)?

[b] Now, look at the graph on page 261 in Appendix B. Discuss with a partner:

- Does this graph surprise you?
- Is it different from the graph you drew?
- Can you think of any ways of overcoming the problem of forgetting what was learnt?
- How important do you think review is?

③ Planning your reviewing – Writing your own review timetable.

[a] Find a diary for this year. A small, pocket-sized one is OK. (If you are near the end of the year, you will need one for next year, too!)

[b] What were the main points, vocabulary etc that you learnt today? Write a reference to them on your year planner or diary for tomorrow, one week from now and one month from now. Do this every day that you have lessons, learn or study anything.

[c] Every time that you study, look at your diary or planner for the things you should review on the days since you last studied. If you do this regularly, you will find that it becomes much easier, and you will be amazed by how much you remember!

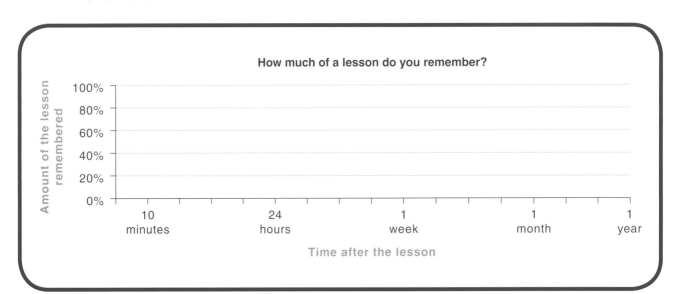

How much of a lesson do you remember?

Amount of the lesson remembered (y-axis): 0%, 20%, 40%, 60%, 80%, 100%

Time after the lesson (x-axis): 10 minutes, 24 hours, 1 week, 1 month, 1 year

GET READY FOR UNIT 4: ACADEMIC AND LITERARY ENGLISH

Read the articles found on the websites below.

*   <http://en.wikipedia.org/wiki/English_for_academic_purposes>
*   <http://en.wikipedia.org/wiki/Literary_genre>

While you are reading these articles, think about:

*   What is the definition of English for Academic Purposes?

*   What are the criteria that define literary genres? Take notes about this.

You may want to make notes of some vocabulary from these readings.

Be prepared to share your answers next time you meet.

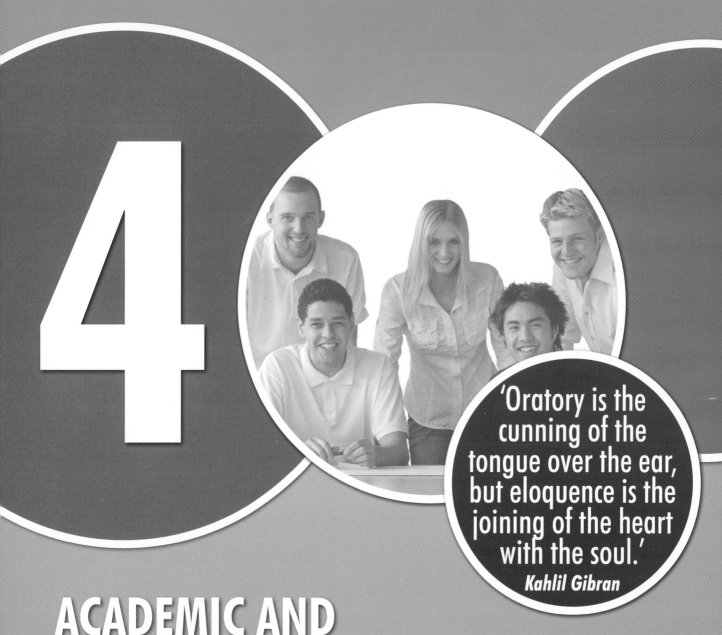

4

'Oratory is the cunning of the tongue over the ear, but eloquence is the joining of the heart with the soul.'
Kahlil Gibran

ACADEMIC AND LITERARY ENGLISH

In this unit, you will move yet closer to academic life in terms of writing, speaking, listening and reading. An authentic university essay around a business topic is your focus for reading, increasing vocabulary, and furthering your understanding of structure and methodology within higher education. Next, you listen to an authentic lecture and are assisted in interpreting every cue that focuses your listening skills. To relax a little, you will be creative in paragraph development using models and then move on to poetry, narrative and creative writing. A native speaker can recognise the different text types of crime fiction, science or a newspaper article with only language clues and a small amount of content. Can you? This unit will assist you to do that.

BY THE END OF THIS UNIT, YOU SHOULD:

SKILL	TASK	PAGE
practise polite turn-taking in English so as to enter discussions, agree or disagree, especially in tutorials	**Speaking 1** *Tasks A, B*	86–87
increase your academic vocabulary	**Reading & Critical Thinking** Reading 1 *Task A*	87–88
know how to decipher difficult vocabulary in context within an authentic university essay and study required organisation of essays	**Reading & Critical Thinking** Reading 1 *Task B*	88–92
know more about the concept of companies' strategic management practice and theory in business	**Reading & Critical Thinking** Reading 1 *Task B*	88–92
understand and use in-text referencing in your own essay writing	**Reading & Critical Thinking** Reading 1 *Task C*	92–93
approach information on the internet and evaluate it for academic credibility	**Reading & Critical Thinking** Reading 2 *Tasks A, B, C*	93–94
become familiar with different text types, their purpose and unique language features	**Reading & Critical Thinking** Reading 3 *Tasks A, B*	95–99
know how to write a paragraph using seven, different methods for development	**Language Spotlight 1** *Task A*	99–103
take notes from books	**Writing** *Task A*	104
learn and use some conventions of poetry, creative and narrative writing	**Writing** *Tasks B, C*	105–106
listen for phrases that signal important points and note-take the points	**Listening & Note-taking** *Tasks A, B* *Tasks, C, D*	107–108 108–111
know, recognise and use discourse markers of cause and effect	**Language Spotlight 2** *Task A* **Further Connections** *Task A*	111–113 115
use ellipsis and substitution, both clausal and verbal	**Language Spotlight 2** *Task B*	113
speak extemporarily	**Speaking 2** *Task A*	114–115

Like oral presentations, tutorials are an important part of university life. You will be expected to be able to initiate, add and take part in discussions around the issues that your lecturers from various faculties have presented. You also will speak with other students about your courses.

You can 'get an idea on the floor' by simply recognising when another speaker is pausing or hesitating and it is appropriate for you to begin speaking. You can also begin speaking by **agreeing or disagreeing** with a speaker, thereby making it your turn to speak. This is called 'turn-taking' and is OK in English. It is not disrespectful if you use the correct cues.

Task A | Taking turns in a conversation

In groups of five, each take a part and read the following aloud. This will give you practice in taking turns, ie 'turn-taking'. Notice some interrupting. This happens in English and is not necessarily rude.

Student 1: *You know, I've been thinking and I think that when people are speaking English, they should just speak English.*

Student 2: *What do you mean by that?*

Student 1: *I mean it annoys me to hear people using their own words in the middle of an English sentence, like words from their own country and then we don't understand it.*

Student 2: *Yes, but everyone does that and it's called world English! I mean there are a lot of things that are just better in your own language. It means more. Makes more sense.*

Student 3: *Yes, I agree with you there. Every language has words that are not really very translatable. English can't say everything in the whole world, you know.*

Student 4: *With respect, if you're talking in one language, then you have to know enough words to speak that language and not be jumping around back and forth.*

Student 5: *I disagree. I think that's utter nonsense. If you're French and have a lot more ways to talk about love,*

then why not use a lovely French word? It happens in writing all the time.

Student 3: *Exactly. I agree. Same thing with Samoans. I think they have a word that talks about where the sky meets the sea – vateoteo – the exact point, and….*

Student 1: *Isn't that the horizon?*

Student 3: *No, not exactly… It's more spiritual than that. It's part of an ancient belief and hard to say in English. So, since there's only that word – horizon –in English then I'd find…*

Student 5: *…find the best word for it in your own language, right?*

Student 3: *Yes.*

Student 1: *Yes, but what about the other people around? I mean like hanging around at the time? If they can't speak Samoan or whatever, then what?*

Student 4: *I agree. You leave people out in the talk.*

Student 3: *I disagree. People could learn something from other languages, don't you think? They could always ask!*

Student 1: *Well, you have a point there, but I think we might just have to agree to disagree on this one.*

Now, examine the table and place the turn-taking cues from the five students into the correct lines: agree or disagree
The cues are on the next page:

AGREE	DISAGREE

Yes, but...	With respect...
You have a point there...	I agree ...
I disagree...	You have a point there, but...
Yes	No

Add the following cues to the columns. Will the speaker agree with the statement made by the previous speaker or disagree?

Hang on a minute ...	What makes you think that?
Certainly ...	We'll have to agree to disagree...
Certainly, but...	Why not look at it like this?
You have a point there...	Well, you have a point there, but...

Task B | Agreeing and disagreeing

In pairs choose one of the following four issues and agree or disagree.

Use the turn-taking cues that you have learned in Task A.

Your teacher will brainstorm ideas for arguing a case for or against.

Issue 1: *It is best for women to stay at home and mind children, not work.*

Issue 2: *There should be one religion in the world.*

Issue 3: *Restaurants should stay open 24 hours a day.*

Issue 4: *Police corruption should be investigated by the police themselves.*

READING & CRITICAL THINKING

Review

Review of some of the features of academic English that you studied in Unit 1.

Academic English:

- uses many nouns and noun phrases
- uses fewer verbs and verb phrases
- uses high lexis (vocabulary) rather than spoken lexis
- if an essay is the text, uses referencing; a bibliography; quotes and paraphrasing
- structures the whole text according to an appropriate schema which includes staging in the introduction, the body and the conclusion
- allows each paragraph to offer supporting evidence for the main theme/s of the essay. These themes are mentioned first in the Preview stage (sometimes called the Scope or Focus stage) which is the final stage of the introduction
- has staging.

READING 1

Examining an authentic university essay

Read the authentic university essay, *Business management*, written by Amy a first year student taking a business and management course towards a bachelor's degree (see page 89). This essay was marked by her lecturer and she received a high distinction. This is equivalent to an A.

The topic is modern strategic management and how organisations can build company vision and work in a global marketplace.

Task A | Definitions in context – Vocabulary

❶ Match the words and phrases in column 1 to the definitions in column 3 by locating them within the text of the essay that follows.

❷ Write the paragraph number where you found the definition. Amy defines each one of these terms, in context, in the essay.

❸ Some words have two or more definitions.

Words	Definitions	Para #
Yin	Big, hairy, audacious goal.	_____
Yang	A company's road map that specifies about technology, customer focus, product and geographic markets, and capabilities it plans to develop.	_____
BHAG	Core ideology – what the company stands for and why it exists.	_____
Strategic intent (3 ways to define)	That through competitor analysis companies are able to stake out less defended markets…and exploit the benefit of surprise in a competitive battle.	_____
Strategic vision	The envisioned future of what a company aspires to become, achieve and create.	_____
Searching for loose bricks	An envisioned future. The direction in which way a business is headed in the long term.	_____
	An active management process that involves the essence of winning, stability, and effort and commitment.	_____
	The strategic intent of the organisation.	_____

Task B | Schema or staging within an essay

Use different coloured highlight pens or box with single, double and triple underlining the following:

Ⓐ Introduction: the three stages within Amy's introduction

   1. General statement
   2. Definition of terms
   3. Scope or Preview of the essay

Ⓑ Body: paragraph 1– Definition of terms/ theme

   1. Write the theme of the essay

   _____

   _____

   2. Does the writer develop that theme?

   _____

   _____

Ⓒ Issues

- Go back to the *Scope* or *Preview* of the essay in the introduction. Write the four issues that the essay promises to discuss.
- Write the paragraph number from the body of the essay where each of those four issues is **first** discussed.

Issue	Para #
1. _____	
2. _____	
3. _____	
4. _____	

Ⓓ Find each of the four issues the essay previewed in the introduction and that you located in question C and highlight them or box them. Write the number and the issue that is being discussed next to the box you create.

Ⓔ Do you understand the development of the essay?

_____

Ⓕ Did Amy cover each of the four issues in the scope within the introduction?

_____

_____

Ⓖ Locate the conclusion and box it.

Ⓗ Does the conclusion reiterate the things that were promised in the scope?

_____

_____

Ⓘ Copy the text from the conclusion (see para 17 below) that summarises the scope of the introduction and that was covered in the body of the essay.

_____

_____

_____

_____

_____

_____

_____

_____

_____

_____

_____

BUSINESS Management

Strategic Intent

Question: Write an essay that outlines what strategic intent means and how it is applied within the management structure of an organisation.

[Paragraph numbers are provided to make it easier for you.]

① Developing an organisation's strategic intent has become a fundamental part of modern strategic management. Strategic intent is thought of as a 'big, hairy, audacious goal' or BHAG, and is generally achieved over the long term. Companies that relentlessly pursue an ambitious strategic objective and concentrate their resources, capabilities and energy on achieving that objective exhibit a strategic intent (Sims, 2006, Week 2). The following essay will discuss how organisations can formulate and build their company vision, strategic intent's role in change and the global marketplace, and the power of catalytic mechanisms and corporate challenges in achieving strategic intent or the BHAG.

② Strategic management can be defined into a simplified framework of five main tasks. The first task is to develop a strategic vision and business mission, followed by setting objectives, crafting strategy to achieve the objectives, implementing and executing the strategy and finally to evaluate performance, monitor new developments and initiate adjustments (Thompson, Strickland & Gamble, 2005, p18). Establishing a company's direction involves the first three strategic tasks and are especially important because they help develop and indicate the strategic intent of a company, for example Canon sought to 'Beat Xerox'. (Reference?)

Lecturer's comment = If this is a quotation, then use quotation marks and reference and page number.

③ Many companies are more familiar with the strategic planning process than strategic intent. Strategic intent can be defined as an envisioned future. Strategic intent also includes an active management process that involves creating the essence of winning, stability, and effort and commitment. Management need to focus the organisation's attention on the essence of winning, eg *for Coca-Cola the strategic intent has been to put a Coke within 'arms's reach' of every consumer in the world*. Employees also need to be motivated by communicating the value of the target, and leaving room for employee contributions. When circumstances change, enthusiasm needs to be sustained through new operational definitions and strategic intent should guide resource allocations (Hamel & Prahalad, 1989, p64).

④ Looking at the first task of strategic management, creating a strategic vision. Strategic vision reflects managers' aspirations for the organisation and the kind of company they are trying to create, strategic vision can be viewed as a company's road map that specifies about technology, customer focus, product and geographic markets, and capabilities it plans to develop (Thompson, Strickland & Gamble, 2005, p29). A well-formulated vision consists of two major components: core ideology and envisioned future. These components complement one another and can be modelled as Yin and Yang.

⑤ Core ideology is the Yin, what the company stands for and why it exists, and is unchanging. The core ideology consists of core values and purpose of the organisation, and *provides the glue that holds the organisation together through time; as it grows, decentralises, diversifies, expands globally and develops workplace diversity*. For example, some core values of Sony are *Elevation of the Japanese culture and national status, being a pioneer – not following others, doing the impossible*. The core purpose of Sony is *To experience the joy of advancing and applying technology for the benefit of the public* (Collins & Porras, 1996, p69).

⑥ The envisioned future is the Yang, what a company aspires to become, achieve and create, and will require change. It consists of ten to thirty years of BHAG, and descriptions of what it will be like to achieve this goal. A BHAG is clear and compelling, highly focused, energising, has a finish line so the organisation knows when it has achieved its goal, and acts as a catalyst for team spirit. Organisations can have many BHAGs at different levels; however a vision level BHAG as it applies to the whole company requires a ten to thirty year effort to complete and is beyond current capabilities and current business environment. The vivid description of the future vision should be visual images people can carry around in their head. Yang can be seen as the strategic intent of the organisation.

⑦ Management of change is an important part of organisation survival and success in today's business environment. The nature of change can be related to the macro and microenvironment and affect the organisation at different levels. Managers therefore have to be able to understand the concepts of change and be able to devise new strategic vision and intent which others will be able to capture. *One approach recognises the importance of holistic abstractions in strategic thinking and communication achieved via the medium of the metaphor* (Pitt, 2001, p7). In organisations, metaphoric thinking helps to simplify complex realities, and shape understandings and actions. Martyn Pitt has identified six metaphors of intent that occur *so regularly that they may well characterise the thinking of many managers.*
1. *Responding:* company's desire to be responsive, strategic intent emphasises need to adapt to situation, eg Jumping on the bandwagon.
2. *Initiating:* company's sustain success from proactive initiating behaviour and first to realise future potentials, eg winning the game, Revolutionising.
3. *Repatterning:* strategic intent is to configure differently what the company presently does, is or knows, and the construction of relationships and networks, eg Rejuvenating, Reforming.
4. *Accumulating:* strategic intent may associate with asset accumulation, increasing net worth, enhancing competitive position through the scale and scope of its activities, eg Investing, Extending.
5. *Learning:* strategic intent emphasises organisational development by experiencing, interacting with and reflecting on new circumstances with the prospect to enable new insights, eg Experimenting, Coping.
6. *Embedding:* strategic intent to assimilate and institutionalise desirable new practices and postures, eg Internalising, Taking on Board.

⑧ The goal of organisations to be competitively successful and sustainable in the marketplace implies managers need to be able to formulate new strategic intent. There are a number of different intents of change, and the use of *metaphors presents an opportunity to conceive, examine and communicate strategic intent in richer, more insightful terms*; (Pitt, 2001, p18).

⑨ In many industries today companies are working hard to match competitors and expand into the international market. Companies with the strategic intent of global leadership need to be able to create tomorrow's competitive advantage faster than competitors mimic the current ones organisations have. One of the most defensible competitive advantages in the global marketplaces is a company's ability to improve existing skills and learn new ones. A company's goal should be not to imitate but innovate competitive advantages, to achieve the strategic intent of global leadership (Hamel & Prahalad, 1989).

⑩ A successful example of the strategic intent for global leadership is Japan's success in the US markets. There are several key approaches evident in the global expansion of Japanese companies, such as Sony, Toshiba, Komatsu, to competitive innovation. Approaches to competitive innovation in global companies include building multiple advantages, searching for loose bricks beyond static analyses of competitors, changing the definition of industry and segment boundaries by establishing new rules of engagement and competing through alliances (Hamel & Prahalad, 1989). It is also important companies understand their own diverse management teams.

⑪ When companies enter into price wars or other competitive battles the wider a company's portfolio of advantages the less risk they face. For example, instead of viewing differentiation or cost strategies as mutually exclusive, Japanese companies such as Mazda have pursued both, by developing a standardised mini van just for the California US market.

⑫ 'Searching for loose bricks' means through competitor analysis companies are able to stake out less defended markets, an uncontested profit segment, particular geographic market or slice of the value chain and exploit the benefit of surprise in a competitive battle. (Hamel & Prahalad, 1989). However due to the often static and domestic nature of traditional competitive analysis tools, such as Porter's Five Forces of Competition or SWPT analysis, it is important companies consider global competitors' national history, government support, probably partnerships, managerial goals, values, and profile their strategic orientation and intent (Hitt, Tyler, Hardee & Park, 1995).

⑬ Another competitive innovation can be changing some of the industry's characteristics, such as entry barriers, by creating new rules of engagement and instead of matching a leading company's capabilities, a company can develop their own.

⑭ In order to achieve the overall strategic intent a company must continually build a resource base over the long term. Establishing alliances, through collaboration, outsourcing agreements and joint ventures, can help achieve this. Sometimes it can even be possible for companies to instantly be number one in the global market without having to enter into a competitive battle. Also in developing alliances a company must understand their potential partner's corporate culture, structure, operating systems, costs and benefits of the alliance, and predict partner's strategic intent for the alliance.

⑮ It is also just as critical for organisations to understand not only their competitor's strategic orientation but also their own diverse and international management teams. This can be achieved by examining the culture of the country and management members, their achievements, previous strategic decisions, and the information gathered can be used to profile strategies (Ibid). Strategic intent is different to the traditional view of strategy. The traditional view of strategy focuses on the degree of fit between existing resources and current opportunities, strategic intent creates an extreme misfit between resources and ambitions (Hamel & Prahalad, 1989, p67). The essence of strategic intent is to become number one in the business so it becomes management's challenge to close the misfit between resources and ambitions by building new advantages. This involves the third stage in the strategic management process, crafting strategy. Strategic intent is specific about the ends, eg reducing product development, but fewer specifics about the means.

⑯ Corporate challenges and catalytic mechanisms are two strategies that organisations can use to help achieve strategic intent. Corporate challenges are derived from analysing competitors and foreseeing the industry life cycle, mutually revealing potential competitive opportunities. Strategic intent is long term and creating a series of short-term challenges can keep the organisation focused on the strategic intent. An example of a challenge one year, may be quality, and the next could be customer service. For these challenges to be successful, the whole organisation, eg individuals and teams must understand and see the implications to their own position. This requires management to complete the following tasks:
- Create a sense of urgency: managers need to create a real crisis by amplifying the signals in the environment that point out the need for improvement.
- Develop a competitor focus at every level through widespread use of competitor intelligence (information).
- Provide employees with the skills they need to work effectively.
- Give the organisation time to digest one challenge before launching another.
- Establish clear milestones and review mechanisms.
(Hamel & Prahalad, 1989, p67).

⑰ In conclusion, strategic intent has contributed to the first three tasks of the strategic management process. The Ying Yang Model illustrates the importance of strategic intent when developing an organisation's vision. In order for managers to deal with change, and devise new strategic vision and intent, it can be helpful to articulate and explore intent via the exchange and adoption of appropriate metaphors. Metaphors make these intentions seem more real in the minds of those involved, and add long term value, and appropriate prescriptions for change. In pursuit of the strategic intent of global leadership, new additions to strategic management have been seen in developing multiple portfolios, searching for loose bricks and changing the terms of engagement. Lastly, corporate challenges and catalytic mechanisms are two strategies that organisations can use to help achieve strategic intent. Strategic intent concerns the direction in which a business is headed in the long term. If identified simply and succinctly it can have a profound effect on the firm's stakeholders, both internal and external. Employees know what they are trying to achieve and therefore how they should make their greatest efforts; customers know what the firm's products and services embody; suppliers understand what the key elements are when dealing with the firm.

REFERENCES*

*Please note: Letters are never placed in front of references at the conclusion of an essay. They are placed here in order to assist you in completing Task C: References.

A Collins, JC & Porras, JI (1996, September-October) 'Building Your Company's Vision'. *Harvard Business Review*, 65-77.
B Collins, J (1999, July-August) 'Turning Goals into Results'. *Harvard Business Review*, 71.
C Hamel, G & Prahalad, CK (1989, May-June) 'Strategic Intent'. *Harvard Business Review*, 63-76.
D Hitt, MA, Tyler, BB, Hardee, C & Parak, D (1995, May) 'Understanding strategic intent in the global marketplace'. *The Academy of Management Executive*, 9, 12-21.
E Pitt, M (2001) 'In pursuit of change: managerial constructions of strategic intent'. *Strategic Change*, 10, 5-21.
F Sims, Al (2006, Week 2) 'Strategic Intent'. *Lecture slides*, 15.
G Thompson, AA, Strickland, AJ & Gamble, JE (2005) *Crafting and Executing Strategy, The Quest for Competitive Advantage: Concepts and Cases*. New York: McGraw-Hill, 18-29.

Task C | References

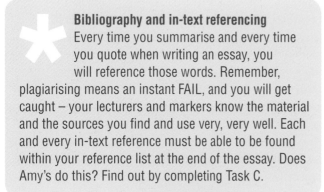

Bibliography and in-text referencing
Every time you summarise and every time you quote when writing an essay, you will reference those words. Remember, plagiarising means an instant FAIL, and you will get caught – your lecturers and markers know the material and the sources you find and use very, very well. Each and every in-text reference must be able to be found within your reference list at the end of the essay. Does Amy's do this? Find out by completing Task C.

❶ Locate each of the references from the References (Bibliography) within the body text of the essay.

❷ Match the numbers of the paragraphs where you find the reference to the letter in front of each reference in the list.

❸ Does Amy include in the text all the references in the reference list?
Answer the following questions:

[a] Which source is quoted the most throughout the essay?

_____

_____

[b] Why do you think Hamel and Prahalad are the authors who are used so extensively within the essay?

_____

_____

[c] Which reference helped Amy to write about the global marketplace? Write the name of the authors; the name of the article and the name of the source that it came from.

_____

_____

[d] Sims, Al, (2006, Week 2), 'Strategic Intent', _Lecture slides_, 15. What do you think this reference refers to?

_____

_____

[e] Which journal is used the most in the essay?

_____

_____

[f] In Reference E, what does 10, 5-21 refer to, ie what does it mean?

_____

[g] Write the publisher and page numbers from Reference G.

_____

_____

READING 2

Evaluating academic credibility of information on the internet

Credibility (n): 1. the quality of deserving to be believed and trusted. (_Longman Dictionary of Contemporary English_, 2003, p 369)

Can internet information be trusted?
What's easier – getting a book published or putting a web page on the internet? Why? Think about whether the information is checked before being published, and whether anyone is going to lose money if the project isn't successful.

Task A | Sourcing material for essay writing, books and the internet

❶ From your answers to the question in the text box above, which do you think is more likely to be true and accurate – information in a printed book or on a website?

_____

❷ If the website is published by a well-respected organisation, would your answer to question 3 change? Would your answer change in other situations as well?

_____

Task B | Critical thinking – Predicting bias and accuracy

Imagine you are reading in preparation for an assignment which asks whether banning firearms (guns) is likely to reduce the number of homicides (murders). Answer the following questions 1–3 for each of the websites (a) to (f) below.

❶ On which websites would you expect a one-sided (biased) view?

❷ On which websites would you suspect the accuracy of the information?

❸ What further questions would you want to investigate before you believe the information you found? (In [b] does the charity have a particular opinion about gun use, eg that carrying a gun deters crime?)

Websites

[a] A firearms manufacturing company.
[b] A charity that helps the families of crime victims.
[c] A pressure group that wants to ban people from using guns.
[d] Someone who has done some research in their spare time. There is no evidence that they have studied the subject carefully.
[e] An investigation, at a well-respected university, into murder rates in countries where guns are banned, compared with countries where guns are allowed.
[f] Police statistics about gun ownership.

Task C | Evaluating website credibility

❶ After completing Tasks A and B, discuss what would you look for in a website before using information from it in an assignment? Does your answer agree with the content of the evaluation forms on the next page?

❷ Continue researching the connection between firearm ownership and murder rates. Try the following sites:

* <www.gunowners.org/> → Fact Sheets → 1999: Firearms Fact Sheet
* <www.abanet.org/gunviol/>
* <www.handguncontrol.org> → Facts

Use the evaluation forms to help you decide which sites are credible enough to investigate further. If you choose to use the information from the site in an essay, what other considerations would you take into account (eg compare the information on the site with information from other sources, or look for information biased in the opposite way)?

You can follow other links but you don't have to go outside the sites.

Credibility

To check truthfulness of websites use **SCOPES**, an organisation which reviews credentials and checks facts on sites for you.

To find the date of the latest update, author, publisher etc of a website, look at the bottom and top of the page/screen.

These evaluation forms can be used with any information source, not just internet sites.

Website evaluation form 1: Looking at bias

professional association a group of people from a particular profession, who support other members of the profession

pressure group an organisation which aims to influence government opinion over a particular issue

institutional affiliation means the organisation who the person is paid by or is a member of

ulterior motive an unsaid reason for doing something

Kind of organisation (eg government, political party, **professional association**, **pressure group**, none (private individual)	
Author's **institutional affiliation**	
Purpose of the page (eg to advertise, entertain, give information, persuade)	
Evidence of **ulterior motive** (eg make money, gain power by promoting a particular view)	
Summary: Can expect a non-balanced viewpoint?	

Website evaluation form 2: Looking at accuracy of information

credentials a person's qualifications, experience and other qualities that show there is a reason to believe the person

Author's **credentials** (eg qualifications, experience)	
Is there a reason to respect the organisation (eg part of government, respected NGO (non-government organisation)	
Are there references? Is it original research?	
When was the site last updated? Is it up-to-date?	
Summary: Can see a reason for lack of accuracy? (Remember that bias can also be a reason for inaccuracy.)	

In English, as in all languages, different texts are written for different purposes and in different ways. The next tasks should assist you to learn about some of the language features that make these texts recognisable. You will try to discover what language features make a crime fiction actually read like a crime fiction, and what different language features make an informative or scientific text an informative or scientific text.

Isn't it all English? Yes, it is all English. But you use different participants (people/no people); different processes (kinds of verbs); there are different circumstances (situations); and they have different social purposes.

Task A | Matching text types

In the following section, you will progressively complete the table on the next page by working through Tasks A, B and C.

❶ Read the following texts 1–7 and make an attempt to match them with the types of texts lettered A–I within the first column of the table on the next page.

This may show you that you can or cannot recognise a type of text from reading it. Further work will show you how to do just that!

TEXT TYPE 2

It was around 5 pm when I reached the front door of the empty apartment building which houses my tiny, rented office. I had had to sleep most of the day after last night's confrontation with Mick and his nasty mates. I needed to touch base and check my answering machine before tomorrow so it didn't really matter how late it was.

When I got inside, I matched the new, black Mazda MX5 convertible parked out front with the petite, pixie-faced young woman standing impatiently outside my office door. It was obvious she was waiting to see me since my office is the only occupied room in the place. I unlocked the door, glancing at my own name – Casey O'Rourke – etched on the glass.

Before speaking, I grabbed the cigarettes off my battered desk, tapped one out of the pack and offered it to her. She smiled briefly, more of a grimace really, said her name was Stacy Beech and took one. I noticed her nails were bitten to the quick.

'How can I help you?'

TEXT TYPE 1

Atalanta was a huntress. She was renowned by both mortals and the gods for her amazing speed in running. She was beautiful to behold and many men desired her. She, however, did not wish to marry and begged her father to allow her to remain free.

Her father refused the swift-running huntress her request and insisted that she choose and marry one of the men who loved her. Since Atalanta would never defy her father, she agreed but convinced him to allow her to arrange a contest so that she might choose the right man.

Because Atalanta could run as fast as the wind, she created a contest whereby any of her suitors who was able to outrun her would be allowed to marry her. But, if she defeated them, the man would have to die.

Many men came to the valley where Atalanta and her father lived. They ran and ran against her, but she always beat them and each one was put to death. Her cruelty became known throughout the land and many people came just to view such a cruel maiden.

One day, Hippomenes came to see the contest. He thought he would despise the girl for her cruelty but once he saw her, he fell in love with her as others had before him. He sought help from Aphrodite, the goddess of love. Now, this goddess decided to help Hippomenes and she gave him three golden apples.

With these in his pockets, Hippomenes told Atalanta's father that he wished to race against his daughter, the girl as swift as a deer and as beautiful as a rainbow.

During the race, Hippomenes pretended to be tired and acted exhausted. While running, he would pant loudly and each time that Atalanta glanced at him, he tossed a golden apple in her path. Knowing how tired this suitor was and knowing that she could beat him easily, Atalanta stooped to pick up the golden fruit once and then twice. The third time she did this, Hippomenes ran with all his strength and just beat her by stretching for the winning post and touching it first. Since Aphrodite was the goddess of love, Atalanta and Hippomenes married happily and Atalanta forgave him for his trickery for she greatly admired the golden apples and thought him clever and handsome to have devised such a trick.

TYPES OF TEXTS	TEXT NUMBER (TASK A, PAGE 95)	LANGUAGE FEATURES NUMBER (TASK B, PAGE 98)	PURPOSE OR INTENTION OF TEXTS (TASK C, PAGE 114) *Write your answer in this column*
A. Crime fiction			To entertain a reader and to describe persons and events around a crime.
B. Fiction			
C. Scientific text			
D. Greek myth			
E. College (university) song			
F. Biography			
G. News story			
H. Abstract for journal article			
I. Recipe			

Text type 3

She dreamed daily of home. There were so many things she missed – the soft eyes of the cattle curiously examining her when she stepped into the grassy paddocks; the early morning mist, white and silent that rested on the mountains then lifted to reveal an enormous blue sky; mute-coloured valley birds hopping, dancing and flying in silhouette, landing on silver-green gums, all these were sweet visions in her mind.

Belle had begun to live for the time she could leave. She hated the frantic pace, the noise and dirt of this tired, greedy city and longed to return to her family and the peace of her father's simple farm.

Text type 4

The relationship between culture and language has increasingly become a subject for exploration as has the classroom goal of modifying student (and perhaps teacher) 'monocultural awareness' (Byram, 1990). Titles such as *Cultural Awareness in the Classroom* (Dink, 1999) and statements such as '... cultural learning is ... preparing the learners for intercultural communication' (Delanoy, 1997, p60) have peppered journals and teaching magazines in the last decade. Intercultural communication both inside and outside the EFL classroom is an important reality.

Text type 5

Last night at 11:00 pm, the driver of a Rexon oil tanker truck lost control on the Houbeen Beach Highway endangering motorists and causing massive pollution when its load was spilled into the Miami Ocean 2 kms north of Brassby. Thousands of litres of oil were dumped and this morning were being contained in a massive clean up operation. 'It's too late for the beautiful birds dead on the beach and for many of our fish which this accident has destroyed', said local resident, Mr Sam Tolafu. Residents of the idyllic island paradise are pitching in to save whatever wildlife they can by cleaning the birds that have survived. All beaches are closed until further notice.

TEXT TYPE 7

O fairest Monticello, we bring to thee our praise;
It is with deepest rev'rence
That we our voices raise,
As on thru life we journey,
Sweet mem'ries will remain,
The years of toil and pleasure,
Replete with wisdom's gain,
Those years of riches measure
That will not come again,
May we be ever worthy,
Standing firm without a fear,
May we your ideals echo,
O Alma Mater dear,
You would join the numbers that form her
* glorious past,*
Pledge yourselves to Monticello, Faithful to the
* last.*

(Source: Monticello College's 105 Commencement, 1943)

Text type 6

The panda is a bear-like carnivore named *beishung* by the Chinese. It has a body about two and a half metres long (six feet) and weighs about 158 kilos (three hundred pounds). It has thick, dense fur which is white except for the black legs and ears, black round the eyes and on the shoulders. It has five toes with claws on each foot. The cheek teeth are broad and the skull is deep with prominent ridges for the attachment of strong muscles needed in chewing fibrous shoots. It lives in the cold damp bamboo forests on the hillsides of eastern Tibet and Szechwan in southwest China.

Pandas live mainly on the ground but can climb trees if they face danger. They are active throughout the whole year, unlike some bears, which hibernate. They are generally solitary animals except in the breeding season when they mix in order to mate and they spend 10 to 12 hours a day feeding. They eat bamboo shoots and grasses, gentians, irises and crocuses and also some animal food. They can flip small fish out of water with their paws.

Genus and species: *Ailuropoda melanoleuca*
Class: *Mammalia*
Order: *Carnivora*
Family: *Procyonidae*

(*Source:* Information based upon facts from *Encyclopedia of Mammals*, BBC Publishing, 1975.)

Task B | Recognising the language features that create a text

Different text types

For a native English speaker, recognising a type of text is possible by recognising the language features of the different writings. They may not be able to say 'why' they know, but they will know which kind of text they are reading. For English learners, you can learn the language features that make up texts. There are certain nouns, verbs, locations and people or things that are part of each particular text.

① Read the boxed *language features* of each text type.

② Read the texts 1 – 7 a second time and find the matching language features.

③ Write the number of each boxed *language features* in the table on page 96 matching it to the correct types of texts.

③ **Language features 3**
- explanation is statement of fact – factual text;
  - participants are non-human;
  - processes (verbs) are relational (to be: is/has, etc);
  - some technical vocabulary;
  - present simple tense.

④ **Language features 4**
- narrator – omnipresent (knows all but is not present);
  - participants are human;
  - processes (verbs) are mental – non-verbal action;
  - description is important.

① **Language features 1**
- first person narrative – the 'voice' of the narrator is evident and clear in the reader's mind;
  - staging – introduction with time, location, setting the scene;
  - past and past continuous tense;
  - processes (verbs) are material and mental;
  - participants are human;
  - location (place) important;
  - time important;
  - descriptive details prominent – of objects and events.

⑤ **Language features 5**
- personal – includes reader as 'we';
  - participants – people, things and events;
  - processes (verbs) – present, present continuous, future; – uses rhetoric.

⑥ **Language features 6**
- authoritative address to reader;
  - participants are outside the text;
  - processes (verbs) are relational;
  - clauses are long and tend to have many nominal groups (more nouns than verbs);
  - presents an argument or proposes a thesis for an educated reader to consider.

② **Language features 2**
- third person narrative;
  - past tense;
  - participants are gods/goddesses of Roman/ Greek origin;
  - processes (verbs) are material and action;
  - content of story imaginary;
  - resolution of story clear (coda);
  - sometimes a moral lesson to be learned.

⑦ **Language features 7**
- headline which signals importance;
  - newsworthy event;
  - verbs of action to retell;
  - processes (verbs) which quote;
  - circumstances of time and place;
  - specific participants.

Purposes and intentions of writers

Each time anyone writes, they have a reason, an intention, a purpose. If you make a list of university books you need to buy, then your intention is to note them down, not to forget and to have it ready when you get to the bookshop so you can buy them. That's the purpose of a list. All the types of texts you have read have purposes as well. It's important for a reader to understand the purpose of texts and intentions of writers. One reason it's important is so that the reader can detect bias and persuasion.

Task C | Purpose or intention of a text

Using the information on the right and the Texts 1–7 write the purpose of the types of texts in the table on page 96. The first one has been done for you.

Purpose or intention of text/author

❶ To provide information about natural and non-natural phenomena.

❷ To provide information about newsworthy events to readers.

❸ To persuade a reader that something is the case and to report on theory and/or research.

❹ To entertain a reader and to describe a particular person or persons in a particular place or places.

❺ To engage a group of people in one act of appreciation in a ceremony using song and to relate historical events.

❻ To entertain a reader and to describe persons and events around a crime.

❼ To entertain and enlighten a reader using ancient stories which may have a moral or warning.

LANGUAGE SPOTLIGHT 1

Outlined below are seven ways for writing a good paragraph. Previously, in Unit 1, you studied how to develop an explanation paragraph.

A method of development means how to write the correct and accurate meaning you wish to express. The seven methods that follow are: *description; giving reasons; giving definitions and examples; cause and effect; listing of details; analogy; comparison and contrast.*

Task A | Seven methods for writing paragraphs: Models

❶ Read and study the following seven paragraphs which use seven different methods of development.

❷ Then write a paragraph using the title next to each model and using the same method of development.

Topic
sentence

Description

Sunset

Sunsets can be magnificent and even inspiring. Every country has them. There are different looking ones in Africa, the Australian and Middle Eastern deserts and the South Pacific. I have been fortunate to see sunsets around the world. One special memory is a sunset that was layered with reds and oranges. The colours changed by the minute as the sun sank lower over the sea. It was an island sunset and they are known for their beauty. As the orb of sun went down beneath the horizon, the colours changed from red and orange to cobalt and indigo blue. The clouds were darkly tinged underneath with orange and pink at the top.

Sunrise

Topic
sentence

Giving
reasons

Reason I'm quitting my job

Being employed is something that is relatively common. Most people are employed in some sort of paid occupation. I'm leaving my current job this week. The main reason is that the boss is difficult to work with. Also, the position is demanding and yet underpaid. I'm often asked to work late and am never rewarded for that. All in all, it's an unhappy situation and life is just too short to hate what you do day in and day out.

Reason I'm studying

3. DEFINITIONS AND EXAMPLES

Topic sentence
Definitions and examples

Recession

Recessions may occur within individual countries and globally. Recessions are generally periods of time when there is a slowdown in economic activity. Businesses contract and production of products fall. For example, the GDP, defined as Gross Domestic Product, is less. A global recession, as defined by the IMF (International Monetary Fund) means economic growth that is less than 3%. By this definition, 2008–2009 are recent years when the world experienced a recession.

DEFINITIONS AND EXAMPLES

Economic downturn

4. CAUSE AND EFFECT

Topic sentence

Cause and effect

Weather and hurricanes or cyclones

Weather is defined as all the conditions in the atmosphere. Events such as temperature, wind, humidity and barometric pressure form weather. Weather causes hurricanes. If it turns to thunderstorms, the result can be a hurricane or cyclone. They are caused by thunderstorms under certain conditions. First, the ocean has to be warmer than 26.5°– Celsius (81° Fahrenheit). Also, heat and moisture from the ocean's surface must combine and this can result in wind. This is the combination that causes a cyclone, heat, moisture and wind from the surface of the sea. In a cyclone, winds are above 64 knots and the movement of those winds is circular, spinning counter-clockwise.

CAUSE AND EFFECT

Earthquakes and tsunamis

Online collaboration

Topic sentence

When businesses collaborate on projects online, there are conversations. How are these managed and what are the rules? There are things such as creating norms, breaking convention, finding insights and conquering fear.

Listing of details

- Creating norms means that there is formal talk and informal talk, and a choice has to be made about what is appropriate where. When product development is at stake, breaking convention may be required.

- In the same way innovative people with innovative ideas work in global teams and conventions may be thrown aside at times.

- Finding insights and placing them in difficult to locate internet places may make them hard to find.

- Conquering fear among experts who do not wish to share hard-earned knowledge is a challenge. Experts consider their value is linked to the information they hold.

Email etiquette

Marriage, like bread...

Topic sentence Analogy

Some say that marriage, like bread, should be made fresh every day. Certainly, fresh bread is delicious and much better on the day it is baked. Marriage is something that is long term so it must mean that each and every day the people in that relationship must rise and begin fresh again. It means people in a marriage ought to work on the present moment of their lives together and make sure it is fresh every new day. All relationships would benefit from this analogy.

Love, like weather...

Topic sentence Comparison and Contrast

Spoken English compared to written English

Grammar in English has evolved to construct the world in different ways than talking does. However, in speaking, distance between speakers can be close, many verbs occur, and there is little need to distil the meaning (to take big ideas and lengthy sentences and boil them down by nominalising words and phrases). In contrast, in writing, especially academic writing, the interpersonal distance must be extended, and whereas speaking allows many verbs, academic writing does not. As well, by comparison to speaking, academic writing uses nominalisation a great deal. In addition, the issues written about are often abstract rather than concrete.

My language spoken compared to my language written

_____

_____

_____

_____

_____

_____

_____

_____

_____

_____

_____

_____

_____

Taking notes from books

At university, your source of information will largely be from books as well as the internet at times. You must take notes from books since it is impossible to read numerous, whole books for each subject. Thus, you need to practise note-taking and using books as a reference.

Task A | Note-taking from a book

1 Choose one chapter from your book to take notes from.

2 *Very quickly* look over the entire chapter.

3 Note down any headings that are in **bold**.

4 Decide upon a method for note-taking – writing numbers 1, 2, 3, 4 etc or letters A, B, C, D etc. You can combine numbers and letters by making the main points or themes either a letter or a number and listing smaller details beneath.

_____

_____

_____

Next is an example of notes taken from the short text titled *Using a library*.

Example of note-taking from the text

Connor, C & Wessley, S (2002) 'Library Systems and Students', *Using a Library*. New York: Randoff Publishers, p 22.

Note that the first thing to do is to be sure to write the source in its entirety and correctly! Don't forget to do this!

Now begin note-taking:

1   Research (2002) Connor, C & Wessley, S
2   Students should learn Dewey Decimal Classification system
   A. Dewey Decimal – def. classify
   B. 10 major subject classes, then divide ideas by 10s.

Notice the word 'def.' in the notes above. It stands for *definition*. It is an abbreviation for the word 'definition'. There are some standard abbreviations but you should also devise them for yourself (just be sure you remember what you decided upon so that you can read your notes and recognise your own abv/s (abbreviations)).

Here are abbreviations that the authors use. Some are commonly known to writers of English.

- U = you
- R = are
- TV = television
- bk = book

- ref = reference
- ref 2 = refer to
- wman = woman
- cond. = condition
- etc = and so forth or so on.

Using a library

We have found over the years that many students do not actually gain the best benefit from their libraries. Our research (2000) showed that many students wander around looking in areas hoping to find what they want after searching for a particular book on a reading list which has been checked out by someone else.

Often, their attitude is that if the book they sought is gone, then they cannot complete their assignment. This article hopes to show students some ways to approach the situation differently.

First, students need to learn that the cataloguing system used is the Dewey Decimal. This is a classification system of classifying books into ten major subject classes and then further dividing ideas by tens, the divisions being represented by the numbers in a decimal system. The most useful thing a student may do is to attend their library orientation class and learn how to access this cataloguing system.

Source: Connor, C & Wessley, S (2002) 'Library Systems and Students', *Using a Library*. New York: Randoff Publishers, p 22.

Creative writing

Creative writing is a form of writing that draws upon your own thoughts, desires and sense of fun. It is meant as a form of expression beyond the strict rules of academia. Poetry is a form of creative writing. Sometimes it has rules and other times it is free in form. That is up to the author. That is up to you.

Robert Gray, a living Australian poet says, 'In a poem, everything is equal'. Think about that. It means that a comma is as important as a word. It means that the form and look of a poem is as important as its subject.

Octavio Paz said that 'Poetry is language making love'.

Poetry does not have to rhyme. Although Task B shows a conventional, Western style of producing poetry, remember to use your own thoughts, feelings and emotions to produce a poem of your own.

Task B | Learning some conventions of poetry, and writing poems

Read and examine the poems and follow the instructions beneath each one.

> ## Love's Emblems
> by John Fletcher 1579–1625
>
> Now the lusty spring is seen;
> Golden yellow, gaudy blue,
> Daintily invite the view:
> Everywhere on every green
> Roses blushing as they blow,
> And enticing men to pull
> Lilies whiter than the snow,
> Woodbines of sweet honey full:
> All love's emblems, and all cry
> 'Ladies, if not pluck'd, we die.'

❶ [a] What is the theme of the poem?

_____

[b] Is there more than one theme? What other theme besides *Spring* is mentioned?

_____

[c] Count the syllables in each line of the poem. How many are there?

_____

[d] Write the last word of every line in a vertical row.

i. _____

ii. _____

iii. _____

iv. _____

v. _____

vi. _____

vii. _____

viii. _____

ix. _____

x. _____

[e] Find the words that rhyme from the words above and note which lines rhyme with each other.

_____

_____

[f] Are there any patterns that you can see?

_____

_____

[g] What conclusions can you draw about typical 16th century poetry?

_____

[h] Write your own 16th century poem in English.

_____

_____

_____

_____

_____

_____

_____

_____

_____

_____

_____

_____

❷ Select words from the circle (or don't) in order to compose poetry of your own. You are not bound by convention or rules. Write as you wish, you do not need to rhyme or have a certain number of syllables per line.

leaving verse

clan love beauty song content unto as a the I thee
sing lonely feed eyes deep drown upon anguish soul pale kissed
temple none now gone among cloudy day or of on be to go my thy your
when her can his in of against fine turning shaded touch voice however
taught soft sweet and birds roses lilies dark banish see when rest quiet all
are know hours dream laid face passion here sweet earth silent
covers cold lift to up but with your alone all beyond
cove core heart fire true grace

Writing to explore an idea
To tell a story, you write a narrative.
Narratives contain description. Your task will
be to tell a story, use description and develop
a main idea.

The narrative below tells about a holiday. It uses past
tense, description and puts events in a sequence.

Task C | First person narrative writing – Description

❶ Read the model which is a descriptive piece of narrative writing.

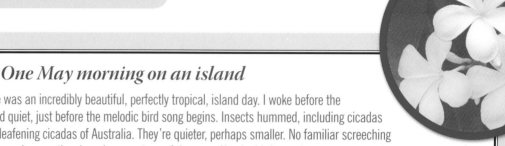

One May morning on an island

In the first week in May, there was an incredibly beautiful, perfectly tropical, island day. I woke before the morning alarm. It was still and quiet, just before the melodic bird song begins. Insects hummed, including cicadas but not like the raucous and deafening cicadas of Australia. They're quieter, perhaps smaller. No familiar screeching cockatoos nor loudly singing magpies, nor the slow, drawn out cry of the crow. No, the bird sounds were sweet and gentle, little calls back and forth to one another… a human's ears not offended nor consumed by it…allowing the mind to travel.

It was a morning when your mind went out and up and on and on, soaring up to the ancient, extinct, volcanic mountain peaks covered in lush, ever-present dark green. Casting about and then lifting over the quietly resting, waveless Pacific. There was nothing to bump against. No high rise buildings, no crowded suburbs with their just awakening inhabitants filling the atmosphere above them with a chaos of thoughts and morning preparations for leaving the house. No distant rumble of traffic or factories. The silence made me acutely aware of the fact that there is not a freeway for 1000s of miles; that there is no rushing traffic, no rush of anything at all.

Driving to work, it was obvious that the day was special. There was the usual bright blue sky with pure white cumulus clouds growing out of the horizon. But the ocean… and the lagoon… both were completely still and reflective. The sea today was more like a quiet lake than the heaving, moaning, crashing South Pacific Ocean. The lagoon was a mirror. It was covered in blue and pink. The surface of the water merged into unforgettable colours. Streaky mist hugged the hips and soft curves of the mountains below the waist, then gave way to brilliant sunshine and shadow over their curved spines. Trees shimmered in the light.

This was poet's territory. But, prosaically, I unlocked my air-conditioned office door and turned for a last look at the glorious morning.

(Source: K Cox, May 2007.)

❷ Describe any special day or thing that has moved you in your life.

_____

_____

_____

_____

_____

_____

_____

_____

_____

_____

_____

_____

**LISTENING &
NOTE-TAKING**

The portion of the lecture you are about to hear was given by Jana Hubata at the College of Natural Therapies, Sydney, Australia, on 29 March 2010. The lecture is called *The human senses*. Like most lecturers, Hubata uses language that tells the listener what is about to come next. If you learn to listen for key phrases and signals that tell you a definition or explanation or summary is about to occur; you will know what to write down and what to leave out. You have been consistently practising this throughout the units in this book.

You heard the introduction to this lecture in Unit 1.

Task A | Listening for phrases that signal points of importance

Listen to the lecture and place a tick in the table each time you hear a word or phrase (as listed below) that signals an explanation, definition or summary.

LECTURER'S STATEMENT	EXPLANATION OR DEFINITION
And the peripheral nervous system included your…	
Now...	
Hyposmia **is** looking at…and anosmia is a complete loss of…	
When you put the perfume on first thing in the morning…	
What I'm talking about here is…	

Task B | Taking notes using phrases that signal important points

CD 1

Listen to the recording a second time. When you hear the following phrases spoken, take notes filling in the gaps with what the lecturer says next.

The first one has been done for you.

❶ *How do we then distinguish different types of smell?*

Every molecule stimulates a different action

potential/like morse code/a known blue print for

smells

❷ *Now, there are certain conditions that are associated with different types of smell and or, uh, the lack thereof…_____, and _____*

❸ *…fresh halt…What I'm talking about is that only a few molecules _____ _____*

❹ *…high threshold that would mean we need many more _____*

5 *So, that's our sense of smell and I will discuss the sense of taste or* _____ .

6 *...part of your um digestion is the time when you are smelling* _____ .

7 *Humans can only detect* _____ *or* _____ *different* _____ .

8 *...and so we know that – sweet,* _____ , _____ , _____ , _____

9 *...and there is actually one more taste ...* _____

10 *Japanese word meaning* _____

Task C | Answering questions from notes from lecture

Look at your notes and answer the following questions in your notebook:

1 How many flavours can humans detect?

2 Gustation means the sense of what?

3 What other sense is gustation interrelated closely with?

4 What nervous system are the brain and spinal cord a part of?

5 Hyposnia means you have no sense of smell.
❑ True ❑ False

6 Name the five different flavours that humans can detect.

7 The spinal nerves exit from which nervous system?
[a] the peripheral
[b] the central
[c] the molecular
[d] the action potential

8 If a person requires many more molecules to make action potential happen they are said to have what kind of threshold for smell. High or low?

9 What Japanese word is now considered part of human's ability to taste?

10 How many types of receptors for smell do humans have?

Task D | Analysis of language when listening

The following is a transcription of a portion of the lecture, *The human senses*, given by Jana Hubata at the Australian College of Natural Therapies, Sydney, Australia.

Work in pairs or listen to your teacher read aloud portions of the lecture to you. Note the linguistic explanations in the left-hand column within the table which introduce key concepts and definitions.

EXPLANATION	LECTURE
Many lecturers use 'Now' to introduce a new topic or a topic shift within a theme. Sometimes it is to summarise, sometimes it is to explain, but it is always important. Here, she introduces the fact that humans 'we' 'don't have many different receptors'.	**Now,** we don't have many different receptors for every different smell that we... you are able to smell.
'Because' signals the reason for the statement above. She will explain or elaborate upon the above statement of fact.	**Because** we uh
'However' tells us the 'answer'... that we have only one type of receptors. Students to note 'one type of receptors'.	uh have so many different types of smells. **However** only one type of receptors.
Rhetorical question. Students listen and she will answer it.	How do we then distinguish different types of smell?
(The lecturer uses a PowerPoint presentation to describe the model.) The lecturer does not define 'action potential' and students should write it down, then aim to decipher it from its own word meaning and context.	Well, as I have shown you on that picture where the (*Unclear*) reacts with olfactory hair, it stimulates the, ah, ah action potential and every molecule will stimulate a different action potential.
'So...' indicates explanation.	**So,** I can liken probably to the morse code...yeah? dot dash dot dot dash.
'So...' indicates explanation	**So,** every molecule will stimulate this blueprint that generates different action potential and that way you also perceive different types of smells.

EXPLANATION	LECTURE
Comprehension checking	OK?
'Now', introducing new information around the same topic. The key phrase is 'certain conditions' and she will define or explain what these conditions are next.	**Now** there are certain conditions that are associated with different types of smell and/or, uh, the lack thereof ...
'is' means a definition is offered. 'is' means the second definition is offered. (This is easier in the real lecture situation because the words are on a screen so students can refer to it for spelling.)	...hyposnia **is** looking at the reduced sense of smell, and anosmia **is** a complete loss of the sense of smell.
Questions students for personal experience. No need to take notes, just listen for the example or explication of her point.	Have you realised that if you have smelled a smell, uh, for the first time after a couple of minutes, actually after one minute, uh, you barely realise it? When you put the perfume on first thing in the morning, um, you smell the perfume, but in the afternoon you can barely notice it, but the people, the people that pass or interact with you, they still can smell that perfume on you.
'This is because' signals an important point or summing up within the lecture. Students should write what follows that phrase 'adapt to smells'.	**This is because** we do actually adapt to the smell.
'Um' here, signals a whole new topic around 'fresh halt'. Students should note 'fresh halt' and wait for an explanation since it is new information.	Um, the olfaction actually does have a fresh halt.
And here is her language signal offering a complete explanation of what a 'fresh halt' means.	What I'm talking here about is ...
Complex explanation created by using cause and effect discourse cues. Students could note 'if'…'then'…	that only a few molecules of chemicals will already generate the action potential so you can smell a small amount of this particular chemical. **If** we have a low threshold **then** just a few molecules will activate the action potential, but if we have a high threshold that would mean we need many more molecules to stimulate the formation of the action potential.
Again, 'if'… signals explanation using cause and effect. 'Then' is ellipsed before the second half of this explanation '… (then) the receptors will adapt very quickly'.	Um, **if** contact with odour and molecules is sustained, as I mentioned, the receptors will adapt very quickly,
Result signalled by 'so'… and she explains 'what they will do is…'	**so** what they will do is down regulate their sensitivity to the molecules and you will pretty much not notice the sense of smell.
'So' offer a summing up…	**So** that's the low threshold
'but also there is…' summing up of 'adaptation'.	**but also there is** the adaptation.
Comprehension checking.	Does that make sense? Huh?
'So …' summing up.	**So**, that's our sense of smell
'And I will.' preview of what will come next: Taste 'or' gustation = definition signalled by 'or'.	**and I will** discuss the sense of taste or gustation.

EXPLANATION	LECTURE
	Gustation works very well and it is very much interrelated with the sense of smell especially when you are eating...
'So...'this is how it is... 'part of your digestion is the time when you are smelling food.'	So...we have not discussed that yet, but when I um discussed with you the digestive system, part of your um digestion is the time when you are smelling food.
'We refer to this as...' definition of terms.	We refer to this as the cefilic (*Unclear*) – part of digestion –
'that means...' explanation/definition.	that means you don't just eat, you smell food, you see food, you taste the food.
	Already at this particular point, your digestive system starts secreting the digestive juices, so they are already present by the time the food ah, um, gets into the stomach and into the (*Unclear*)
Statement. Students to note down.	Humans can only detect four or five different flavours
'so we know that...'(even if you don't know, this means more statements of fact).	so we know that sweet, salty, sour, bitter and there is actually one more taste that has been recognised and
'...that is called...' definition. ' It's a ...' definition. '...and pretty much means...' definition.	that is called *umami*. It's a Japanese word and pretty much, uh, means delicious. And in a lot of Asian cuisine,
'...you know that...' statement of fact coming.	you know that monosodium glutinate is used,
'...so...' explanation coming.	so it's the taste of monosodium glutamate that distinguishes the ah taste.
Statement of fact.	The sense of taste depends upon these five, primary flavours first,
'but also...'adding to information.	but also the texture of the food.
'And, of course, ...' (now an explanation will be offered). '...because...' explanation. ...'so that way you are not only...' (but must come and give the complete picture, which it does).	And, of course, the odorant molecules that are released from the food and pass through the mouth, because as the food passes through the mouth and into your throat – the passage in the throat is for both the food and the air – and the odorant molecules from the food as you are swallowing it, will still be able to pass into the nasal cavity, so that way you are not only smelling as you are inhaling,
but ....'(Here, the lecturer is not too clear. The meaning is clear in that you should understand now that as you are eating the food, you are also smelling it.)	but as you are inhaling the smell of the food on your plate, but as you are eating the food.
'Um... olfaction is...' explanation.	Um, olfaction is much more sensitive, uh then gustation uh
'...that we call...' definition.	the receptors for gustation are located in parts of the tongue that we call the taste buds.

EXPLANATION	LECTURE
'Uh…they are, of course,…(Here, she reiterates and explains further.)	Uh, **they are, of course,** found on the tongue and some of them are also found on the soft palate, that is pretty much the roof of the mouth…not the hard part…if you put your tongue um
(She pauses in the middle of asking you to do something in order to offer a definition) 'we call that…'.	on the roof of your mouth, you can feel a hard… **we call that** the hard palate and if you follow your tongue to the back of the roof of your mouth, you can feel the soft palate.
'And that is where…' offering additional information and explanation. 'Of course…' she uses 'of course' to signal definitions throughout this lecture. Lecturers have their little speech habits and students should listen for them so they understand what will come next and the importance or non importance of it. 'But, I will mention that a little bit later…'the set up to future talks. No need to note down.	**And that is where** some of those taste receptors are also located. Of course in the pharynx, which is the throat [definition] and the larynx, which is the divided part between the respiratory system and the digestive system [definition]…**But, I will mention that** a little bit later when we get to the respiratory and digestive system.
'Again, there are …' definition or statement of fact …but… signals contrast to above. Note that number will decline with age.	**Again,** there are nearly 10 000 taste buds on the tongue of the young and adults, **but** the number will decline with age.
'And you probably would know….' she gives anecdotal evidence here. Students can just listen.	**And you probably would know** from your grandparents that they say, 'Oh, I can't taste the food, it's not, it's no taste.'
'And again….' statement	**And again,** with age, most of the bodily functions slow and that also relates to these special senses,
'so…' summing up and conclusion to this part of lecture.	**so** the sense of taste as well as the sense of smell, along with other senses will decline with age.

LANGUAGE SPOTLIGHT 2

. . . .

Cause and effect: discourse markers or signals

When writing, talking or reading about *cause and effect* the following types of cues or signals may occur:
- contrast and comparison
- condition and consequence
- reason.

Other cues are addition/example as discussed in Unit 3.

Task A | Discourse cues

The following exercises help you to notice and use discourse markers and understand how they function in texts.

❶ Examine the following table, then ⟨circle⟩ every discourse cue which indicates contrast, comparison, condition, consequence or reason that you find in the text *World languages and world writers* (on the next page).

CONTRAST	COMPARISON	CONDITION	CONSEQUENCE	REASON
conversely	similarly	if	as a result	since
while	likewise	unless	thus	as
in comparison	correspondingly	provided that	so	so
in contrast	equally	for	therefore	because (of)
whereas	in the same way	so that	consequently	due to
instead	in the same manner	whether	it follows that	owing to
on the contrary	equally important as	depending on	thereby	the reason why
but			then	
			in that case	
			admittedly	
			accordingly	
			hence	
			leads to	

❷ Read the text a second time and circle all the cues you can find. Place each cue in the table under the appropriate heading.

- **Ellipsis** means the omission from a sentence of a word or words that would clarify meaning. Ellipsis means words are left out. The reason words are left out is to avoid repetition.

- **Substitution** means to use one word in place of another. And we use substitution in English for the same reason – to avoid repetition. Getting used to ellipses in English will help you to understand written texts that you read.

World Languages and World Writers

When reading books from world literature you will find new language. The books are largely in English but the new language is called 'world language'. This language is created by the gifted writers, who, as a consequence of coming from countries that were mostly former British colonies, began adding to the language and bringing to it the richness of their own traditions. Thus, the works are often called post-colonial writings. As the language of the powers was English, the result is a combination of original language, but grounded in English. For example, from Africa comes Chinua Achebe. Achebe brings African mythology and proverbs into his writing; then there is the Indian writer RK Narayan who paints a wonderful and quite funny portrait of everyday Indian life in novel form. The Caribbean brought Jamaica Kincaid and Derek Walcott. Kincaid has written about family relationships, in contrast to Walcott who writes poetry. There is also the Russian novelist, Alexander Solzhenitsyn. He stated, 'I am encouraged by a keen sense of World Literature as the one great heart that beats for the cares and misfortunes of our world, even though each corner sees and experiences them in a different way…a living, heartfelt unity reflecting the growing spiritual unity of mankind.'

CONTRAST	COMPARISON	CONDITION	CONSEQUENCE	REASON	ADDITION	EXAMPLE

Task B | Ellipsis and substitution

Read the examples below.

> **Example 1**
>
> *I enjoyed the lunch very much, but I thought the lunch was a little expensive. The lunch was special and we ordered the lunch a day in advance.*
>
> Although correct, it reads with too much repetition. Four 'lunches' in two sentences is too many!

- Read the following using ellipsis and substitution:

                 (the lunch)   **(the lunch)**   **(the lunch)**

I enjoyed the lunch very much, but I thought (it) ^ a little expensive. (It) ^ was special and we ordered ^ a day in advance.

'It' substitutes for 'lunch' in the first instance and there is an omission in the last instance. The reader must carry the information forward in their mind in texts. Substitution and ellipsis go together.

> **Example 2**
>
> *If your friends don't want to speak English, how can you encourage your friends to speak English?*
>
> If your friends don't want to speak English, how can you encourage them?

                                    (your friends)

                                (to speak English)

If your friends don't want to speak English, how can you encourage them ^ ^ ?

> **Example 3 ( ) = what is ellipsed**
>
> *Life is never easy and it is difficult to be happy all the time. People seek happiness in many ways and we all need to learn how to be happy.*
>
> Life is never easy and it is difficult to be happy. People seek happiness in many ways and we all need to learn how ^ (to be happy).

Task C | Locating ellipsed words and substitutions

Read the following excerpt from a young adult story and find the omissions or ellipsed words, and note the substitutions.

The howling simply would not stop! I lay in my bedroom listening to the wind, certain, however,

    (1)   (2)

that it ^ came from a different source ^.

          (3)

I had heard it ^ before, one dark night when both my parents went to a dinner party and left me

         (4)   (5)

home alone. I had insisted ^ because at thirteen, I am certainly old enough ^!

       (6)   (7)   (8)   (9)

What was it ^? And why was it ^ so eerie? I decided to contact my best friend, Sam, and ask him ^ to listen ^ over

        (10)   (11)   (12)

the phone. I picked it ^ up and waited for the dial tone. There was none ^. Strange ^, I thought. I decided to use my

      (13)

mobile phone^ instead.

Now things got even stranger. My mobile had a message on the screen that said 'Welcome to the Howling'!

                                                    (14)

I absolutely freaked out and threw the phone across the room before realising that answering ^ was the only way I might

                                         (15)   (16)

ever find out what was really going on. I raced across the room, picked it ^ up, then realised that I didn't know how ^!

1 _____   2 _____

3 _____   4 _____

5 _____   6 _____

7 _____   8 _____

9 _____   10 _____

11 _____   12 _____

13 _____   14 _____

15 _____   16 _____

SPEAKING 2 •••

Extemporary speaking

You cannot always count on a rehearsal to speak. These one minute exercises in speaking without practice and preparation are to help you move forward in speed and confidence when called upon to talk. Relax and have fun. Speak loudly and clearly.

Task A | Speaking 'from the hip'!

Here are some speech ideas – Get on your feet! You have one minute to choose a topic and:

❶ Explain why you're late to class.

❷ Describe the greatest gift you have ever received.

❸ Talk about the most wonderful teacher you have ever had.

❹ Talk about the worst teacher you have ever had.

❺ Tell us how your dream lover looks and acts.

❻ Tell us your idea of the most wonderful place on earth.

❼ Explain how being the richest person in the world would be wonderful.

❽ Explain how being the richest person in the world would be terrible.

❾ Explain how you might save the world from an alien space landing.

❿ Convince us that the ipad is the best invention of the 21st century.

Task A | Cause and effect

Fill in the blank spaces in the reading below using discourse signals/markers of cause and effect.

Most people would agree that one major key to success in study of any kind is application. _____ a person applies her or himself to a task, _____they have a better chance of success _____ someone who does not. Another important aspect is motivation. _____ a person is motivated, they will study and _____ they are more likely to remember what they are studying.

The _____ that both application and motivation are important has been researched over many years. ___ __ _____ __ this research, students can be confident that their efforts will be rewarded __ they only apply themselves and really want to learn. _____ __ this fact, teachers continue to try to motivate.

GET READY FOR UNIT 5: THE NEWS

Read the following articles to help you get ready for Unit 5.

- <http://www.computerworld.com/s/article/9173922/Wikipedia_founder_praises_Google_over_China_decision>
- <http://www.huffingtonpost.com/2010/03/29/new-wikipedia-layout-2010_n_517007.html>.

Consider the following questions about the sites.

- What makes news?
- What makes a news announcement?
- Why has Wikipedia been announced in the huffingtonpost.com website?

While reading, make notes for yourself and find and write down any new vocabulary.

5

'We demand freedom of speech and freedom of press, although we have nothing to say and nothing worth printing.'

Kahlil Gibran

THE NEWS

In this unit you are going to think. You will think about issues of newsworthy importance around the world in the fields of sociology and psychology, and read, listen, discuss and write about these issues. You will examine linguistic ways to recognise, then deal with persuasion, opinion, bias and fact. You must see the differences between these forms of writing and speaking in order to critically consider what the writer or speaker is offering. You will learn extended paragraph writing, conquer perfect tenses and revise material presented in previous units. To extend vocabulary, there is also independent work around university word lists.

BY THE END OF THIS UNIT, YOU SHOULD:

SKILL	TASK	PAGE
have increased general knowledge about the current world-wide issue of refugees and critically considered it	**Speaking 1** *Task A*	118
	Reading & Critical Thinking *Tasks A–F*	118–122
	Speaking 2 *Task A*	140–141
have increased knowledge around the field of psychology and social learning theory and critically considered it	**Listening & Note-taking** *Tasks A, B*	133–134
practise the staging within an oral presentation	**Listening & Note-taking** *Task A*	133
learn language differences between fact and opinion in writing and speech	**Reading & Critical Thinking** *Tasks A–F*	118–122
recognise bias and persuasion and how written and spoken language functions to create it	**Reading & Critical Thinking** *Tasks B–G*	119–123
	Listening & Note-taking *Tasks C, D*	134–135
read and think critically	**Reading & Critical Thinking** *Task G*	122–123
know more about register and apply that knowledge to your own writing	**Language Spotlight 1** *Tasks A, B*	123–124
track main ideas/participants through a text to increase comprehension in reading and understand the use of pronominal referencing	**Language Spotlight 1** *Tasks C, D*	125–126
study a university word list and increase vocabulary	**Language Spotlight 1** *Task G*	127
know how to write an extended introductory paragraph	**Writing** *Tasks A, B, C*	127–130
paraphrase main ideas from a reading	**Writing** *Task D*	131–133
when listening to a lecture, know where you are within the stages of the talk in order to keep on task and not get lost	**Listening & Note-taking 1** *Task A*	133
understand how to listen for fact versus opinion and take notes of important points	**Listening & Note-taking** *Tasks B, C, D*	134–135
use perfect tenses	**Language Spotlight 2** *Tasks A, B*	137–140
review narratives, participant tracking, processes and tense	**Language Spotlight 2** *Tasks C, D*	140
critically consider information and events posted on a website	**Further Connections**	142

Considering some issues around refugees

Most countries in the world today are facing migrations of people who are displaced from their own countries by war, famine, natural disasters or persecution. These seekers of a new life are some times referred to as asylum seekers. They are refugees. *refugee(s)* (n)

❷ Does your country accept refugees?

❸ If you answered 'yes' to the question above, from which countries do the refugees arrive?

❹ What are some of the reasons that people become refugees?

❺ Do you believe that a country has a humanitarian responsibility with regard to people from another country who are under threat of death if they remain in their own country?

❻ What is your personal opinion about refugees or asylum seekers in the world today?

Task A | Refugees and your country

Ask your partner the following questions:

❶ Does your country accept applications from refugees?

READING & CRITICAL THINKING

Fact and opinion

Two opposing points of view are presented from two fictitious newspapers. They are written as if from the editor of papers.

Bias and persuasion mean that people have an opinion and sometimes attempt to present their opinion as fact. There is a difference between opinion and fact. The work you do in this section will teach vocabulary, acquaint you with important issues and help you learn how to distinguish fact from opinion.

Task A | Vocabulary

❶ Try to match the vocabulary in the columns to their definitions.

Editorial 1 from *The Social Left Herald* '*Stranded refugees lose again*' (on the next page) contains all the vocabulary words. If reading the article does not explain the vocabulary enough, then use your dictionary as a last resort.

Word	Meaning
[a] stranded (v)	an accusation
[b] determination (n)	the political party not in power
[c] asylum seekers (n)	a person who migrates into a country for permanent residence
[d] refugee (n)	to drive aground on a shore, esp. of the sea, as a ship, a fish, etc.; to bring into a helpless position
[e] humanitarian (adj)	to follow a course of action
[f] indictment (n)	people seeking a refuge or a sanctuary – a safe place
[g] opposition (n)	a going out; a departure or emigration, usu. of a large number of people
[h] interned (v)	the act of coming to a decision: the fixing or settling of a purpose; the settlement of a dispute by authoritative decision
[i] pursue avenues (v)	to diminish or destroy the purity of
[j] tarnish (v)	one who flees for refuge or safety, esp. to a foreign country, as in time of political upheaval, war, etc
[k] immigrant (n)	obliged to reside (stay or live) within prescribed limits and not allowed to leave them, as prisoners of war or enemy aliens, or troops who take refuge in a neutral country
[l] exodus (n)	having regard to the interests of all mankind

Task B | Reading and understanding implication

Read the editorial and answer the questions that follow.

Editorial 1

The Social Left Herald

News for those who care about the real issues

Stranded refugees lose again ...

1. It is unfortunate, if not downright illegal, when a country assumes a position outside international and United Nations determinations. Today, another boatload of desperate people has been towed out of waters near our shores. This country has created a tarnished reputation for itself with regard to the handling and treatment of refugees attempting to enter the country via boats. Asylum seekers are referred to by the current government as 'illegal immigrants', which is ridiculous and incorrect as one cannot be an immigrant when one is a refugee. Additionally, this government most definitely appears to have as an agenda, the elimination of participation in policies which allow new people into the country via any means other than visa application.

2. The editor of this newspaper recalls the 70s when the Vietnam War necessitated an exodus from some regions of that country via similarly dangerous means as that used by the current people fleeing war-torn countries. Leaking boats were rescued by the military (which currently has quite a different agenda) from the seas nearby our shores, humanitarian care was taken with these asylum seekers and processing of their claims for refugee status was carried out efficiently and quickly.

3. Not so today. This government has gone so far as to engage the military to 'guard' our shores in a so-called 'border protection policy' and to send ships (even leaking) loaded down with people onwards, rather than allowing them to pursue the avenues that should be open to them. Worse still, if they do get onshore, the processing times for their claims for refugee status have taken years! The asylum seekers are being interned; they are kept in camps in hostile environments with little or no stimulation. Additionally, children are housed with adults without schooling or entertainment. This is rapidly becoming a human rights issue and is a sad indictment of our government which is heartless at the very least and racist at its worst.

4. The opposition is not offering solutions through new policies either. Thus, our only power as a people is to question and, ultimately, reject both parties and to place support with the Left Greens Democracy Party which has made public its humanitarian and legal policies regarding this issue.   *Bill Bradley*

❶ Using your dictionary, define the word 'issue'.

_____

_____

❷ What does the bold lettering beneath the name of the paper say and what does it mean?

_____

_____

❸ After reading the headline, what issue do you believe is going to be discussed in the article?

_____

_____

❹ Examine the headline and write what else you think the article is going to discuss.

_____

_____

❺ From the headline, can you guess which side of the issue the editorial will take?

_____

_____

❻ What does the headline 'Stranded refugees lose again ...' imply?

_____

_____

7 Identify the author of the editorial and write the name.

_____

_____

8 Examine the name of the newspaper. Are there any clues in the name of the paper that might give you an idea of what the editor may say in this article?

_____

_____

9 Who is the possible audience for this editorial?

_____

_____

10 Do you know what the term 'left' implies in Western politics?

_____

_____

Task C | Vocabulary

1 Try to match the vocabulary in the columns to their definitions. Editorial 2 from *The Finance Review*, 'Weekly world financial indicators' contains all the vocabulary words. If reading the article does not explain the vocabulary enough, then use your dictionary as a last resort.

Word	Meaning
[a] commotion (n)	government expenditure which exceeds the money available; also called 'in the red'
[b] financial (adj)	to deter/discourage through fear or doubt about proceeding
[c] budget deficit (noun group)	to set upon with arguments, pleading, entreaties
[d] deterrent (n)	requests using pleading
[e] influx (n)	concerning money
[f] assailment (n)	the arrival of people in great quantity
[g] entreaties (n)	improve by alteration, substitution, abolition
[h] reforms (n)	political or social disturbance

Purpose or intention of writer: identifying bias, connotations and attempts to influence
Bias indicates looking at something in a way that is one-sided or prejudiced in its presentation. Bias is an opinion disguised as fact.

Task D | Reading and thinking about the intention of the author

1 Students should read Editorial 2 that follows.

Editorial 2

The Finance Review

Weekly world financial indicators

1. Despite the current commotion raised by a small minority surrounding the government's policies concerning illegal immigrants, thankfully, there is a wiser, more financial view.

2. The cost burden of processing illegal immigrants has and is becoming an increasing encumbrance upon the taxpayers of this country. The government's sensible border protection policies, although lifting the defence budget considerably and creating a temporary budget deficit, are preferable. Engaging in border protection will prove a deterrent to other illegal immigrants and discourage people smugglers.

3. This country could ill afford an influx of the magnitude that other less prudent policies might give rise to. The continuous assailment upon the government and entreaties from a few bleeding hearts to alter these policies is not viable. Financial markets have responded strongly to the government's stance in a positive way.

4. This editor has observed national division around this issue widen. The press is divided and individuals have strong opinions concerning who has the right to apply to live in their country. The fact is that illegal immigrants are queue jumpers. Diplomatic representation in countries of origin, which support the international coalition of nations is the proper procedure to follow. Additionally, many of the claimants are not actually refugees and are merely seeking to shortcut an established process.

5. As polling has demonstrated, there is confidence in the wider community and markets will continue to reflect this confidence in the current government and its reforms.

Task E | Purpose, intention, bias, persuasion

Discovering a writer's purpose

Now that you have read the two opinion pieces which both concern a particular government's policies around refugees entering their country, try to examine the purpose of each writer within each editorial. Begin with *The Social Left Herald*.

1 What opinion does the topic sentence in the introductory paragraph express?

_____

_____

_____

2 Write the adjectives and noun groups used to express this opinion.

_____

_____

_____

3 Write the adjective from sentence 2 that describes the editor's opinion of the people seeking refuge.

_____

_____

4 Write the adjective from sentence 3 that describes the editor's opinion of the country's reputation.

_____

_____

5 What does the writer imply and intend you to think about the military in para 2 when he or she writes 'Leaking boats were rescued by the military (which currently has quite a different agenda) from the seas nearby our shores …'?

_____

_____

_____

6 When you read 'humanitarian care was taken with these asylum seekers and processing of their claims for refugee status was carried out efficiently and quickly', does the past simple passive 'was taken' and 'was carried out' imply that this is not happening now but it did happen in the past?

_____

_____

7 In para 3, what is the implication of using ' ' (quote marks) around the word *guard*?

_____

_____

8 In para 3, ' ' are used again around '*border protection policy*'. Why?

_____

_____

9 Why does the author choose to write '*so-called border protection policy*' rather than simply '*border protection policy*'?

_____

_____

10 In para 3, find the exclamation mark and explain what is implied by its use.

_____

_____

_____

11 In para 3, what is the writer's view of the government?

_____

_____

12 In the final paragraph, what <u>statement</u> does the writer make concerning the opposition party?

_____

_____

13 How does the writer attempt to influence the reader?

_____

_____

14 In the last paragraph, the intention of this writer is revealed. Look at the text after the summation or conclusion cue – 'Thus'. Write what the author believes is our only option.

_____

_____

_____

15 Based on your reading of the entire editorial comment, what was the author's intention? In other words, why was this article written? You may choose from the following comments:

[a] to criticise the current government's policies around refugees

[b] to encourage support for the Left Greens Democracy Party

[c] to appeal to the public for support for international refugees

[d] to question the humanitarian nature of internment

[e] all the above.

Task F | Opinion vs fact – Persuasive writing

Editorial 2 shows how language creates meaning and how language choices help a writer to express an opinion. Editorial 2 also tries to persuade the reader to think as the writer does. Certain language choices have been made for that purpose.

Answer the following questions based on Editorial 2.

1 What opinion does the topic sentence in the introductory paragraph express? _____

_____

② Write the nouns and noun phrases used to express this opinion. _____

_____

③ What purpose does the word 'Despite' serve as the first word in sentence 1? _____

_____

④ What purpose does the word 'thankfully' serve in sentence 1? _____

_____

⑤ The writer uses an argument beginning in para 2. How does this argument begin? _____

_____

⑥ What does 'sensible' refer to? _____

_____

⑦ What is the writer's view of the government's border protection policies? _____

_____

⑧ What is the financial effect of the government's border protection policies according to the writer?

_____

_____

⑨ Since the writer says that the policies will lift the defence budget (more money will be spent) and create a budget deficit (the country will be in debt), he or she still argues that they are a good thing. What one key word signals to the reader that this is going to be the argument? _____

_____

⑩ Why are the border policies preferable? _____

_____

⑪ Is the statement 'This country could ill afford an influx of the magnitude that other less prudent policies might give rise to' a fact or an opinion? _____

_____

⑫ Is the above statement in question 11 worded like a fact? How do you know that it is not necessarily factual? _____

_____

⑬ What evidence is there that refugees are actually 'queue jumpers' as the editor states? _____

_____

⑭ How does the writer attempt to convince the reader to agree with him/her in the last paragraph? _____

_____

Task G | Reading critically; thinking critically

Critical reading

Reading critically means to question what you read. Read with thought and consider who wrote what you are reading and why they wrote it. Also consider the language used within the text. Do you accept the 'naming of things' that is there? For example, if you read the following sentence what would you think? *The low class Zinahossies are ruining the cities and suburbs where they have moved. These people are different, with different customs and habits.* Do you see words that indicate the writer's opinion? Can you see bias? Who is this writer to make such a statement? Words such as 'low class' and 'different' are value judgments – 'Different' from whom or what? The reader does not have sufficient information to agree or disagree. The reader may agree, but it's important to know that this writer has not necessarily written fact, only opinion. If the writer goes on to prove these statements with facts, figures, historical analysis, then the reader may make a decision based on that.

Read the text *Language as power* on the next page and answer these questions.

① What is the main point of the article? Choose from the options below.

    [a] The main point is that language is constructed.
    [b] The main point is that readers must not believe all they read.
    [c] The main point is that people speak different languages.

② What does the writer want from readers? In other words, what is the writer hoping to teach the readers to do? _____

_____

③ Who constructs the rules around language and what institutions does language serve? _____

_____

④ What does social convention have to do with language and its construction? _____

_____

⑤ **[a]** Look at para 5. Can you list a few examples of when people are supposed to speak only a certain length of time? _____

_____

    [b] Can you list some examples of a situation where a writer is not allowed to write or where a writer might write something, but it would not be read?_____

_____

    [c] List some examples of a situation where a writer's work is not allowed to be read. _____

_____

⑥ What is one way that you can become a critical reader?

_____

Language as power

1. Why does language matter? Except for people speaking different languages, don't we all accomplish the same thing with language – communication? No, because some people have power and others do not. Language serves those in power very well and they are often the ones who make the rules as to how language must be used.

2. Social conventions about who has power are maintained largely through language. When you examine the feminist movement in the West from the 60s onwards, language had to be changed in order to stop the 'norm' always being male. Textbooks defined scientists, teachers, everyone, really as '... A *man* who ...'. Gender was and (often still is) a determiner in power relations. The naming of things creates our feelings about them and determines how we think about these things. If you refer to a woman as a 'woman', it is correct and direct. If you refer to a woman as a 'chick' or a 'slut', then the name means something else. 'Chick' often means 'young or sexy' and 'slut' means a 'woman of loose morals' (note that 'slut' is almost never used for a man in English.) These names have power to hurt or offend, yet they all mean woman.

3. Whether power is maintained by gender, race, wealth, politics, education or any number of other factors, it is largely maintained by 'dominant meanings' (Janks, 1993) which are often not challenged. When people do challenge the dominant meanings the status quo could be altered.

4. Language rules about who is allowed to speak or write and when, how people are addressed and how long people can be listened to are all governed by social conventions. Language is constructed. It is constructed by making choices from the range we have. It is not natural, nor inherent. It is learned and created and it serves the interests of the users, if they know how to use it.

5. Students of English as well as native speakers, by becoming critical readers, may gain insight into language as power and become more empowered themselves. 'Critical readers resist the power of print and do not believe everything they read' (Janks, 1993, iii).

Reference

Janks (1993) *Language, Identity and Power.* Johannesburg: Hodder & Stoughton.

LANGUAGE SPOTLIGHT 1

Remembering register

▶▶ **SB P. 20**

Register means all the factors that go into any discourse. In other words, everything that influences language choices in writing or conversation. It matters *who* is involved, *where* they are involved and *what* method is being used to communicate.

When register is correct, you hardly notice it. It means that language and grammar are presented correctly for the type of text or conversation. When register is incorrect, you notice that the language doesn't match the type of text or conversation. A student essay that started with a sentence such as 'I reckon that most countries have really stupid leaders…' would make the reader stumble, for, although this may be a possibly correct statement, it would be written in the wrong register for a student essay.

Task A | Considering register when you read

Read the following 'news story' and comment upon the register by answering the questions at the end of the story. Why do you think the words *news story* in the sentence above are between the punctuation marks called single quotation marks? Can you guess? It is not a quote.

Student debt continues to soar with no hope in sight

Governments in a lot of countries just keep on charging students more and more fees to go to university. They say that they are helping because the students can take out student loans. But the loans have interest to pay and, as well as that, I reckon when you graduate you're not exactly instantly rich so it's hard to pay back all that money.

I know people who live in countries where, as soon as they start working, the government takes out money from their salary to pay back their student loan. It might sound fair, but then again, it can go on for years, so really, we are having a situation where people who first join the work force are poor and stay poor to pay for their education.

❶ Does the article read like a news story? _____

❷ What is the usual format for reporting the news? Fill in the spaces using the story and then comment upon what is missing or different in this 'news' item.

[a] Headline _____

_____

[b] Name of reporter _____

[c] Summary of the event _____

_____

[d] Time and place stated _____

_____

[e] Background to the event _____

_____

❸ What sort of grammar is used:

[a] action verbs? _____

_____

[b] processes (verbs) of thinking and feeling? _____

_____

❹ Is higher lexis (vocabulary)/written language used?

_____

_____

❺ If it is not a 'news story', what does it read like?_____

_____

Task B | Considering register when you write

❶ Rewrite the story in the space below, making it a news story.

- use appropriate register
- remember to include the essential ingredients of a news story
- the author will be you – so write your name as the 'by-line'
- your teacher will provide a model for you to compare your writing with after you complete the writing.

Student Debt Continues as a Worldwide Issue

_____

_____

_____

_____

_____

_____

_____

_____

_____

_____

_____

_____

_____

_____

_____

_____

_____

_____

Task C | Tracking the main idea throughout texts

Pronominal referencing and participant tracking

When reading, you need to keep track of the main idea. That main idea is the main participant. Participants may be nouns, noun phrases, pronouns and substitute words for the main idea. In writing, you need to ensure it is clear to the reader who the participant(s) is or are.

❶ Identify the main participants and track (follow) them using underlining or highlighter.

❷ Read the news story below and identify the main participant. For example, in the previous sentence, the main participant is *the news story*.

Woman Missing in Lake Como

[1] The vehicle of an Italian woman was found on the river bank at Lake Como on Friday night. [2] The woman was last seen driving the car along the road above the lake, near the ferry stops late Friday afternoon. [3] The 2010 red Suburu was identified by her husband who stated that his wife was Mrs Viola Martese. [4] He said that his wife had taken the car around 7 pm. [5] She and her husband were holidaying in the area. [6] Mrs Martese is still missing. Police are investigating.

Here is another way to show and keep track of the main participant. In this case, we will use 'an Italian woman'.

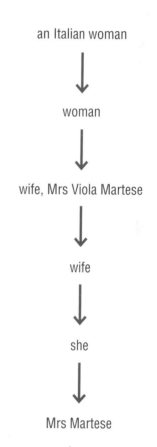

an Italian woman

↓

woman

↓

wife, Mrs Viola Martese

↓

wife

↓

she

↓

Mrs Martese

❶ Name the two main participants mentioned in the news story in the first sentence

_____

❷ Write the word that refers to *the Italian woman* in the second sentence. _____

❸ Write the word that refers to *the vehicle* in the second sentence. _____

❹ Write the word that refers to *the vehicle* in the third sentence. _____

❺ Write the words that refer to *the Italian woman* in the third sentence._____

❻ Write the word that refers to *the Italian woman* in sentence 4. And the vehicle? _____

❼ Write the word that refers to *the Italian woman* in sentence 5. _____

❽ Write the word that refers to *the Italian woman* in sentence 6 _____

Brief explanation of substitution in English

The vehicle of an Italian woman is a noun phrase; *The woman* is the same noun, *she* is the pronoun substituted for *woman* which refers back to *'an Italian woman'* and *Mrs Viola Martese* is the proper noun in the form of the woman's name.

The important point here is not the grammatical names, rather, how the grammar works. The reader must keep track of the person or idea/s that the writer introduces.

Task D | Tracking more than one participant simultaneously

Read the next news story below and track the following participants using the grid that follows the texts:

❶ Australian firefighters

❷ the scene of a factory fire

❸ five workers

❹ work

You can colour code, underline or number them as you track them the first time. Do one at a time.

Chemical Blaze Challenges Firefighters

1   Australian firefighters rushed to the scene of a factory fire, saving lives in West Wollongong on
2   Saturday night. The firefighters fought the chemical blaze for over seven hours. The brave and
3   tired men rescued five workers who were working overtime on the premises.
4   They were overcome by smoke and were lying on the factory floor when firefighters broke the
5   doors to enter the blazing building to check if anyone was inside.
6   The premises were presumed empty, but the workers had the key and had arranged with one
7   another to complete work there to meet a deadline. This work was crucial for a major overseas
8   contract for the company. The men in red said they were 'just doing their job correctly' by
9   checking the building for people. No charges are to be laid against the men.

Write each reference to the four participants found in the news item in the table below.

AUSTRALIAN FIREFIGHTERS		THE SCENE OF A FACTORY FIRE		FIVE WORKERS		WORK	
Line No	Reference	Line No	Reference	Line No	Reference	Line No	Reference

Task E | Main participants = theme

❶ Read the beginning of the next news story and locate the main participant/s.

> In the USA, a shocking, recent death penalty study of 4578 cases in a 23-year period (1973–1995) concluded that the courts found serious, reversible error in nearly seven of every ten capital sentence cases that were fully reviewed during the period (Moore, 2001).

List here:

[a] _____

[b] _____

[c] _____

[d] _____

❷ Now track a *death penalty study of 4578 cases in a 23-year period (1973–1995)*

_____

_____

❸ Now track a *23-year period*.

[a] _____

[b] _____

Task F | Referencing to avoid plagiarism revisited

You have studied in-text referencing involved in research, previously in Unit 1. (That was the kind of referencing that refers to source material, not the pronominal referencing just examined – ie she for woman, or he for man, or man for Mr Smith, etc). You have also studied the writing of references or bibliographies that are a requirement in essays and occur as the final section within any researched essay. You have examined these features in every unit of this book so far. The word 'reference' has referred to three different things.

Now, here is some helpful information on how to organise references as you gather them from books in a library. This technique works for internet references as well, since you must include information from websites as part of your bibliography or reference list at the end of your essays.

How to be organised when gathering source material
1. When you are in the library, photocopy the cover and the inside page (where the date of publication and publishing company name appear) from every book you refer to as well as the pages you are going to read.
2. For example, if you used pages 50 through 57 from a chapter in a book edited by Smith, and the writer of the chapter or unit was McPhee, you would photocopy:
   - the first page of the chapter;
   - all the pages you are going to read (beginning with the last page and working forward to the first page) – this will mean the pages come out in the correct numerical order on the photocopier;
   - the cover of the book;
   - the inside page where the publisher and publication date appears.
3. Carry a stapler with you. Staple all these pages together and this will be ONE of your references.

When you begin to complete your bibliography, you can find the information very easily!

Task G | University word lists

At university and in other academic contexts, it will help you to learn the higher lexis (vocabulary) that is commonly used by native English speakers at this level.

❶ Type the words 'University word list' in any search engine, OR go to the following website <http://www.latrobe.edu.au/lasu/eslresour/vocab.html>

❷ Find the red underlined words 'Academic Word List' and click on them.

❸ Examine the headwords of the 'Academic Word List' found at this site.

❹ Locate the sublists which are numbered beside each word. Make a list of the family of words beginning with *access*.

_____

_____

_____

_____

WRITING ••

Extended paragraph writing, including introductory paragraphs
A paragraph in English is like a little essay all on its own. It has an introduction, a body and a conclusion. The introduction is the topic or initial sentence, the body is made up of sentences which provide concrete, supporting evidence of the topic or about the topic, and the conclusion is the last sentence of the paragraph.

Previously, in Unit 4, you studied paragraph writing and methods of developing paragraphs. This section introduces you to extended paragraph writing, ie writing a more lengthy paragraph.

An extended paragraph has more detail. **You add details**. These details are facts. They support what you are writing about. Write factual details to extend your paragraph.

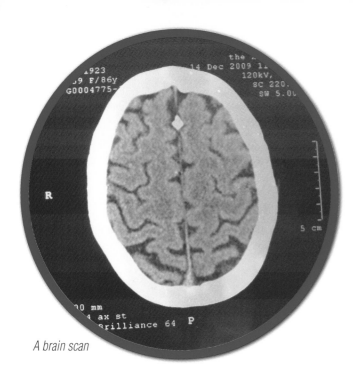

A brain scan

Task A | Study a model for extended paragraphing

Read the *model* text that follows about memory. It contains extended paragraphing. Note the following:

1 There are *two main participants*; the person being discussed and the topic of memory.

2 The method of paragraph development (Unit 4) is by *giving examples*. These examples are details and they are factual.

3 It is an introductory paragraph and has the usual staging: (a) General introductory statement (main idea);(b) Definition of terms and positioning the reader; and (c) Concluding sentence that may introduce the next paragraph.

Memory – An unusual case

General statement	→	There is a 41-year-old woman, an administrative assistant from California known in the medical literature only as 'AJ', who remembers almost every day of her life since age 11.

This explains or defines above, in addition there are a great many <u>details</u> and the addition of these details extends the paragraph... makes it longer

→ AJ states, 'My memory flows like a movie-non stop and uncontrollable. She remembers that at 12:34 pm on Sunday, August 3, 1986, a young man she had a crush on called her on the telephone. She remembers what happened in *Murphy Brown*, a television program, on December 12, 1988. And she remembers that on March 28, 1992, she had lunch with her father at the Beverly Hills Hotel. She remembers world events and trips to the grocery store, the weather and her emotions. Virtually every day is there. She's not easily stumped.

This develops the thinking further by giving examples – the introduction is extended.

→ There have been a handful of people over the years with uncommonly good memories. Kim Peek, the 56-year-old savant who inspired the movie *Rain Man*, is said to have memorised nearly 12 000 books (he reads a page in 8 to 19 seconds). 'S', a Russian journalist studied for three decades by the Russian neuropsychologist Alexander Luria, could remember impossibly long strings of words, numbers, and nonsense syllables years after he'd first heard them. But AJ is unique. Her extraordinary memory is not for facts or figures, but for her own life. Indeed, her inexhaustible memory for autobiographical details is so unprecedented and so poorly understood that James McGaugh, Elizabeth Parker and Larry Cahill, the neuroscientist at the University of California, Irvine, who have been studying her for the past seven years, had to coin a new medical term to describe her condition: hyperthymestic syndrome. AJ is an extreme on the spectrum of memory.

Task B | Extended paragraphing – Schema as per sequence or sentence order

1 Carefully read the paragraphs on the next page. Some sentences are not in the correct sequence or order. They are numbered though, for discussion with your teacher after you complete the supported writing.

2 Arrange and write/copy the sentences in the extended paragraph/s in order.

3 Study how the paragraph is extended and note why.

4 Remember, each one (A and B) is one, long paragraph.

5 When finished, go on to the second paragraph (B) and do the same.

Paragraph A

Archaeology in the field

① Every detail should, therefore, be recorded in the manner most conducive to referencing later. ② Between 1880 and 1890 he conducted a series of excavations on Cranborne Chase in southern England and published his results in four detailed monographs (1887–1898). ③ Pitt-Rivers insisted on careful, disciplined excavation and a total record of the finds. 'Excavators', he wrote, 'as a rule record only those things which appear to them important at the time, but fresh problems... are constantly arising'. ④ Although Worsaae and other famous explorers/discoverers – including in the eighteenth century Thomas Jefferson, third President of the United States, and in the nineteenth century Heinrich Schliemann (1822– 90), the discoverer of Troy, and Sir Flinders Petrie (1835–1942) – were pioneers of archaeology in the field, it was General Pitt-Rivers (1827–1900) who transformed excavation into a precise and meticulous technique.

Source: Whitehouse, D & R (1975) *Archaeological Atlas of the World.*

London: Thames and Hudson, p 13.

Archaeology in the field

Paragraph B

The white pond lily

① Each seed is in a little bag, which the botanists call an 'aril', and which serves to float the seed off for some distance from the parent plant. ② The aril finally decays and the seed falls to the bottom where, if the conditions are favourable, it develops into a new plant. ③ It has been stated that pond lilies, in the state of nature, have an interesting way of opening in the early morning, closing at noon, and opening again toward evening. ④ If the habits of the insects which pollinate these flowers were better known, we should possibly have the key to this action. ⑤ Each flower opens usually for several consecutive days, and the first day of its blooming it opens about an hour later and closes an hour earlier than the days following. ⑥ After about two months the pod bursts, letting the seeds out in the water. ⑦ In our ponds in parks and grounds we find that each species of pond lily opens and closes at its own particular time each day. ⑧ After the lilies have blossomed, the flower stem coils in a spiral and brings the ripening seeds below the surface of the water.

Source: Comstock, Botsford A, (1961) *Handbook of Nature-Study.* Cornell, Ithaca, NY, USA: Comstock Publishing, pp 496-97.

The white pond lily

Task C | Extended paragraphing

1 Write an extended paragraph of 200 to 250 words. Use the guide below to assist you. The writing is based upon personal information, so you will use your own experience and life to write it. It should still follow the format of an extended paragraph and be written in as academic a manner as possible.

TOPIC I am a student

Phrases that may help you:

In the past, my studies were conducted by or at …

After that, …

Following that, I…

Next, …

There were many schools I attended…

(or) There were many subjects I studied over the years, such as…

General statement: _____

_____

_____

_____

Adding details from the past: _____

_____

_____

_____

_____

_____

_____

_____

_____

Concluding statement: _____

_____

_____

_____

_____

❶ Read the text below *Population explosion over time*. Then paraphrase the main idea/s in each paragraph 1–9 by writing a short summary of each paragraph using your own words and some of the words from the text.

> The following phrases may help you:
>
> *was the result of/gave rise to/ demonstrates that…*

Population explosion over time

1. Let's examine the human population, its relationship to the world around it (its environment) and its growth over time. Until around 10 000 years ago, people ate wild plants and animals. Then, there was a climate change, and the new weather made it easier to plant things and establish small crops. People began to grow their own food and they also domesticated animals. Animals, such as the pre-cursor to the dog became friends of hunters. This change or transition from hunter-gatherer status was a great turning point in the history of humans. Humans related to nature in a different way, food supplies were more abundant, and this relationship now fostered a very rapid increase in population.

2. Thus, **population growth** is not a new thing on earth. The era referred to above has two names, the first is the **Neolithic era** but it could also be called the first **Agricultural Revolution**. Archaeologists discovered new tools from this time that provided evidence that people were cultivating crops. The relationship between food and population is what is known as a *constant* in biology.

3. Population increased relatively slowly until about the mid-1600s, when approximately 500 million people inhabited Earth. The population doubled to 1 billion within the next 200 years, doubled again to 2 billion between 1850 and 1930, (80 years) doubled again by 1975 (45 years) to over 3 billion and now, in 2007 (33 years), it has doubled yet again to 6 billion people.

    If the Agricultural Revolution is true, then the model of population growth known as **logistic** makes sense. More food gives rise to more people;

conversely, when many people compete for fewer resources, the population will decrease. That is the logistic model of population growth. For example, in the logistical model of population growth, there is the major biological assumption that increasing population density reduces the resources available for individual organisms, ultimately limiting population growth.

4. There is competition between individuals of the same species for the same limited resources. As population size increases, competition becomes more intense, and the growth rate declines in proportion to the intensity of competition. In other words, population growth is **density dependent**. How many people there are in relation to available resources will determine how many people can survive. Either the birth rate is decreased or the death rate is increased, or both.

5. Flies in a jar demonstrate density-dependent regulation in laboratory populations. For example, when a pair of fruit flies are placed in a jar with a constant amount of food added each day, population growth fits the logistic model. After a rapid increase, population growth levels off as the flies become so numerous that they outstrip their limited food supply. Each individual in a large population has a smaller share of the limited food than it would in a small population. Also, the more flies, the more concentrated the poisonous wastes become in the jar.

6. There are those who posit (or think and offer their position) that there is an analogy between human and the fruit flies in the experimental jar. As the world population rapidly increases at near

exponential levels, some offer a logistic model for the inevitable slowing down of population expansion. Our population on earth has doubled in 40 years. And, although food production methods have improved and increased the supply of food to many, it is undeniable that wide-spread famine exists. 854 million people across the world are hungry, up from 852 million a year ago. Everyday, almost 16000 children die from hunger-related causes – one child every five seconds. (Black, Morris & Bryce (2003) 'Where and Why Are 10 million Children Dying Every Year?'. *The Lancet*, 361: pp 2226–2234.)

7. It appears that increasing population density amongst humans reduces the resources available for individual organisms, ultimately limiting population growth. The 'ultimately' has not arrived because at the moment the population is still growing. Will there be ever increasing hunger, death and poverty for those humans not living in countries that have access to resources outside their own boundaries in order that population growth slows down?

8. The regions experiencing the most severe environmental degradation and in many cases hunger are the same that are experiencing the most rapid population growth. These countries, the so-called 'developing countries', are getting some assistance with conservation of their bio diversity from organisations such as Conservation International who work with the support of USAID (United States Agency for International Development).

9. But, the question remains, will humans overcome their biological destiny and 'conquer nature'? And, if so, how will they do this? Could resources be shared more equitably so that countries with ancient traditions that are being developed by richer nations participate in a more prosperous way? Is it true that 'living simply' might allow others to 'simply live'? Is this another turning point in history? Will the death rate exceed the birth rate in order to *level* population growth? What part will you play wherever you exist on the planet?

Source: Adapted from (Pearson Longman text)

Paragraph paraphrases

1. _____
   _____
   _____
   _____

2. _____
   _____
   _____
   _____

3. _____
   _____
   _____

4. _____
   _____
   _____

5. _____
   _____

6. _____
   _____
   _____
   _____

7. _____
   _____
   _____

8. _____
   _____
   _____

9. _____
   _____
   _____

② Next, match the paraphrases below to each paragraph within the text by placing its number in the blank provided.

Model paraphrases

A ____ Comparisons between populations are possible. One comparison uses a laboratory model about fruit flies and humans. When members of the same species compete for food (or other resources) some die.

B ____ The first example of population growth was demonstrated thousands of years ago by the relationship of humans to the earth and this was the result of climate change.

C ____ Population density gives rise to the slowing down of population growth as resources become more scarce.

D ____ Emerging or developing countries have the fastest rates of population growth and also have the most degraded environments.

E ____ In the laboratory, experiments demonstrate that populations are density dependent.

F ____ The first Agricultural Revolution gave rise to the first population explosion.

G ____ Population growth has continued since the 1600s. There is a model of growth called 'logistic'.

H ____ Can humans be an exception to nature and natural forces?

I ____ In a logistic model, population is density dependent.

③ Finally, match your own paraphrases to the paraphrases above and compare them.

> ### Writing by paraphrasing – Read and write
> To paraphrase means to put another person's words into your own. You gather an idea from reading and then try to state that idea in different words from the original. It's a small summary. You paraphrase it. Why? Sometimes, it needs to be shorter. Also, it means you can interpret the thinking and make it your own. It is useful when you don't wish to copy word for word exactly what another author has written.
>
> When you paraphrase, you often use the ending of a sentence as the beginning of your paraphrase. Think about the **idea** and put that idea in your own words, don't simply copy words from the text.

LISTENING & NOTE-TAKING

Staging in lectures and presentations

In English, most all lectures or presentations will follow a pattern that is recognisable to a native speaking listener. If you are giving a presentation, then you must follow that pattern. When listening to a lecture, you will hear discourse cues or signals that will clearly indicate what stage of the lecture you are about to hear. Your comprehension and processing of information is enhanced by understanding these stages.

Task A | Reviewing discourse signals for predicting a speaker's stage within a presentation

Before you listen:

❶ Ask your partner to read out half of the oral discourse cues or markers.

Discourse cues/markers

Today, I would like to …
In conclusion...
There are three main points …
In 2002, Barker and Johnston …
To summarise …
In order to define 'cactus', it is important to consider …
This talk will cover two current theories around the topic of …
Thus, it is obvious that the government should provide …
It is beyond the scope of this presentation to include
   everything around the topic of forestry, so …
It would appear that one solution might be to …
Actually, there is not a great deal of research that has been
   carried out around this subject …
Let me begin by …
A great deal of research has been carried out around this
   aspect of the subject since 1922 …
Next
However
It is worth considering …

Task B | Markers and stages

❶ Match the oral discourse markers in Task A to the correct stage of a presentation by filling out the table below. Now, change roles and you read the cues.

> **Stages of a presentation**
>
> **Introduction** – this is the stage where you explain the title of your talk, give background information, provide definitions of terms and the scope of what you will cover.
>
> **Body** – this is the stage where you show the research you have accomplished, make relevant points if you have an argument to put forward, counter other arguments and name your sources.
>
> **Conclusion** – this is the stage where you summarise each main point (state again) and give a recommendation for the future.

INTRODUCTION	BODY	CONCLUSION

Task C | Using the language you know to prepare for listening

If you were attending a lecture today in any of the fields of Sociology, Psychology, Economics, Business or Science, you could come across the following information. Your lecturer will have prepared you by having a course outline with the dates for various lectures. The title of the lecture is *Bandura's social learning theory as it applies to observation of acts of media violence*. Albert Bandura was and still is, a famous psychologist. You can find the actual 1965 footage of his Bobo Doll Experiment on YouTube.com by searching *Bandura Bobo Doll*. Professor Bandura from Stanford University introduces it and explains his findings. This lecture is based upon those findings and outlines what a Bobo Doll is and what his experiment entailed.

❶ How do you think you could prepare for this lecture?

❷ Try to define the vocabulary words on the next page as they relate to social learning using what knowledge you have around the subject. If you have web access or a dictionary, look up the words. Your teacher has the definitions for you to check against.

Vocabulary

psychology (n) _____

_____

social learning theory (n group) _____

_____

conditioning (n) _____

_____

aggressive (adj) aggressive behaviour/He's *aggressive*. _____

_____

procedure (n) _____

_____

exposure (n) _____

_____

inconsistent (n) or (adj) _____

_____

consistent (n) or (adj) _____

_____

Task D | Note-taking instructions and practice

CD 1

❶ Listen to the recording *Bandura's social learning theory* and write down the types of behaviour the lecturer describes. Make notes for the definitions and fill these in later more thoroughly.

KEY PHRASES/INCLUDING LECTURER'S OPINION	TYPES OF BEHAVIOUR	DEFINITIONS AND EXPLANATIONS
_____	_____	_____
_____	_____	_____
_____	_____	_____
_____	_____	_____
_____	_____	_____
_____	_____	_____
_____	_____	_____

Task E | Understanding what you heard in the part lecture

1 What experiment proved that children will copy violence when it is modelled or shown to them?

_____

_____

2 What is a Bobo Doll? Paraphrase the experiment with the doll in the laboratory from your notes.

_____

_____

3 Which sentence tells you there are other views concerning the influence of media violence? A,B or C?

A. _Bandura researched social learning theory, but his first attempts were not concerned with media violence._

B. _There are thousands of experiments which have concluded that violence in children has increased; however, it is difficult to link this increase to violence within society._

C. _The link between violence presented in the mass media and aggressive behaviour has been established in laboratory conditions; however, there are still inconsistent findings._

_____

_____

_____

4 The lecturer states that _Unfortunately, many early behaviouralists did not link thought processes to behaviour._ What key word gives you an opinion? What is the opinion of the speaker then?

_____

_____

5 Bandura believed there were three main influences in people's lives. This lecture covers one. What is the influence discussed here?

_____

_____

6 According to the lecture, what group of people were Bandura's main interest?

_____

_____

7 Social learning is based upon what main idea?

_____

_____

8 The children in the Bobo Doll Experiment had a choice of materials to play with the doll after watching a model of behaviour. What did they choose to do with Bobo after observing?

_____

_____

9 What conclusions came out of this experiment and social learning theories concerning media violence and watching of violence?

_____

_____

10 What do you think the lecturer's opinion is about media violence?

_____

_____

11 State some phrases that the lecturer used that showed his opinion.

_____

_____

12 The lecturer stated that some of the findings were inconsistent and that fact makes the debate around the issue of media violence 'a _____

_____

_____

13 How does the lecturer support his statement of opinion that 'Children are more violent than before'?

_____

_____

14 According to the lecturer, the psychologist Bandura was very respected. What evidence do you have to prove this? Use logic to deduce this answer.

_____

_____

15 What do you think about watching acts of violence repeatedly? Do you believe it influences the mind?

_____

_____

Bandura

_____

_____

Bobo Doll

_____

_____

_____

_____

_____

_____

Bandura's theory

_____

_____

_____

Experiment

_____

_____

_____

_____

_____

_____

_____

Theory of

_____

_____

LANGUAGE SPOTLIGHT 2

Perfect tenses

These activities will assist you to understand the past perfect tense and revise the genre of narrative or recount.

Past, past perfect and past continuous tenses are used in the following narrative, which is based upon a true story about a whaling ship called the *Essex*. The *Essex* is famous because it is the only whaling ship ever sunk by a whale. The ship was built in 1796 in Salem, Massachusetts, which is now part of the USA and her last whaling voyage in the Pacific Ocean took place in November 1819.

The account is an extract from the book Owen Chase wrote on the wreck of the *Essex*. He was first mate on the ship and was 23 years old. He later became a captain and wrote a book titled,

Narrative of the Most Extraordinary and Distressing Shipwreck of the Whaleship Essex.

The narrative is a factual recount of the events. This is followed by the story of what happened to the crew while their ship was sinking. Both texts are true stories and, because they are recount, will contain certain grammatical features and structure:

- time and date
- place
- chronological order with temporal sequencers
- description of events, but not many feelings
- specific participants
- verbs of action.

Narrative of the Most Extraordinary and Distressing Shipwreck of the whaleship *Essex*, by Captain Owen Chase, 1821

1. The whaleship *Essex* left Nantucket on her last whaling voyage to the Pacific on August 12, 1819, under Captain Pollard. It carried a crew of 21 men, one was a boy of only 15.

2. The *Essex* sailed from the Galapagos Islands. Presently a whale rose and spouted a short distance ahead of my boat. I made all speed towards him, came up with him and struck him with a harpoon. Feeling the harpoon he threw himself in an agony over towards the boat and giving a severe blow with his tail struck the boat near the edge of the water amidships and stove a hole in her. I immediately took up the boat hatchet and cut the line from the harpoon to disengage the boat from the whale which by this time was moving off with great velocity. I succeeded in getting clear of him with the loss of the harpoon and line and finding the water pouring fast into the boat, I hastily stuffed four or five of our jackets in the hole, ordering one man to keep constantly bailing and the rest to pull immediately for the ship. We succeeded in keeping the boat free and shortly gained (arrived at) the ship.

3. The boat which had been stove was immediately hoisted in … I was in the act of nailing on the canvas when I observed a very large spermaceti whale, as well as I could judge about 85 feet [26 metres] in length. He broke water about 20 rods [100 metres = 110 yards] off our weather bow and he was lying quietly, with his head in a direction for the ship … In less than two or three seconds, he made directly for us at the rate of about three knots. I ordered the boy at the helm to put it hard up, intending to sheer off and avoid him.

4. The words were scarcely out of my mouth before he came down upon us with full speed and struck the ship with his head, just forward of the fore-chains. He gave us such an appalling and tremendous jar as nearly threw us all on our faces … We looked at each other with perfect amazement, deprived almost of the power of speech. Many minutes elapsed before we were able to realise the dreadful accident … The whale started off in a direction to leeward (away from the ship).

5. … I dispatched orders … I again discovered the whale, apparently in convulsions … He was enveloped in the foam of the sea … and I could distinctly see him smite his jaws together, as if distracted with rage and fury. He remained a short time in this situation and then started off with great velocity across the bow of the ship to windward. I was aroused with the cry of a man at the hatchway: 'Here he is – he is making for us again'.

6. I turned around and saw him, about 100 rods directly ahead of us, coming down apparently with twice his ordinary speed and, it appeared to me at that moment, with tenfold fury and vengeance in his aspect. The surf flew in all directions about him, and his course towards us was marked by white foam a rod in width, which he made with the continual violent thrashing of his tail. His head was about half out of water, and in that way he came upon and again struck the ship. He struck her to windward, directly under the cathead, and completely stove in her bow …

In Text 2, which follows below, the writer is not giving a first hand account in the past, but is telling the reader about known past events, and for this reason, the past perfect tense is used a great deal.

Text 2

What happened to the crew of the *Essex*?

1. The crew were in three whale boats while their ship was sinking. They had had time to gain access to the other boats. There was plenty of time while the crew sadly watched their ship, its decks awash, slowly sinking. Before the *Essex* went down, however, members of the crew had gone aboard several times to collect food, water and other things. They had taken as much as they had room for in the boats.

2. They had sails and masts in all boats and were more than 1600 kilometres away from the nearest land mass. Those who were rescued eventually, were rescued three months later.

3. They told their rescuers how in great storms and in the darkness the three boats had become separated. The winds had blown them off course. They told how supplies of food and water in their boat had run low and how at the time of their rescue they were living on a handful (70 grams) of bread each per day. They told how one after another their crew mates had died of starvation and thirst until there were only three survivors left out of seven. Day after day, week after week, they had looked in vain for a sail. They told how they had eaten parts of the dead men's bodies in order to stay alive. They told how the huge waves in great storms had threatened to sink their boat and how they had had to keep bailing to keep afloat. Only their trust in God's goodness had saved them from the hopelessness and despair which leads to death …

Source: Text 1 and 2 compiled from and with the permission of GA Pittman (1983) *Whales and Whaling in the Pacific*. New Caledonia: SPC, pp 77–88.

Task A | Locating verbs (processes) in recounts

❶ Underline or circle all verbs (processes) in each recount narrative.

❷ Make a list of each of the verbs (processes). Include the noun so that you have a phrase, not just an isolated verb. For example, in line 1 of the first text, you would write: The *Essex* <u>sailed</u>; a whale <u>rose and spouted</u>;

❸ Next to your list, note which tense is used.

❹ Go back to each sentence and examine the verbs in their context. Why do you think the simple past is used in the first recount?

❺ Why is the past perfect used in the second recount? Note: the past perfect tense expresses a past action that was completed before another past time or event.

❻ Create a paragraph of a story and then another paragraph which tells about that story and which uses these two tenses? For example, tell (or write) a story about a famous tragedy in your country. Write it as the person to whom it happened. Then, write a sequel to your story explaining the story further, but not in the first person.

An interesting note: It was a son of Owen Chase, himself a whaler following his father's trade, whom Herman Melville spoke to and to whom the son gave a copy of his father's book (about the sinking of the *Essex* by a whale). Melville used the story in his masterpiece *Moby Dick*, which you may have heard about or read.

Task B | First person vs third person

❶ Compare the first person account, *Narrative of the Most Extraordinary and Distressing Shipwreck of the Whaleship* Essex, to the third person narrative, *What happened to the crew of the* Essex?

Use the table on the next page to help you. The first one has been done for you.

FIRST PERSON NARRATIVE		THIRD PERSON NARRATIVE	
Narrative of the Most Extraordinary and Distressing Shipwreck of the whaleship Essex, *by Captain Owen Chase, 1821*		*What happened to the crew of the* Essex?	
Author	Owen Chase	Author	Unknown
Target audience	Present day historians; anyone interested in whaling	Target audience	The same audience

Task C | Language features of narratives

❶ Refer to the items below, which were pointed out at the beginning of these narratives. Next to each one, write evidence of them from either of the two texts.

- time and date _____

  _____

- place _____

  _____

- chronological order with temporal sequencers _____

  _____

- description of events, but not many feelings _____

  _____

- specific participants _____

  _____

- verbs of action _____

  _____

Task D | Participant tracking

❶ Track the participant – *the whale* – in Text 1, *Narrative of the Most Extraordinary and Distressing Shipwreck of the Whaleship* Essex.

Use any format you wish – circle all participants, or make a list of the words – draw lines from each reference to the next.

SPEAKING 2 •••

Task A | Refugees – What are they? Who are they? Where are they? What do they have to do with me?

❶ You have examined and read a little bit about refugees and some opinions related to 'asylum seekers' in this unit. In pairs, or groups, research the current state of affairs using the WWW and following the instructions in the table. Discuss your findings with one another and see where you agree and disagree with the questions.

QUESTIONS	WEB SEARCH AND LINKS/INSTRUCTIONS	ANSWERS
Who or what is a refugee?	Enter – What is a refugee? Define: refugee 1. An exile who flees for safety <Wordnetweb.princeton.edu/perl/webwn> Scan the definitions. Locate the definitions that refer to refugees and not bands and songs by bands or in movies. En. <wikipedia.org/wiki/refugees>	Choose a definition and write it here
How many Belgian refugees are estimated to be in Britain?	Enter – Refugees in England. Query – <nytimes.com/gst/abstract.html>	
What is NERS?	<www.refugee.org.uk/welcome.htm>	
On the NERS page, locate Statistics and click the link. Who is NESPARS?		
How far back do the statistics go from NESPARS?		
On the main page of the North of England Refugee Service, what does the Chief Executive Officer, Daoud Zaaroura say about refugees? Do you agree or disagree with that statement? Why?	<www.refugee.org.uk/welcome/htm>	
What does Amnesty International say about Refugees' Human Rights?	Enter – Refugees in Australia Amnesty International <www.refugeesaustralia.org/directory.htm www.amnesty.org.au/refugees/>	
What do you think should be done about refugees in the world? Do you believe countries have responsibilities to other people who are fleeing their own country?	Research this question using your own ideas.	
What does the sign show above the words 'Situation dire for refugees in Malaysia' on the home page of the site you are on now? (Amnesty International)		
What, according to campaign coordinator Dr Graham Thom has happened to many Burmese refugees who flee to Malaysia?	Click – 'View all Features' under 'Situation dire for refugees in Malaysia'.	
	Enter your own country and find out about refugees.	

Task A | General knowledge, comprehension and critically considering information (a news announcement) from a website

Read the following announcement and answer the questions.

The Global CIO Summit Virtual Event

Companies in every industry and in every country need to be able to design, source, build, market, sell and support products around the globe and around the clock. In that context, global CIOs need to create IT systems and processes that are powerful, flexible and secure enough to achieve that daunting goal, and they need to do so quickly. And in today's customer-driven economy, CIOs and their teams need to deliver global infrastructures and applications that squeeze out extra costs and time.

In light of these challenges, the first Global CIO Summit Virtual Event will be held in Oct 2009. This immersive, online environment will feature presentations, research, and collaboration sessions that address these and other issues.

Among six key note speakers are; Ralph Szygenda, Corporate CIO, General Motors and Toby Redshaw, Global CIO, Aviva plc, London.

To register, go to <techweb.com/globalciosummit>.

---

❶ When will the Global CIO event be held?

_____

❷ Where is it to be held?

_____

_____

❸ Who is in charge of this event?

_____

❹ What are their qualifications for organising and running it?

_____

❺ Does the information provide explanations for words like CIO?

_____

❻ What do you think a CIO is?

_____

❼ The announcement states that this is the 'first' summit held. Can you know if this is true?

_____

❽ Who are the two key note speakers listed and what positions do they hold?

_____

_____

❾ How would you research the key note speakers' credentials?

_____

❿ What is the web address provided for registration to the event?

_____

⓫ If you can, type in virtual events calendar and see what's currently happening.

_____

⓬ What are some advantages of this type of conference? (ie a 'virtual' conference held online rather than in a particular place).

_____

_____

⓭ What are some possible disadvantages?

_____

_____

Task A | Extension

Consider the question below:

The 21st century has seen the advent of an incredible amount of technology. Choose one form of technology and trace its origins, development and current state. Discuss its impact upon society and determine whether it is part of the global marketplace.

Task B | The 'Greenhouse effect'

Read the following articles to help you get ready for Unit 6:

*   <www.simple.wikipedia.org/wiki/Greenhouse_effect>

*   <www.simple.wikipedia.org/wiki/Global_warming>.

While you are reading, think about:

*   What is the 'Greenhouse effect'?

*   Why does the 'Greenhouse effect' occur?

*   What are the likely results of the 'Greenhouse effect'?

Also, make notes of some vocabulary from these readings about global warming and the 'Greenhouse effect'.

6

ENVIRONMENT AND LIFESTYLE

'As between the soul and the body there is a bond, so are the body and its environment linked together.'
Kahlil Gibran

In this unit, you will look at a topic that affects every aspect of our lives as well as touching on many academic disciplines, including business. It is also a common topic on international English language exams. In this context, you will practise distinguishing between facts and opinions. You will follow and make predictions, and will describe numerical information from graphs and charts before carrying out and writing up a small research project. You will take notes from, and summarise, a detailed spoken explanation and will learn some further ways of reporting the work of others. Then you will practise debating opinions.

BY THE END OF THIS UNIT, YOU SHOULD:

SKILL	TASK	PAGE
have gained confidence about discussing environmental issues and have expanded your vocabulary in this topic area	Entire unit	146–166
have gained further practice of a range of reading skills	**Reading & Critical Thinking** Reading 1, 2 and 3 *All tasks*	147–152
have practised distinguishing between facts and opinions	**Reading & Critical Thinking** Reading 1 *Task A*	147–148
have practised avoiding emotional language	**Reading & Critical Thinking** Reading 1 *Task B*	149
have investigated the plausibility of some claims on the internet	**Reading & Critical Thinking** Reading 1 *Task D*	149
have developed a plan for extensive reading outside class	**Reading & Critical Thinking** Reading 2 *Task A*	150
be able to identify written predictions	**Language Spotlight 1** *Tasks A, B*	153
be able to choose appropriate tenses and verbs for future predictions	**Language Spotlight 1** *Task C*	153
have practised writing descriptions of numerical information expressed in graphs and charts	**Writing** Writing 1 *Task A*	154–157
have carried out a small research project	**Writing** Writing 2 *Task B*	160
be able to write research reports	**Writing** Writing 2 *Task A* Writing 2 *Task C*	157–160 161
be able to write abstracts	**Writing** Writing 2 *Task D*	161
have practised taking notes from detailed spoken explanations	**Listening & Note-taking** *Task A*	162–163
be able to write summaries of information from spoken explanations	**Listening & Note-taking** *Task B*	163
be able to use a range of reporting verbs in spoken and written referencing	**Language Spotlight 2** *Task A*	164
have practised useful expressions for refuting, exemplifying, requesting further explanation and checking understanding	**Speaking 2** *Tasks A, B, C*	165–166

Task A | Sharing knowledge about environmental issues

❶ **[a]** Copy the table below onto a large sheet of paper (one per group), leaving plenty of space to write in each cell.

[b] In small groups, share your current knowledge to fill in the table. Add additional environmental issues at the bottom of the table; you can make your table as large as you like. The pictures in this unit may help you think of ideas.

NAME OF ISSUE	WHAT IS THE ISSUE?	CAUSE OF THE ISSUE	POSSIBLE SOLUTIONS BY GOVERNMENT	POSSIBLE SOLUTIONS BY INDIVIDUALS	ASSOCIATED VOCABULARY
Deforestation					
Global warming					
Pollution					

❷ Compare your table with another group's. How similar are they? Explain anything that is in your table but not in theirs.

❸ Back in your original group, add to the table extra information that you learned from the other group.

❹ As a group, rank the issues in order of seriousness. Then, explain your rankings to the class, giving justifications.

READING 1

Task A | Distinguishing between facts and opinions

❶ Discuss in pairs the following questions:

[a] List at least five words you associate with the word 'nuclear' and five that you associate with 'poison', around the circles below. Use a dictionary and/or thesaurus, or check with your teacher. Explain to your partner any words that you know but your partner doesn't.

nuclear

poison

[b] Is nuclear power used in your country? If so, what for?

[c] What are the advantages of nuclear power?

[d] What do you know about the dangers of nuclear radiation?

[e] Have you heard of any nuclear accidents? What do you know about their consequences?

❷ Read the essay *Our world is one place* on the next page to gain an overview of the main ideas.

❸ Tell your partner what you think the main ideas are. Does your partner agree with you?

❹ Answer these questions by yourself. Then discuss your answers with your partner.

[a] As a first impression, do you think the essay expresses facts or opinions, or both?

_____

[b] Facts can be things which are commonly known or understood and are accepted as fact, eg humans need air to breathe. Find a point which you believe is factual. Why do you think it is fact?

_____

_____

[c] Find at least one point that is clearly a personal opinion.

_____

[d] Find at least one point that could be a fact or could be an opinion. What additional information would help you decide?

_____

_____

[e] How many points are referenced? Do you think this is sufficient for academic writing? Why?

_____

_____

[f] Can you find out more about the referenced point, and check to see whether the author has interpreted his/her sources correctly? Or is something missing?

_____

[g] Can you believe the non-referenced points, other than those that are common knowledge or are clearly opinions?

_____

[h] Find at least one point which is stated as true but could easily be proved wrong with just one example. How could you change the wording to make the statement stronger (ie harder to prove wrong)?

_____

_____

[i] Do any points sound too extreme to be true?

_____

[j] Do we know who the author is? When you read texts that claim to give facts, is it important to know who the author is? Who is the author working for? Is this information also important?

_____

_____

_____

Our world is one place

① The world is interconnected. One country's activities influence others and transgressions against nature affect us all. One country's practices not only influence itself but also impact upon every other country.

② One example comes from the highly dangerous and unclean energy source, nuclear power. The risk factor in this industry, despite attempts by its proponents to minimise it, is beyond belief. For example, regarding the 1986 disaster when the Chernobyl nuclear power plant in what is now the Ukraine experienced an explosion and a fire, Gordon and Suzuki (1990, p57) report that radioactive particles travelled as far as Sweden within days and eventually as far as Canada's Arctic. Radioactive dust poisoned the city and surrounding rural areas and caused problems such as miscarriages in pregnant women, and cancer to other unborn as well as living children and adults.

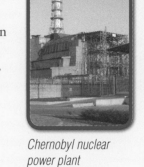

Chernobyl nuclear power plant

③ In this major wheat-growing area, crops within a huge radius were contaminated, bringing financial ruin to farmers and food shortages for the Ukrainian people. Children who were poisoned and who now have cancers as a direct result are called *the children of Chernobyl*. Since this accident occurred in 1986, more than one generation is affected. Some of the children of Chernobyl visit the US and Australia each year under sponsorship programmes so they can enjoy sunshine and holidays before they die of the cancers transmitted from the Chernobyl nuclear power accident. Estimates concerning how long the soil will remain contaminated range from 100 years to 250 000 years.

④ Another example of one country's activities seriously impacting upon another's is the notorious Ok Tedi mine, a uranium mine in Papua New Guinea which previously belonged to BHP Billiton of Australia. This mine was of extreme importance to the country's economy, providing over 25% of Papua New Guinea's export earnings. However, careless management of hazardous waste (known as *tailings*) resulted in the destruction of an entire river and subsequently all the communities that relied upon that river for fishing. Almost every plant, fish and living organism died as a result of the tailings leaking out of ponds. Soil could no longer grow anything, people could no longer eat any of the fish and soon there was no fish left to eat. The ponds (which leaked in heavy rain and ruined the water and plant life) were simply dug out of the earth with no linings on the walls; this was the management system of highly radioactive and poisonous waste by a multi-billion dollar company. While the mine employed a large number of people, 50 000 had their livelihood destroyed by the mine. A total of 1300 square metres of land was destroyed. Eventually, the company was forced, by courts of law, to compensate and relocate villagers who were affected by the problems.

⑤ Meteorology provides another example of world interconnectedness. A question has been posed – *Might a butterfly flapping its wings affect the weather in another part of the world?* Some scientists answer a definite 'yes' to this research question. This is an example of how some scientists believe that all parts of the globe are linked together.

⑥ The earth is a sphere and all parts are connected; we inhabit it together. Regardless of culture, class, race or religion, humankind remains a biological organism co-existing with and dependent upon nature in order to survive. Oxygen and water are as essential to humans as they are to fish, dogs and cats.

⑦ Our interdependence as a species with other living organisms is unquestionable, yet both elected and non-elected governments around the world continue to allow and indeed pursue courses of action which are ruining the balance between us and the earth. This balance is a matter of survival for the human race.

⑧ In conclusion, in the past 200 years a new technological age has begun, led by Western consumerist, capitalist countries and followed by all developing nations. This model sets out to enslave nature – not work with nature in harmony but to control nature. It is this writer's opinion that nature will not be controlled; nature refuses to be the slave of humankind and will retaliate by simply eliminating the species from the planet.

⑨ A major nuclear accident or war would cause worldwide damage to our environment, from which no person would survive. Continued irresponsible mining of uranium and no facilities for safe waste disposal will contaminate the earth to the extent that all water is poisonous and land unproductive and unfit for food production. Arid wastelands and more desertification will occur as a result of global warming along with rising sea levels which will take whole countries out.

⑩ People need to unite and fight for their planet. Governments that continue to pollute the earth with no regard to the future should be removed from office. Scientists need to gain the respect of decision makers and be listened to, so that the planet and its peoples have a chance for a future where we are not wearing gas masks to breathe nor protective suits to shield us from the polluted air and rain. Will we end up underground or in domed cities like stories of science fiction? Is this what you want?

Task B | Academic style – Avoiding emotional language

> ### Emotional connotations
> Connotations are feelings associated with words. Two words with quite similar meanings might have very different connotations. For example, 'eat' and 'consume' can have the same meaning, but 'consume' can have a more negative connotation; if we say 'people consume a large amount of tuna', we might have a feeling of people using up the tuna fish that's available. If we say 'people eat a large amount of tuna', the connotation is much more neutral.

1 With a partner, discuss these questions about the text in Task A.

[a] How passionate do you think the author is about the subject? Highlight or mark the text which provides evidence for your answer.

[b] What other techniques does the author use to make the text emotional?

[c] Do you think the passionate language and techniques are normal in academic writing?

[d] Do you think that academic writing could be shocking or surprising? If so, how?

2 Paraphrase the language you identified in question 1a to make it more academic in style. Then, compare your paraphrases with a partner's and discuss them. In this instance, you may use any of the non-passionate vocabulary from the text in your paraphrases.

Task C | Reactions to the text

1 Discuss with a partner or in small groups:

[a] Do you agree with the author's thesis? Why (not)?

[b] What are some of the issues around the following:
- nuclear power
- mining for minerals
- mining for coal.

[c] In your opinion, should nuclear power and mining be banned, allowed in certain circumstances only, or allowed freely? Give reasons for your answer.

[d] In what ways has the text in Task A affected your opinion?

2 Choose a thesis relating to something you talked about in question 1. Discuss the supporting ideas you could use with your partner. Then, write a discussion or argument essay around that thesis/issue.

Task D | Investigating the plausibility of claims on the internet

Work with a partner and answer these questions:

1 Look at the Wikipedia page about:
- The Chernobyl disaster
- The Ok Tedi environmental disaster
- The butterfly effect.

Find:
- three points that appear to be facts and for which there are no references
- three facts or opinions that are referenced.

2 For the three points that are referenced, follow the references. Decide:
- Is the source credible?
- Why do you think so?

3 Do an internet search for the same key word. Go to one of the pages found by the search.
- Are references provided?
- Can you follow the references easily?
- Can you find out who wrote it?

READING 2

Task A | Reading practice outside class

1 With a partner:

[a] List as many reasons as you can why reading practice outside class is important.

[b] Think of useful aims for your reading practice.

[c] Write the ways that you already read outside class in the top row of the table.

[d] For each, give a mark out of 5 for enjoyment, ease of use and usefulness.

READING ACTIVITY (EG READING NOVELS IN ENGLISH)	MARK OUT OF 5 FOR		
	ENJOYMENT	EASE OF USE	USEFULNESS
Your ideas			
Other good ideas			

2 Join with another pair. Compare your tables and discuss the marks you gave. Choose the ideas from the other pair you like best and that fit your aims. Write them in the bottom row of your table (leaving space for more).

3 Swap your tables with another group. Discuss them as before. When you get your book back, add new ideas to your table.

4 Decide which ideas are best for you and try them out. Next week, you will tell your group which ideas you tried out.

5 After you have tried out these ideas, you may reject some, change others or try new ones.

6 Make a plan for your future extensive reading.

READING 3

Task A | Further skimming and scanning practice

In this section (page 152), you will read a text *Waste disposal in Asia* which is an extract from a United Nations report in which various predictions are given for the future of the environment in South-east Asia. It is taken from the end of a chapter on Asia and the Pacific.

❶ Discuss these questions with a partner.

   [a] What kind of waste do you throw away regularly?

   [b] What do you know about what happens to it after you throw it away?

   [c] What issues with waste disposal have to be overcome?

   [d] Can humanity continue throwing things away forever?

❷ Skimming race. Read the ideas below. Race to be the first to write down the paragraph numbers in which you might find each idea.

   _____ **[a]** How countries are improving waste disposal in cities.

   _____ **[b]** Amount of waste generated in a particular country.

   _____ **[c]** Population growth in a particular country.

   _____ **[d]** Predictions for growth in waste from cities.

   _____ **[e]** Effects of dangerous untreated chemicals.

❸ Scan the text to answer the following questions.

   [a] How many contaminated sites are there in New Zealand?

   _____

   [b] What problems are affecting the South Pacific?

   _____

   [c] Which Chinese cities are 'Environmental Star Cities'?

   _____

   [d] What percentage of Asia's solid waste is expected to be produced in East Asia in 2010?

   _____

   [e] What's the expected total population of Chinese cities in 2025?

   _____

   [f] What's the average proportion of GDP spent on water and sanitation in Asia?

   _____

❹ Work with a partner to answer these questions:

   [a] Complete the table using points made in the text.

   [b] What does the text imply are the root causes of these problems?

   [c] Which of the problems mentioned do you think is:
     • most important
     • most difficult to deal with

   [d] Which problems exist in your country, that you are aware of? Which are most important? Which are most difficult to deal with?

PROBLEM MENTIONED IN THE TEXT	ARE THEY BEING DEALT WITH? IF SO, WHERE? AND WHERE NOT?
rapid increase in the amount of waste	

Waste disposal in Asia

1   The total waste generated in the region amounts to 2 600 million tonnes a year, of which solid waste accounts for 700 million tonnes and industrial activities generate 1 900 million tonnes (UNESCAP/ADB, 1995). The East Asian sub-region generated 46 per cent (327 million tonnes) of the region's total municipal solid waste in 1992–93; this proportion is projected to increase to 60 per cent by 2010 (UNESCAP/ADB, 1995). The Republic of Korea produced a 50 per cent increase in industrial waste in the period 1991–95 alone (Government of Republic of Korea, 1998). In New Zealand, many of the country's estimated 7800 contaminated sites are in urban industrial areas (New Zealand Ministry for the Environment, 1997).

2   A large percentage of industrial wastes in South-east Asia, including hazardous chemicals, are discharged without treatment. These wastes affect not only the health of workers who handle them but also residents living near factories. However, many countries now have effective legislation for the safe handling, treatment and disposal of these substances (ASEAN, 1997).

3   Many urban waste disposal systems are inadequate. Disposal of untreated waste water is spreading water-borne diseases and damaging marine and aquatic life. In response, investment in domestic waste water treatment systems has been accelerated in many South-east Asian countries, including Malaysia. High rates of urbanisation in the island states of the South Pacific have also resulted in serious waste management and pollution problems, particularly with respect to their impacts on groundwater resources. Environmentally safe disposal of solid waste and sewage is a major concern for the island states of the region where land and therefore available disposal sites are limited and sewage systems are lacking.

4   In most countries, the urban population is likely to grow threefold in the next 40 years (UNESCAP/ADB, 1995). China alone is expected to have 832 million urban residents by 2025.

5   As urban areas, especially megacities, expand further, increases in traffic congestion, water and air pollution, and slums and squatters settlements can be expected. Most large Asian cities already face an acute shortage of safe drinking water and a fivefold increase in demand is anticipated within the next 40 years (UNESCAP/ADB, 1995). Public expenditure on water and sanitation is around one per cent of GDP for most countries of the region, and is likely to rise.

6   In East Asia, many governments are attempting to reduce the growth of their primary cities by curbing rural-urban migration. A new trend for Chinese cities is represented by Dalian, Zhuhai and Xiamen, Zhangjiagang, Shenzhen and Weihai, the Environmental Star Cities, where great efforts are being made to emphasise urban environmental planning and pollution prevention amid economic development (SEPA, 1998).

7   Urbanisation is one of the most significant issues facing Asia and the Pacific. How to deal with increasing amounts of urban and industrial waste is a major concern for most of the region. While the proportion of people living in urban centres is still lower than that in developed countries, it is rising rapidly, and is focused on a few urban centres.

References

ASEAN (1997) *First ASEAN State of the Environment Report*. Jakarta: Indonesia ASEAN Secretariat.

Government of Republic of Korea (1998) *Environmental Protection in Korea*. Kwacheon, Republic of Korea Ministry of Environment. New Zealand Ministry for the Environment (1997) *The State of New Zealand's Environment 1997*. Wellington, New Zealand: GP Publications.

SEPA (1998) *Report on the State of the Environment in China 1997*. State Environmental Protection Administration of China. Beijing, China: China State Environmental Science Press.

UNESCAP/ADB (1995) *State of the Environment in Asia and the Pacific 1995*. United Nations, New York, USA: United Nations Economic and Social Commission for Asia and the Pacific, and Asian Development Bank.

Source: United Nations (2000) *Global Environmental Outlook 2000: UNEP's Millennium Report on the Environment*. London: Earthscan Publications, pp 92, 93. Reproduced with permission.

Vocabulary

discharge (v)   allow something (usually a liquid or gas) to escape into the outside world; *discharge* (n for the substance discharged)

sewage (n)   waste from human bodies that is carried away from houses; *sewer* (n) = the pipes through which sewage flows

curb (v)   to reduce the amount of something (usually something harmful); a *curb* (n)

Discharge

Predicting the future

Task A | Tenses for future predictions

❶ The text *Waste disposal in Asia* in the previous reading section talked about the past, present and future. Work with a partner to answer the following questions.

[a] Complete the table using the text to analyse which verb forms are used to refer to **future events**.

VERB FORM	NUMBER OF TIMES USED ONLY WITH FUTURE MEANING
'will'	
present simple active	
present simple passive	
present continuous	
'be' verb + (adverb) + infinitive	

[b] Do you find anything surprising?

[c] Make a list of the verbs used in the text to express future predictions. How many more, with similar meaning, can you add to your list?

[d] What differences can you see between the following?
- 'is predicted not to …'
- 'isn't predicted to …'.

Task B | Reading to identify predictions

❶ Find a newspaper article or web page that looks at future trends. Use your knowledge of tenses and verb choice to locate the phrases of prediction.

❷ Tell other students the predictions you found and discuss them. Also share your list of language to express predictions. Try to use these expressions in your own writing in the future.

Task C | Writing and speaking to express future predictions

❶ Write a short report to summarise what you found in Task B. Pay particular attention to verb and tense choice with the predictions expressed. Don't use phrases from the article!

❷ Think about the questions below, and plan how you might respond to them using expressions from Task A. Then, with a partner, discuss the questions:

[a] How do you think your lifestyle will be affected by environmental problems in the future?

[b] How well do you think the world will deal with environmental problems?

WRITING 1

Task A | Describing/reporting numerical information from charts and graphs

❶ **[a]** Look at the following numerical information relating to multicultural aspects of a fictional country, Govirmda. Which figure is:

  i. a pie chart? _____

  ii. a line graph (often just called a graph)? _____

  iii. a bar chart? _____

[b] Look at the titles of Figures 6.1 to 6.3. What information do they include (eg place, reason, person for whom the research was done, time, or what the figures show)?

Small hydroelectric power station

Fig 6.1: Greenhouse gas emissions from various sources in Govirmda, 1990–2010 and projection to 2020

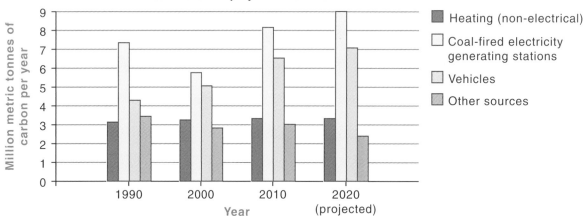

- Heating (non-electrical)
- Coal-fired electricity generating stations
- Vehicles
- Other sources

Fig 6.2a:	Fig 6.2b:	Fig 6.2c:
Percentage of electricity generated by various methods (1980)	**Percentage of electricity generated by various methods (2000)**	**Percentage of electricity generated by various methods (2020)**

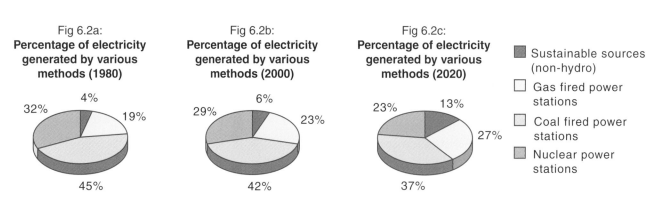

- Sustainable sources (non-hydro)
- Gas fired power stations
- Coal fired power stations
- Nuclear power stations

Fig 6.3: Levels of air pollution in various cities in Govirmda, 1990–2010 and projection to 2020

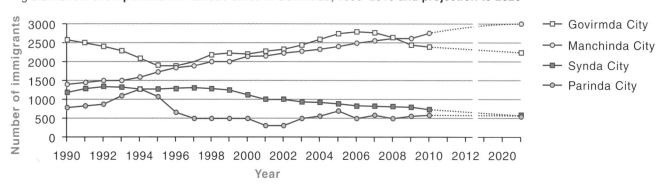

- Govirmda City
- Manchinda City
- Synda City
- Parinda City

[c] Write a sentence or two for each graph or chart to explain what it represents. The first has been done for you as an example.

Figure 6.1 – *This bar chart shows the amounts of greenhouse gas emissions in Govirmda from different sources, in 1990, 2000, 2010 and forecasts for 2020.*

Figure 6.2 – _____

_____

_____

_____

Figure 6.3 – _____

_____

_____

_____

[d] Compare your answers with a partner's. Are the meanings the same, even if the words are different?

❷ **Features of written descriptions of numerical information.**

Read a description of Figure 6.1 in the text below. While reading, think about which language features might be characteristic of numerical descriptions.

❸ Answer the following questions, which focus on identifying common features of written descriptions of numerical information.

[a] What main point is represented in each body paragraph?

Para 2 _____

Para 3 _____

Para 4 _____

Para 5 _____

[b] How do you think the author chose the order of paragraphs?

[c] Which tenses are used in the following situations:
- to describe the actual chart, not the data on it?
- to describe the data in the bars representing 1990, 2000 and 2010?
- to describe the data in the bars representing 2020?

Greenhouse gas emissions in Govirmda

1 Govirmda generates greenhouse gases from a range of sources, some of which have increased emissions since 1990 and some of which have seen a reduction in that time period. This report will look at some of the details about these changes. Figure 6.1 shows three main sources of greenhouse gas emissions (heating, coal-fired power stations and vehicles), together with 'other' sources, which are grouped together.

2 The most common source of emissions during this period was coal-fired electricity generating stations. Despite a significant fall from nearly 7.5 million tonnes of carbon in 1990 to just below 6 million ten years later, the trend over the whole period covered by the chart was towards a general increase, with emissions of over 8 million tonnes in 2010 and around 9 million tonnes projected for 2020.

3 Emissions from vehicles also showed a strong upward trend. In 1990, only 4.3 million tonnes of carbon were emitted from this source, but this figure rose to 5.1 million in 2000 and 6.6 million in 2010. A figure of 7.1 million is projected for

2020, which would mean a considerable increase of nearly two-thirds over the 30-year period.

4 Emissions from heating and other sources showed the least noticeable changes. Heating resulted in 3.2 million tonnes of carbon emissions in 1990, rising minimally to 3.4 million in 2010. No further increase or decrease is forecast over the next five years. The contribution of the 'other sources' was the only fall over the whole period. In 2000, emissions from 'other sources' were approximately half a million tonnes lower than they had been in 1990, at around 2.8 million tonnes. Emission levels were virtually constant over the next ten years, reaching 3 million in 2010. However, a small drop to 2.5 million is anticipated by 2020.

5 The data demonstrates that, overall, carbon emissions in Govirmda have increased over the last 30 years, and that this trend is expected to continue until at least 2020. Of especial concern is the rise in emissions from vehicles and coal-fired power stations.

[d] Locate words from the text which describe change and no change, then complete the table.

	VERBS	NOUNS
to go up	_____	_____ _____
to go down	n/a	_____ _____ _____
to have no change	_____	n/a

[e] Fill in the boxes in the diagram below using the following words.

climb	gentle	rapid	sharp	decline
gradual	reach a peak	slight	drop	increase
remain constant	slow	fall	level off	remain stable
steep	a fluctuation	peak	rise	fluctuate

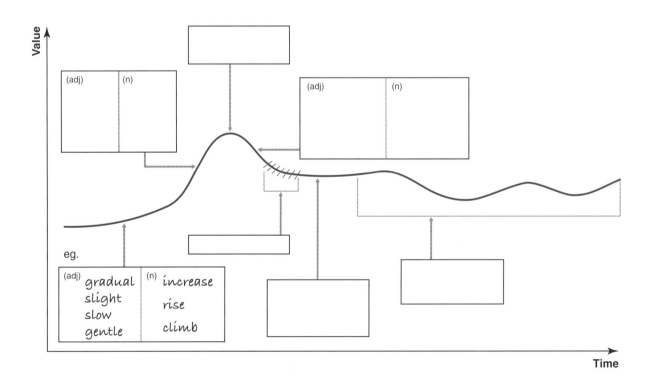

eg.

(adj) gradual slight slow gentle	(n) increase rise climb

④ Common mistakes to avoid. With a partner, find and correct the problems with the following, which relate to Fig 6.2. They are all grammatically correct; the mistakes are in the vocabulary and/or logical meaning.

[a] The percentage of electricity generated by nuclear power stations dropped down between 1990 and 2000.

[b] Less power was generated by nuclear power stations in 2000 than in 1980.

[c] Sustainable sources increased between 1980 and 2000.

❺ Writing to describe numerical information.

[a] Write a description of:
  i. Figures 6.2a, b and c together.
  ii. Figure 6.3.
  Use the work you did previously in this section to help you.

[b] Swap your writing with another student. Check whether your partner has included the features from Step 2 above.

[c] Exchange ideas about how each other's writing can be improved. For example, you could suggest different words to increase the variety of vocabulary.

[d] Write a second draft, incorporating ideas from your partner that you like.

WRITING 2

Task A | Introduction to research and research report genre

Research reports

As the name suggests, research reports describe research projects. Research drives most academic disciplines, and although different disciplines may report research in different formats, there are many similarities. Some common kinds of research include:

- *Experimental research*: Common in science; experimental researchers set up situations to test whether an idea (an hypothesis) is true
- *Observation*: In this, researchers watch in a systematic way what people, animals or natural phenomena do, and describe the patterns they see.
- *Library research* (sometimes called *secondary research*): You will most likely do a lot of this at university. It involves drawing information from existing publications.
- *Survey research*: Here, researchers ask questions of lots of people, and use statistics to find out averages, etc

In this section, you will read a basic survey research report, carry out your own small survey research project, and write up the results as a research report.

❶ With a partner, answer these questions based on what you know now. It may be useful to think back to research you did in your previous studies – such as experiments in science lessons, or surveys.

[a] What would you do first in a research project?
[b] What other steps are required?

❷ **Stages in a research report.** Complete the following with a partner.

[a] Put these stages in the order you might expect to find them in a research report.

_____ Findings (= what was discovered).

_____ Background (= background and context of the research, including why it was done).

_____ Method (= how the research was done).

_____ Aims (= what the researcher wanted to find out).

_____ Conclusions (= what the results mean).

Using modern, environmentally friendly transport

[b] Check your answers by looking at the headings in the research report written by an undergraduate student for an assignment, on page 159.

[c] Sometimes, these stages have different names. Match the words below with the heading with the same meaning in question 2[a].

Results	Introduction
Context	Procedure

[d] Are reports written in your language divided in the same way?

[e] Each stage may have sub-stages. For example, the Findings stage of the report you just looked at has sub-stages *4.1: Findings regarding knowledge*, and *4.2:*

Findings regarding behaviour. Look at the following sub-stage headings and decide what stage you would expect to find them in.

Definitions	Research design	Commentary
Discussion	Questionnaire design	Analysis
Data collection	Recommendations	Implications
Literature review	Data analysis techniques	

[f] This report (but not all research reports) has an abstract. Read the abstract on the next page and then the rest of the report and compare the two. What do you think the purpose of the abstract is?

❸ Identifying language features of reports. Work through the following with a partner.

[a] Read the report again. Complete the table with the tenses most often used in each section, and the reasons why you think they are used.

STAGE	TENSE OR VERB FORMS OFTEN USED	REASON
Background		
Aims		
Method		
Findings		
Conclusions		
Recommendation		

[b] Highlight the discourse signals in a different colour. Do you notice particular types of discourse signals in particular stages?

[c] What words are used to refer to the people who took part in the survey?

[d] What other research-related vocabulary can you find?

Vocabulary

implement (v)	if you implement something, you do it; *implementation* (n)
awareness (n)	if you *have awareness* of something, you know that it exists; *aware* (adj)
NGO (n)	Non-government organisation: an organisation that is separate from government. Usually they exist for charity or campaigning purposes and don't exist to make a profit
consumption (n)	buying or using things, especially things that are not really necessary; *consume* (v)
modify (adj)	if you modify something, you make changes to it to improve it; this word often has positive connotations; *a modification* (n)
devise (v)	to invent a new way to do something
elicit (v)	get someone to tell you
discrepancy (n)	an unexpected or illogical difference

Knowledgeable but slow to change? An investigation into the relationship between environmental knowledge and behavioural change.

Abstract
With increasing awareness around the world of the need to deal with environmental problems, it is useful to know how members of the public incorporate environmentally-friendly habits into their everyday life. In this study, 52 respondents were surveyed about their knowledge of and the extent of their implementation of the three Rs (Reduce, Reuse, Recycle). Results indicate that environmental advice should be re-directed towards providing practical ideas that can be cheaply and conveniently implemented by the public. Further, if efforts are made to reduce the cost and increase the convenience of environmentally sustainable behaviour, this will lead to greater adoption of such behaviour by the public.

1. Background

Environmental awareness has been increasing over the last few decades, due to campaigns by environmental NGOs and governments as well as education to encourage people to modify their behaviour along more sustainable lines. At the same time, some (but by no means all) businesses have supported this trend by developing and promoting 'green' or 'environmentally friendly' products. However, the trend towards increasing consumption has continued, resulting in increased use of packaging and energy. For example, large cars, especially four-wheel drives, with significantly increased fuel consumption, are becoming more popular. It is useful then to know how effective the educational campaigns have been, not only in increasing the public's knowledge but also in modifying their behaviour towards greater sustainability, and also to find out how campaigns can increase their effectiveness further.

2. Aims

The purpose of this research was first to investigate how much knowledge a representative sample of people actually have about environmentally sustainable behaviour and, secondly, to find out the extent to which this knowledge has led to a positive change in behaviour. A final aim was to look at the factors that are most effective at encouraging people to make their behaviour more sustainable, so that future campaigns can be targeted effectively.

3. Method

3.1 The sample

The sample size was 52. These respondents were selected from a variety of age, gender and socio-economic backgrounds. They were all residents of urban areas.

3.2 Data collection

This was carried out through the use of a questionnaire. Initially, the questions were trialled with a sample of 10 people. A new improved questionnaire was then devised. This comprised 10 questions and focused on some of the most common behaviours. It attempted to elicit frequencies of particular behaviours such as re-using items even when buying new ones was more convenient, and choosing to buy goods with less packaging than their competitors.

4. Findings

4.1 Findings regarding knowledge

Knowledge of what the three Rs represent was reassuringly high. Forty-five of the respondents (87%) could say what the three Rs were. However, only a much smaller proportion (23%, or 12 respondents) could say accurately that reduction of waste and consumption was the most important of the three. As for more practical knowledge, all participants knew how to recycle, but only two-thirds of the respondents (35 respondents) were able to give, without prompting, ways in which they could reduce their consumption. The weakest area of knowledge was in techniques for reusing, with only 16 respondents (31%) able to come up with unprompted ideas. However, when given suggestions such as taking used supermarket bags to the supermarket instead of being given more new ones, or buying reusable instead of disposable products, a high 90% said the idea was familiar.

4.2 Findings regarding behaviours

Turning to what people actually do rather than just know about, recycling was the largest category, with 79% saying they do this as much as possible and 88% of respondents claiming to do it from time to time. Reducing waste and consumption, however, was a very different matter, with only 69% doing anything in this regard. For example, just over half of all respondents (52%) said they had in the past bought an alternative product because it had less packaging, and 32 (58%) claimed that the energy consumption of products was a major factor in their purchasing decisions.

Re-using again was the least common behaviour, with only 62% able to cite examples of having done this. Just over one-third (18 respondents, or 35%) had reused supermarket bags, despite the high level of awareness of the importance of this, and only 38% of respondents said they never bought disposable products when reusable ones were available.

Despite having knowledge, almost everyone was aware of ideas for following the three Rs that they didn't actually do. Reasons given were as follows:

Inconvenient: 56%
Too expensive: 52%
'Uncool' or 'no one else does it': 18%

(Note: These figures add up to more than 100% because respondents were able to specify more than one reason.)

5. Conclusions

5.1 Commentary

It is clear that there is a discrepancy between knowledge of the three Rs, knowledge of how to follow them, and the extent to which people actually do follow them in their actions. It is interesting that many respondents who couldn't suggest a way to follow the three Rs were not only able to do this after prompting, but realised they actually did do it themselves. This suggests that a lot of knowledge is subconscious. However, it is disappointing that many people, despite knowing how to recycle, reduce and reuse, don't actually do it. Expense and lack of convenience are the biggest obstacles to environmentally sound behaviour.

5.2 Recommendations

Because such a large proportion couldn't name ways to reduce or reuse, the most important of the three Rs, it is recommended that campaigns shift their focus from recycling and highlighting the three Rs to actually providing concrete, practical suggestions for how to implement them. These suggestions should be as convenient and cheap as possible for the public, in order to reduce the obstacles to their implementation.

Task B | Mini research project

In this section, you will conduct and write up a small research project.

> **Group assignments**
> Many university courses include group assignments, in which the mark for each member of the group depends on how well the whole group works as a team. This section gives you experience at doing this.
> Because you are working in a group, you will have to negotiate in almost every step of this project. Everything you learned in previous units about discussion and tutorial participation skills will help.

❶ A research project often tries either to:

- answer particular questions (called research questions), or
- present a statement (called a *hypothesis*) and try to find out whether it's true or false.

What are the research questions in the research report in Task A?

❷ Work in small groups.

[a] Choose a topic for your research within the field that your teacher gives you.

[b] Decide on a research question or hypothesis.

[c] Write a questionnaire with between five and eight questions to investigate your research questions or test your hypothesis. For example, in the questionnaire used for Task A's research report, one of the questions may have been 'How often do you recycle?'

[d] Trial your questionnaire (conduct a pilot survey) in your class. This is to identify any problems there may be with the questionnaire. For example, there might be more than one way of understanding the question, or you might find it's impossible to draw conclusions from the answers to some of the questions.

[e] After looking at the results of the pilot survey, discuss how to adjust the questionnaire. Then revise the questionnaire.

[f] Carry out the main survey

[g] When finished, help each other to collate answers and draw conclusions. A group secretary should record the conclusions.

Abstract
When using published course book... materials to their particular teaching... a co-author of an EAP text book, w... have always intended that user... something borrowed to course boo... for an international audience o... freelancers, and it is intended that boo... where by interpretative course should...

Task C | Writing a research report

❶ Write a report of the research carried out in Task B. Your report should:

- be well staged
- use tenses and discourse signals appropriate to research reports
- use the language for future predictions from Language Spotlight 1
- use your own words; do not copy from the example research report in Task A
- accurately reflect your research project and its conclusions.

Do not write an abstract at this stage: that is covered in the next task.

Task D | Paragraph development – Abstracts and executive summaries

❶ Read some abstracts of research papers in your field. Your teacher will help you find them. Then:

[a] Work out roughly how many words are in each.
[b] Circle the nominalisations.
[c] Box sections that:
- explain why the research area is significant
- state exactly what was researched (eg research question or hypothesis)
- explain how the research was carried out
- state what the conclusion was.

[d] Explain and discuss what you found at [a] to [c] with another student.

❷ Write an abstract for your research report, including the features listed in the box below.

❸ [a] Read the research reports written by some other students in your class. Write an abstract for each.

[b] Discuss the abstracts that other students wrote for your report with the students who wrote them.

What is an abstract?
You will see many abstracts in your academic reading. You may have to write them for longer assignments such as theses and dissertations.

Abstracts in published papers have the following purpose:
- To help potential readers decide quickly which articles are relevant to their needs, and worth looking at in more detail

Abstracts have these key features:
- They are very short, usually less than 150 or 200 words
- They contain only the most important information in the paper
- There is plenty of nominalisation, to help keep their length short
- They often follow similar stages as the paper they summarise, eg
  – reason for the research → method → results → conclusion

They usually answer these questions very briefly:
- Why (the research area is significant)
- What (exactly was researched) – for example, the research question or hypothesis
- How (the research was carried out)
- What (the conclusion was).

If you are intending to study a business-related subject, you may have to write **executive summaries** rather than abstracts. An executive summary provides all the important information from the report, so that busy managers can get the most important information quickly without having to read the complete report. For this reason, executive summaries are sometimes a little longer than abstracts.

Writing abstracts
One useful process for writing an abstract is:
- write the key words or a sentence from each main section of your report
- join them together into a cohesive whole, making adjustments where necessary; this is your first draft
- refine your first draft.

Task A | Taking notes from detailed spoken explanations

❶ Work with another student.

[a] Mark the following on the map:
- the Arctic
- the south of Spain
- the Caribbean Sea
- the Mediterranean Sea
- the east coast of North America
- the Atlantic Ocean
- Iceland.

[b] What do you know about the climate of each of these places? Which places are cold in winter? Which are warm in winter? How about summer? Which place would you prefer to visit for a holiday?

CD 1

❷ Listen to the lecture titled *Oceanography: Ocean currents and climate change*. As you listen:

[a] follow on the map the places the lecturer talks about. You can draw arrows or other symbols if you like; and

[b] make a list of the main ideas of the talk next to the map.

❸ Compare your notes with a partner's.

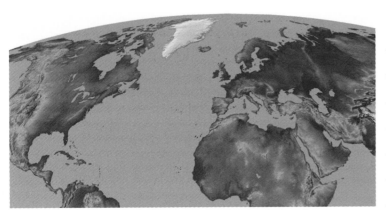

Main ideas

_____

_____

_____

_____

_____

_____

_____

❹ With another student, place these words in the correct place in the vocabulary box.

Vocabulary

_____ (n)	a line that goes around the Earth at a certain distance from the equator; *line of* _____ (n)	
_____ (n)	powerful movement of water in a particular direction	
_____ (n)	not changing for a long time; _____ (adj)	
_____ (adj)	judged in comparison with something else; eg _____ *to a sumo wrestler, 100 kg is quite light*	
_____ (n)	weight compared with size; _____ (adj); eg *iron has greater* _____ *than plastic*	
_____ (n)	continuous movement around something else; _____ (v); eg *the* _____ *of blood around the body*	
_____ (n)	a terrible disaster	
_____ (n)	if something has this, people believe it to be true; _____ (adj)	

... mageddon   circulate

circulation   credence

credible   current

dense   density

latitude   relative

stability   stable

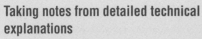

Taking notes from detailed technical explanations

In most disciplines, you will hear technical explanations from time to time; whether it's how a particular research process is carried out, how to use a piece of equipment or some computer software, or how to use a particular technique.

During technical explanations, the speaker often moves from one idea to the next very quickly. Thus, writing linear notes is often too slow. Therefore, it is often a good idea to:

- draw diagrams and annotate (write words in) them
- use any handouts that you can, and annotate them
- write down the technical words
- read through your notes as soon as possible after the lecture, so that you can add anything you've missed out while you still remember it
- meet with other students after the lecture, and
  - compare notes
  - try to explain some of the more difficult parts to each other.

5 In earlier units, you have seen various formats for taking notes.

[a] With a partner, discuss which ones might be suitable for this lecture.

[b] By yourself, choose the one that you will use. It doesn't have to be the same as your partner's.

[c] Prepare your format. Make sure there is enough space to draw diagrams. You may put in it the main ideas you identified at question 2b, on the previous page.

6 Listen to the lecture again, taking notes while you listen. Draw diagrams, maps and charts where appropriate.

CD 1 · 8

7 Compare and discuss your notes with a partner. Take it in turns to explain the following processes to your partner:

- how the THC works
- what the computer modelling shows
- what the observations show

Paraphrasing and summarising from lectures

In some ways, paraphrasing from lectures is easier than paraphrasing from readings, because it isn't usually possible to quote directly – few people can take notes quickly enough for that! But still, if you're asked to write a summary of a lecture or any other form of paraphrase, here are some tips:

- make sure your notes are detailed; comparing notes with others students will help
- only include points that are important for the explanation
- if possible, read explanations in textbooks, in handouts, online or elsewhere of what you're going to summarise
- use your own words
- check your writing after the first draft to make sure it's clear; perhaps ask someone else to read it
- write more than one draft.

Task B | Writing summaries of detailed explanations from lectures

1 Write short explanations of the following, using your notes about the lecture and following the tips below.

- how the THC works
- what the computer modelling shows
- what the observations show.

2 Compare your explanations with a partner's.

[a] Are there any points that one of you has included but not the other?

[b] How important are these points to the explanation? Could any be missed out?

[c] Are all words the writer's own?

Task C | Critical thinking about the lecture content

1 In small groups discuss these questions about the lecture. Use your notes from Task A.

[a] The lecture talks about the North Atlantic Ocean. If these issues happen there, could they also happen in other parts of the world?

[b] The lecture mentions some quite dramatic changes, such as ocean currents changing direction quite significantly. How much does this concern you? Why?

[c] How strong do you think the evidence is that the THC will change stop?

[d] How strong do you think the evidence is that the THC may change?

2 In different groups, discuss how your lifestyle would change if the climate in your area changed radically. Think about such things as:

[a] How changes in the weather might affect your leisure activities, including holidays

[b] How changes to the weather might affect crops and thus the price of food

[c] How changes to the climate might affect a job that you can imagine yourself doing in the future.

Task A | Reporting verbs used in referencing

1 Look at the referenced idea from the essay on p 148, reproduced below. Can any of the words be changed without changing the meaning?

Gordon and Suzuki (1990, p 57) report that radioactive particles travelled as far as Sweden within days and eventually as far as Canada's Arctic.

2 The following verbs can be used to report ideas. Add to the list by looking at articles in academic journals and noting the verbs that are used.

ask	assert	claim
deny	maintain	report
suggest		

3 Listen to the *Oceanography* lecture again, ticking off the reporting verbs used and adding any that aren't already in your list

CD 1

8

4 Match the words with the following tags, to show the differences in meaning. Some of the tags will match more than one reporting verb, and some reporting verbs don't match any of the tags.

- strong
- not certain
- continue to believe
- doubt
- disagree.

5 Re-write the following as referenced ideas and remember to paraphrase.

[a] The end of civilisations in the past has often been caused not by political or economic change as previously supposed, but by climatic change. Harvey Weiss and Raymond Bradley, 2009.

[b] The question we should examine is whether logging in the north-west of Govirmda should be allowed to continue. J Chakraverty, 2006.

[c] Due to climate change, many plants in the UK are flowering many weeks earlier every year than they did 40 years ago. A & R Fitter, 2010.

[d] I would like to propose the concept of shifting taxation from positive transactions (such as the receiving of income) towards transactions with more negative impacts such as the purchase of products which are bad for the environment. Özlem Aksu, 2011.

[e] Recycling is not the best way to solve environmental problems because the process uses plenty of energy in itself – reducing consumption would be much more effective. Hwa Jin Lee, 2009.

[f] Due to human activity, the amount of carbon in the atmosphere has risen to 390 parts per million by volume. This figure must quickly return to below 350 parts per million if we are to avoid serious consequences from global warming.

Environmental protest to raise awareness of the need to reduce greenhouse gas emissions to 350 parts per million

You are going to debate the following proposition:

We should take steps now to deal with climate change.

You will do this in groups of around six students; in each group, half will be for the proposition and the other half will be against the proposition. Your teacher will decide which side you will take.

> **Taking a position**
> As has been mentioned before, discussing and refining opinions based on evidence is important in many academic disciplines. A good way to do this is to think through the arguments and evidence that can be used for the opposite position to your own.
>   In this section, you may be asked to take a position which is very different from your own. Think of this as an opportunity to refine your ideas about the topic.

Your debate will follow this procedure:

- toss a coin to decide which side talks first.
- take it in turns to make a short speech in support of your position (for example, if the 'for' group wins the toss, one of their speakers talks first, then the first speaker of the 'against' group, then the second speaker of the 'for' group, etc). Your teacher will give you a time limit for each speech.
- after each speech, the next speaker may give arguments against the previous speaker's ideas, as well as presenting their own ideas.
- after all speakers are finished, the members of both groups hold a discussion in which they ask further questions about the ideas they heard.

Task A | Preparing for an informal debate

Work in the groups in which you will debate.

1. Brainstorm ideas that could be used to support your position.

2. Research these ideas, perhaps on the internet. Try to find supporting evidence for your ideas.

3. Discuss the ideas you found in your groups.

4. In the debate, each person will have to talk explain a particular point (or more than one point), giving evidence. Decide who will give each point.

5. Prepare and practise your speeches.

Task B | Refuting, exemplifying, requesting further explanation and checking understanding

1. Write the bold words from the list of functions next to the appropriate useful expression.

> **Useful expressions**
>
> _____ *When you said that …, did you mean that …*
>
> _____ *You mentioned before that … but what about …*
>
> _____ *Do you mean that …*
>
> _____ *But, if what you say is true, then …*
>
> _____ *So you mean …*
>
> _____ *I see. And I think some further evidence for that is …*
>
> _____ *But, you said earlier that …*
>
> _____ *I can see why you're saying that, because …*
>
> _____ *If it's the case that …, why can't …*
>
> _____ *Well, I think we should also think about …*
>
> _____ *Could you give me an example?*

> **Function**

- Contradicting or **refuting** the previous speaker's idea
- **Giving an example** supporting a previously mentioned idea
- **Asking for further explanation** or information
- **Checking understanding**

② Practise using the expressions from Task B by discussing any of the topics in the list:

A student should monitor each discussion and mark the table each time an expression is used for one of the functions (the expressions used don't have to be those in the Useful expressions box).

Topics

- *I am (am not) environmentally friendly in my everyday life because I …*
- *I think the environment is (isn't) important because …*
- *I think we should ignore environmental problems and just do what we want, because …*
- *The hardest environmental problems to deal with are …*
- *People don't know enough about how to deal with environmental problems. The government needs to educate people and businesses better about how they can help.*

FUNCTION	1ST TOPIC	2ND TOPIC	3RD TOPIC
Contradicting or refuting the other person's ideas			
Giving an example supporting a previously mentioned idea			
Asking for further explanation or information			
Checking understanding			

Task C | Debate

① Hold your debate according to the procedure at the start of this section, according to your preparations from Task A. Use the language in Task B for the final (open discussion) stage of the debate.

FURTHER CONNECTIONS

Task A | Business connections

① Discuss and/or write about one or more of the following topics:

- Can companies gain an advantage over their competitors by being environmentally friendly?
- How are environmental issues likely to affect the industry in which you are working or would like to work in the future?
- Some people say that companies have not tried hard enough to reduce their contribution to environmental problems, and that the government should intervene to ensure that companies do more. To what extent do you agree with this point of view?
- Consumers have enormous power to ensure that companies minimise their environmental footprint. To what extent do you agree with this opinion?

GET READY FOR UNIT 7: LEARNING ON CAMPUS

Go to the website of the university you intend to apply to, or any university you have heard of in an English-speaking country. Find the main page for international students (with most universities, it is a link on the front page) and then find the page or pages about services for international students.

Think about:

- What support services are available to overseas students

- Which of those services might be useful to you

- How you can access them.

You may want to make notes of some vocabulary from these readings.

Be prepared to share your answers next time you meet.

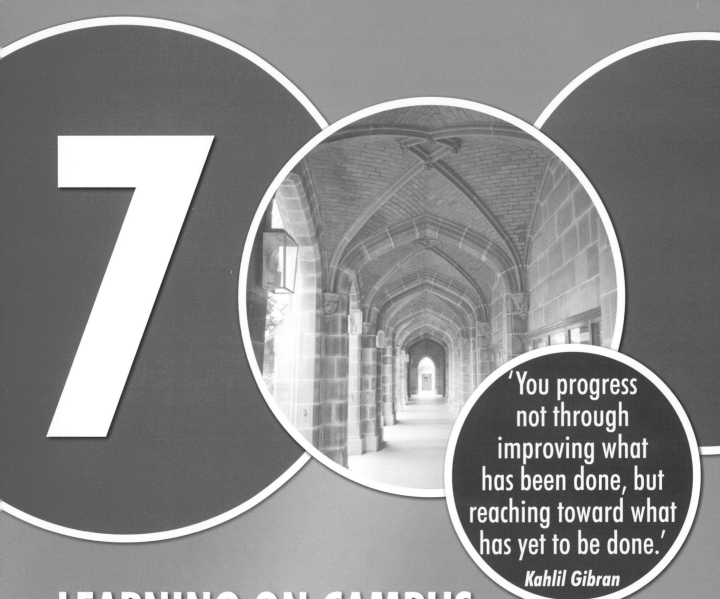

7

'You progress not through improving what has been done, but reaching toward what has yet to be done.'
Kahlil Gibran

LEARNING ON CAMPUS

In this unit, you will have a further look at the topic of education, to further assist with preparation for your tertiary studies. You will further extend your tutorial participation skills, and will also practise reading from different points of view. You will refute arguments in writing, and practise note-taking from a new angle: annotating the PowerPoint slides that are now so often used by lecturers. There will be opportunity for practice of speculating, and there is also a focus on the kinds of requests you may have to make of lecturers and other staff during your further studies.

BY THE END OF THIS UNIT, YOU SHOULD:

SKILL	TASK	PAGE
have gained confidence in discussing topics around education and learning and have expanded your vocabulary and knowledge of this topic area	**Speaking 1** *Tasks A, B* **Speaking 1** *Task D* **Reading & Critical Thinking** *Task A* **Writing** *Task A* **Listening & Note-taking** *Task A* **Speaking 2** *Task A* **Further Connections** *Tasks A, B*	170 172 172–175 177–179 179–181 184 187
have further developed tutorial discussion skills, and have expanded your repertoire of useful expressions for such situations	**Speaking 1** *Task C, D*	171–172
have gained further practice of a range of reading skills	**Reading & Critical Thinking** *Tasks A, B, C*	172–176
have practised using texts to assist in making and supporting judgements	**Reading & Critical Thinking** *Task B*	175–176
have practised reading from different points of view	**Reading & Critical Thinking** *Task C*	176
have further developed skills in writing in academic registers by avoiding personals	**Language Spotlight 1** *Task A*	176–177
be able to effectively refute arguments in paragraphs and essays	**Writing** *Tasks A, B*	177–179
have practised annotating computer slides while listening to a lecture, and using those notes	**Listening & Note-taking** *Tasks A, B*	179–181
have practised listening to identify the speaker's attitude	**Listening & Note-taking** *Task C*	182
have practised choosing appropriate verb forms in hypothesising, speculating and other uses of conditionals	**Language Spotlight 2** *Tasks A, B, C*	182–183
know how to appropriately make academic requests and replies in appropriate situations	**Speaking 2** *Task B*	185–186
have developed a plan to practise speaking even outside class, including after the course finishes	**Speaking 2** *Task C*	187

Task A | Extending campus vocabulary

❶ In pairs, look at each set of words below and try to decide whether they are the same or different. If different, what is the difference? If necessary, use a learner's dictionary or ask your teacher.

[a] department/faculty/school of …
[b] arts/humanities/science/social science
[c] applied science/pure science
[d] prerequisite/core subject/compulsory/elective (AuE), option (BrE)
[e] Bachelor/Honours/Master's/Professional Doctorate/ Doctorate/PhD
[f] semester/trimester/term
[g] pass/credit/distinction/high distinction; third, lower second, higher second, first class honours degree
[h] exams/assignments/continuous assessment.

❷ Discuss your education system with your partner using the vocabulary from question 1 to guide your discussion.

Task B | Discussion and predicting

You are going to listen to an undergraduate tutorial in which two students, Eleanor and Hamid, discuss who should pay for education, and whether all subjects should be funded the same way. They are studying Arts Management, a subject offered to students in the School of Management as well as the Arts Faculty.

❶ In small groups, discuss these questions:

[a] Should higher education be available to all students with sufficient academic ability? Why/Why not?

[b] Who should pay for higher education? The students themselves? Parents? Governments?

[c] What are the advantages and disadvantages to your answer to [b] for:
- equity of access to university; and
- cost to the country of universities?

[d] Why might people choose to study:
- arts subjects, such as literature and history
- pure science subjects, such as astronomy and maths
- vocational subjects, such as business and law?

[e] If the government provides some funding for university study, should it depend on the subject to be studied? Why/Why not?

[f] With a student from a different group, predict arguments on each side of the discussion you're going to hear by completing the table below.

ALL HIGHER EDUCATION STUDY SHOULD BE FUNDED BY GOVERNMENTS	ARTS AND PURE SCIENCES NEED NOT BE FUNDED BY GOVERNMENT

Task C | Noticing tutorial discussion techniques

1 **Listening for main ideas.** Listen to the tutorial conversation *Funding for education* and in the table in Task B:

CD 1

- tick the items already written that you hear
- add any other points that you hear.

2 **Listening to identify tutorial discussion techniques**

[a] Read the functions in the table below. Then, with a partner, add any expressions you can think of to the right-hand column of the table. You could:
- use words you remember from the recording
- add expressions you already know; and
- try to create new expressions from your own knowledge of English.

CD 1

[b] Listen again and tick the 'function used' column for each function you hear.

[c] The script of the conversation is in Appendix B on page 259. With a partner, mark the functions listed on that page.

[d] Add to the table below any other expressions from the script that reflect the functions.

3 With a partner, speculate about the following:

[a] Why do you think the tutor doesn't speak much?
[b] What ideas might the two speakers use to continue their discussion?

Outdoors tutorial

FUNCTION	FUNCTION USED? (✔)	EXPRESSIONS OR LANGUAGE POINTS FOR THIS FUNCTION
Asking a question that expects agreement in reply		• tag questions (with falling intonation)
Indicating understanding, but not agreement		
Steps in a logical argument		
Illustrating using a hypothetical situation		
Making a new point		
Supporting a point with examples		
Showing understanding by restating the other person's point in own words		
Referring back to a previous argument		

Task D | Tutorial discussion practice

1 **[a]** Work in groups. Prepare a conversation, similar to a tutorial discussion, that you can present to the class.
- Choose from the list of discussion topics at the end of the unit (Further Connections, Task A or B, page 187), or your own topic.
- Try to include in your discussion as many of the functions listed in the table as you can. You could use the 'own group' column to keep track of them.

FUNCTION	OWN GROUP	OTHER GROUP 1	OTHER GROUP 2	OTHER GROUP 3
Asking a question that expects agreement in reply				
Indicating understanding, but not agreement				
Steps in a logical argument				
Illustrating using a hypothetical situation				
Making a new point				
Supporting a point with examples				
Showing understanding by restating the other person's point in own words				
Referring back to a previous argument				

[b] Present your conversation to other groups. Your audience will tick off the functions in their table as they listen.

[c] Discuss these questions:
- Which group used the greatest number of functions?
- Which group had the strongest arguments?
- Why were these the strongest?
- Which way of presenting a point impressed you?

2 Choose another topic (your own choice or from the list at the end of this unit), to carry out further discussions. Ensure that you (and each other!) use a variety of functions from earlier in this section. Feel free to suggest expressions to each other!

READING & CRITICAL THINKING

Task A | Discussion and reading – Discrimination and harassment at university

1 With a partner or in groups, discuss the following questions:

[a] What behaviours do you think can lead to disciplinary action being taken at university?

[b] List as many kinds of discrimination as you can.

[c] For each, give an example (eg discrimination against women: a company may be reluctant to promote women with children because it thinks they will have too much focus on their family to work hard).

[d] What does 'harassment' mean? Use a dictionary if necessary and give examples.

[e] What are the problems in the following situations? Do you think they are examples of discrimination, harassment or neither?

i. *A well-qualified and experienced woman is trying to get a job but, again and again, instead of her, a man is chosen. She is in her late twenties and recently married.*

ii. *A man with good qualifications and experience but a scruffy hairstyle and rough manner is finding it difficult to get a job.*

iii. *A male student often touches female students on the arm and the back – this is considered 'normal' in his culture. The male student doesn't realise that one particular female hates this. In her culture, people smile in all situations and, in public, hide any negative feelings they have.*

iv. *Someone who has a different political opinion from her boss is repeatedly passed over for promotion.*

v. *A male in an office makes sexual jokes in front of female colleagues, and forwards emails containing similar jokes to many colleagues, both male and female.*

vi. *A student who has to use a wheelchair is told that he can't do a particular course because lectures take place in an old, historic building with no wheelchair access.*

vii. *A student and a lecturer become romantically involved with each other. At the end of the course, several students apply for a scholarship to a higher level course, including the student who's involved with the lecturer. One important factor in getting the scholarship is a reference from the same lecturer. Only one scholarship is available.*

viii. *A university course has a high fee, which only the rich can afford.*

❷ Carry out these instructions by yourself, then discuss your answers with a partner.

[a] Read only the headings in the following text, to familiarise yourself with the structure of the text (30 seconds). It is from a university's student handbook.

[b] You have two minutes to find and circle definitions of:
- discrimination;
- direct discrimination;
- indirect discrimination; and
- harassment.

[c] What punishments are given for harassment?

[d] What does the text say you should do if you're a student at this university and you feel you're being harassed?

[e] For each of questions [a] to [d], did you skim, scan or read in detail?

Preventing discrimination and harassment

1 What is discrimination?

1.1 Direct and indirect discrimination

Both direct and indirect discrimination are unlawful in all aspects of employment and education at this institution. Discrimination means treating someone unfairly because they happen to belong to a particular group of people.

1.2 Direct discrimination is the result of beliefs and stereotypical attitudes some people may have about the characteristics and behaviour of members of a group. It occurs when a person or group is harassed or excluded because of a personal characteristic such as gender or ethnic origin. For example:

- a selection committee refusing to consider applicants with family responsibilities
- refusing to employ or enrol Aboriginal people or people whose first language is not English
- assuming that a person with a disability would not be able to undertake a course of study because of their disability.

1.3 Indirect discrimination occurs where a rule, work practice or decision is made which applies to all persons equally and appears to be non-discriminatory, but which in practice significantly reduces the chances of a particular person or group of persons from complying with it. For example:

- recruitment or promotion based on length of service may indirectly discriminate against women applicants, because women are more likely to have taken career breaks to accommodate family responsibilities
- selection criteria requiring a specific number of years of previous experience may also constitute indirect age discrimination.

Consideration of indirect discrimination means that the university must look not just at the intention but also the impact of any rule changes. However, indirect discrimination is not illegal if the condition, requirement or practice which indirectly discriminates is seen to be reasonable in the circumstances.

1.4 Areas of discrimination

The university is committed to ensuring the elimination of any discrimination or harassment in employment, education and service delivery on the grounds of:

- sex
- race, colour, descent, national or ethnic origin, ethno-religious background

- marital status
- pregnancy or potential pregnancy
- family responsibilities
- disability (includes physical, intellectual, psychiatric, sensory, neurological or learning disabilities and illness such as HIV/AIDS)
- homosexuality
- transgender status
- age
- political conviction
- religious belief.

The Equity and Diversity Unit provides confidential, equity-related grievance advice to both students and staff who feel they may have been discriminated against or harassed on any of the grounds listed above.

2 What is not unlawful discrimination?

- **Administrative action.** Managers and university staff frequently have to make difficult decisions, for example, course changes. These decisions may not please everybody but they do not normally constitute discrimination.

- **Student assessment.** Academic staff have a responsibility to students to assess their work fairly, objectively and consistently across the candidature for their particular subject/course. A poor assessment is not discriminatory, provided the criticism is reasonable and constructive. Giving appropriate criticism and taking appropriate corrective action when an individual's assessment is unsatisfactory is a standard part of academic life.

- **Consensual relationships.** A relationship of a sexual nature based on mutual attraction, friendship and respect does not constitute discrimination, **providing the interaction is consensual, welcome and reciprocated**. However, consensual relationships may lead to conflict of interest (see later).

3 University policy on the prevention of harassment

The university is committed to ensuring that all students and staff are treated fairly and equitably, and can work and study in an environment free of harassment. Discrimination, harassment and victimisation are unlawful, undermine professional relationships, diminish the experience of university life, and will not be tolerated at this institution.

All students and staff have a responsibility to contribute to the achievement of a productive, safe and equitable study and work environment by avoiding practices which lead to, support or condone harassment.

3.1 Legislation

Provisions relating to unlawful harassment are outlined in both federal and state anti-discrimination laws. These laws prohibit discrimination and harassment in employment, education and service delivery on the grounds previously listed. The legislation also prohibits racial, homosexual, transgender and HIV/AIDS vilification, dismissal because of family responsibilities, and victimisation resulting from a complaint.

3.2 What is unlawful harassment?

Unlawful harassment is any unwelcome conduct, verbal or physical, which has the intent or effect of creating an intimidating, hostile or offensive educational, work or living environment, and which happens because of a person's sex, pregnancy, race or ethno-religious background, marital status, age, sexual preference, transgender status or disability.

Unlawful harassment can include:

- verbal abuse or comments that put down or stereotype people
- derogatory or demeaning jokes intended to offend on the basis of stereotyped characteristics
- offensive communications (such as posters, letters, emails, faxes, screen savers, websites)
- offensive telephone or electronic mail or other computer system communications
- insults, taunting, name calling, innuendo or bullying
- persistent or intrusive questions or comments about an individual's personal life
- unwelcome invitations especially after prior refusal
- activities that involve unwelcome sexual, sexist, racist or other discriminatory behaviour
- non-verbal behaviour such as whistling, staring and leering
- uninvited sexual or physical contact such as embracing, kissing or touching
- intrusive questions about sexual activity
- demeaning jokes of a sexual nature

- promises, propositions or threats in return for sexual favours
- engaging in behaviour which is embarrassing, humiliating or intimidating
- derogatory comments about race, religion and customs
- teasing or offensive language and racist behaviours
- mocking customs or cultures.

The offensive behaviour does not have to take place a number of times: a single incident can constitute harassment.

What is important is how the behaviour affects the person it is directed against. Unlawful harassment can occur even if the behaviour is not intended to offend. Students and staff should be aware that differing social and cultural standards may mean that behaviour that is acceptable to some may be perceived as offensive by others.

4   Procedural guidelines

The university's procedures for handling complaints are based on confidentiality, impartiality, procedural fairness, protection from victimisation and prompt resolution. Any complaints of harassment or discrimination will be dealt with promptly, seriously, and without victimisation of those involved.

Disciplinary action may be taken against students or staff who are found to have harassed other students or staff. Breaches of the policy will be considered to be 'misconduct' or 'serious misconduct' in the case of employees, and 'non-academic misconduct' in the case of students, and may result in the most serious cases in permanent expulsion (for students) or dismissal (for staff). Formal warnings about inappropriate behaviour are a common outcome for first offences, unless the behaviour is of a very serious nature.

4.1   What to do about harassment?

Students should seek advice from the Equity and Diversity Unit (if the complaint relates to unlawful harassment) or the Student Services Unit (for counselling and support). The Students Association also provides advice and advocacy for students.

Source: Adapted from: UTS Equity and Diversity Unit (no date given) 'Preventing discrimination and harassment', UTS Equity and Diversity Unit, Sydney. Internet site available at: <http://www.uts.edu.au/div/eounit/unit/discrim.html> (25/08/02). A variation is also published in Lambert, T & Barreto, L (2001) UTS Students' Association *Postgraduate Handbook 2001*. Sydney: UTS Students' Association, pp 36–39.

Task B | Using texts to assist in making and supporting judgments

In this task, you will use the text from Task A to make and support judgments about the situations you discussed in that task.

❶ For each situation [i] to [viii] on pages 173–174, mark any relevant section of text.

❷ Using the text you marked, make a judgment about whether the situation involves:

- discrimination
- harassment
- neither.

according to the university's policies as described in the text. Use the table to record your judgment.

SITUATION IN TASK A, Q1[e]	DISCRIMINATION?	HARASSMENT?	NEITHER?	NOT DISCUSSED?
i.				
ii.				
iii.				
iv.				
v.				
vi.				
vii.				
viii.				

❸ Compare and discuss your judgments with someone you spoke with in Task A.

❹ Answer these questions in small groups.

[a] Did anything from the reading surprise you?

[b] Would a university have similar policies in your country? What, if anything, would you expect to be different?

[c] Do you think that ideas of what constitutes discrimination should vary from culture to culture, or are they universal, that is, do they apply to all humans? Why?

Task C | Reading from different points of view

❶ Your teacher will divide the class into two.

Students A: turn to p 260. Make a list of points from the text in Task A that are relevant to the question you see there.

Students B: turn to p 261. Make a list of points from the text in Task A that are relevant to the question you see there.

❷ With another student from your group, compare your notes.

❸ Work with a student from the other group. Compare your questions. Explain your notes and their relevance to your assignment question.

❹ How important do you think it is to know why you're reading, before you start reading? Discuss with your partner.

LANGUAGE SPOTLIGHT 1 •••

Task A | Avoiding personals

❶ Work with a partner.

[a] Find parts of the text on pages 173–175 that have the same meaning as the following:

- *Discrimination is when you are unfair to someone because of something like their skin colour or how old they are – you know, like if you don't give a man a job because you think men aren't good at that kind of job.*
- *Well, harassment is when you're making someone feel upset because of what you're doing.*

[b] Which do you think are more spoken in style: the definitions in [a] or the definitions in the text? More written in style? What clues to this can you find in the choices of language used?

❷ With a partner, compare the two paragraphs below. Work out three ways in which personals have been removed.

Paragraph 1

More and more young people like me are travelling overseas to study. If you go to the airport, you'll see many people my age going to other countries – travelling as backpackers or going to study overseas. In my opinion, this trend seems to be increasing. I believe that this is very beneficial for society, because if we go overseas, we can learn more about the world, we can understand other cultures better and the kinds of experiences that we have when we travel can help us to learn more about ourselves.

Paragraph 2

More and more young people are travelling overseas to study. At the airport, many young people going to other countries can be seen travelling as backpackers or going to study overseas. This trend seems to be increasing. This is very beneficial for society, because if people go overseas, they can learn more about the world; they can understand other cultures better and the kinds of experiences they have can help them learn more about themselves.

Personals

Personals are words which include the writer or speaker, or the reader and listener. These include personal pronouns (such as *you* and *us*) and possessive adjectives, such as *my* and *our*. They also include the general *you*, roughly equivalent to the *one*.

Academic writing in most disciplines avoids personals; in other words, by avoiding personals, you are on the way to achieving a good academic style.

❸ By yourself, remove the personals from the following. Try to keep the meaning as close as possible to the original. Then, compare your answers with a partner's. Did you use the same techniques to remove personals?

[a] It is my opinion that the world is more interesting because there are different cultures.

_____

_____

[b] When you travel to other countries, you should respect the culture of the country you're visiting, and you should be careful not to do things that may be normal in your country but which might cause offence in your new country.

_____

_____

_____

_____

_____

[c] You shouldn't touch people's heads in Thailand; if you do, you will offend people because it's against their culture to do this.

_____

_____

_____

_____

[d] In my experience, the more you understand the local culture, the better the experience of travelling overseas is.

_____

_____

_____

[e] If you're interested in helping the local people in developing countries, try to stay in family hotels rather than ones owned by international organisations, and shop in local stores and markets rather than fast food restaurants and supermarkets. That way, you'll help the profits to stay in the country.

_____

_____

_____

_____

_____

❹ **Review.** The paragraphs you read in question 1 were introductions to essays answering this question:
To what extent do you think that the trend for young people to travel overseas is a positive one?

[a] With a partner, mark the stages of the introduction (General statement, Thesis and Preview/Scope) on Paragraph 2.

[b] Individually, write your own essay response to this question. Use the techniques from question 2 in your writing.

WRITING •

Task A | Paragraph development – Refuting arguments

❶ Discuss with another student:

[a] What subject are you going to study in your university or college course?

[b] What were the factors in your choice of that subject? Which of these were the deciding factors?

[c] Which is usually a stronger factor in students' choices of tertiary study?
- personal interest in the subject; or
- the salary and status of the job(s) that the qualification usually leads to.

❷ Read the two paragraphs below, which are an extract from a textbook. Then, discuss with your partner from step 1:

[a] What is the main idea of the second paragraph?

[b] Is there anything in the two paragraphs which surprises you?

[c] Which part of the second paragraph agrees with your answer to 1c above? Draw a box around it. Also, draw a box around the part of the paragraph that disagrees.

[d] Underline the part of the second paragraph that separates the two parts you identified in 2b.

[e] Find an expression near the beginning of the second paragraph that 'distances' the writer from the idea he/she later refutes. Double underline it.

[f] Brainstorm other ways you could write that separating stage (hint: it doesn't have to be a whole sentence). Write them in the refuting arguments box, facing, for future reference.

1. Motivation is also a big factor in adult learning. The motivations of adults are often quite different from those of children. Adult motivations are usually divided into two categories: intrinsic motivation and extrinsic motivation. Intrinsic motivation exists when a person wants to do something because they naturally find it interesting in itself; the motivation comes from inside the person. So, for example, it's intrinsic motivation that causes a sports fan to attend his or her favourite team's matches. Extrinsic motivation, on the other hand, is motivation that comes from outside the person. Examples of extrinsic motivators include the possibility of a pay rise, a higher-status job or a threat of punishment.

2. The question then arises as to which of these types of motivation is stronger. Some people instinctively believe that extrinsic motivation works best. Many companies, for example, base their remuneration packages and staff retention strategies around pay scales, bonuses and other extrinsic strategies. In the case of staff who are apparently under-performing, they often enforce punishments such as pay freezes and denial of promotion. Similarly, universities often give prizes for high achieving students. Unfortunately, though, there is a problem with this. Research shows that it is more often the case that intrinsic motivation is more powerful than extrinsic. Interest in a particular subject of study usually leads to greater success in study than extrinsic factors such as the thought of higher salaried jobs at the end of the course. Incidentally, it has also been found that intrinsic motivation usually provides a higher level of enjoyment than extrinsic motivation – in other words, students who choose a subject because they find it interesting have a better time than those who choose a subject because of the future job prospects.

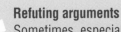

Refuting arguments
Sometimes, especially in an argument essay, it may be useful to look at a view that opposes yours, and show why it is wrong. The second paragraph on the previous page is a good example of this. One advantage of this strategy is that you can show that you understand the other side of the argument, but have a good reason not to agree with it.

Examples of useful language for refuting arguments include:

_____

_____

_____

With this kind of language, though, try to use your imagination! At this stage in the course, you should try to avoid relying too much on formulaic language.

❸ **[a]** In small groups, brainstorm ideas which can be used to refute the following arguments.
[b] Individually, write paragraphs in which the argument is presented and then refuted. Avoid using personals in your paragraphs.

- *All university students should study a language.*
- *Universities should allow rich people who can afford to pay full fees to study even if they don't achieve the entry requirements.*
- *University education should be free for everyone who meets the entry requirements.*

Task B | Argument essay in which ideas are refuted

❶ For the question below:

[a] Brainstorm as many ideas as you can with a partner, both for and against.
[b] Write an argument essay in which you mention but refute views that oppose the thesis. Avoid using personals in your essay.

> *The benefits of overseas study outweigh the costs and other disadvantages.*
>
> *Do you agree or disagree with this view? Give reasons for your answer.*

LISTENING & NOTE-TAKING

Task A | Note-taking by annotating computer presentation slides memory

❶ **Orientation to the lecture topic.** In small groups, discuss these questions:

[a] How good do you think your memory is?
[b] Are you better at remembering some things than others? For example, phone numbers, birthdates or places you visited a long time ago?
[c] Do you think there might be different types of memory?
[d] What do you think is the best way to study for exams?
[e] What strategies do you know of to improve your memory? Have you used any of them?
[f] Can you keep many things in your mind at the same time – for example, when multi-tasking?

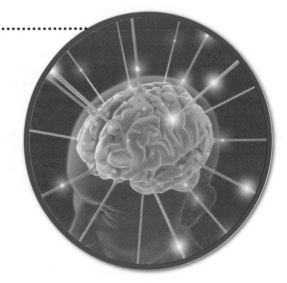

❷ Look through the slides on the next page. Then, speculate with your partner about what the lecturer will say.

Computer presentation slides
Often, lecturers will make the slides (eg PowerPoint slides) from their lectures available to students, perhaps as handouts or on their website. Sometimes, you will be able to obtain them before the lecture. If this is the case, then it is a good idea to do so! Reading them before the lecture will help you follow it.
Also, annotating (adding comments to) slides during the lecture is a good way to take notes – many of the main points and some details will already be written on the slides!
Be careful! While the points usually appear in the same order in the talk as in the slides, you may still have to make some minor jumps.

Memory

- Types of memory
- How memories are formed
- HM as an example

1

HM

- Severe memory problems
- Some memory tasks OK
- Brenda Milner has studied him

2

Procedural memory

- Motor skills
- Not fully conscious
- Several types

3

Declarative memory

- Episodic
- Semantic

4

Three box model for memory formation

- Sensory memory
- Working memory
- Long-term memory

5

Sensory memory

- One type for each sense
- Very short lasting
- Medium capacity

6

Working memory 1

- Short lasting
- Small capacity
- Lifetime can be extended – a little

7

Working memory 2

- Consciousness
- Memories easily lost
- Multi-tasking issues
- Filter to long-term memory

8

Vocabulary

conscious (adj)	if you notice or are aware of your thoughts, they are *conscious*; *consciousness* (n)
a muscle (n)	the parts of your body which move
a hormone (n)	a chemical produced inside your body which controls growth, mood, etc
multi-tasking (n)	doing several things at the same time; *multitask* (v)
linear (adj)	a process in which one thing happens at a time, in sequence rather than at the same time, is *linear* (adj)

Long-term memory

- Long lasting
- Very large capacity
- Like muscles

9

How to remember

- Stress
- Make connections
- Sleep

10

Further notes

- Probably an over-simplification
- Probably not linear

11

CD 1

❸ Listen to the lecture *How memory works*, and annotate the slides as you go.

❹ Compare your annotations with another student's. Add any information you missed to your slides.

10

Task B | Using notes from annotated computer presentation slides

❶ In pairs, decide whether these situations use sensory, working or long-term memory. If they use long-term memory, decide whether it is procedural, episodic or semantic. Use your annotated slides.

____ **[a]** Listening to music
____ **[b]** Listening to song lyrics and writing them down
____ **[c]** Remembering your first day at school
____ **[d]** In a shop, remembering what your friend asked you to buy when you were outside the shop, three minutes before
____ **[e]** Remembering your girlfriend's or boyfriend's birthday
____ **[f]** Riding a bicycle for the first time in five years
____ **[g]** Writing up your notes after a lecture
____ **[h]** Taking an exam
____ **[i]** Knowing the rules of a sport
____ **[j]** Being very good at a sport.

❷ From your notes, decide whether these are most likely to be true or false, according to the lecturer. Correct the false statements.

[a] HM had good sensory memory
[b] HM had good working memory
[c] HM had good long-term memory

[d] Sensory memory for sounds is the same as sensory memory for images
[e] Working memory can hold around seven items
[f] We notice easily when something slips out of working memory
[g] Exercise of the memory wears it out, causing memories to fade
[h] Being somewhat excited about something helps you to remember
[i] Sleep is better for such things as studying for an exam than for learning to play a sport well
[j] All cognitive scientists agree that the three-box model is accurate and complete.

CD 1

❸ Listen again, and check your answers to 2. You may want to adjust or add to your notes.

10

❹ Using your notes, write a short paragraph about two of the following. Then, swap with another student. Which points in the paragraphs do you think are correct? Discuss with your partner.

- Why it's a good thing that sensory memory lasts only a short time.
- Why driving and using a mobile phone at the same time is dangerous.
- What effect stress has on memory.
- How to remember things more effectively.

Task C | Listening to identify the speaker's attitude

 Attitude
Attitude includes any way of showing feelings about a topic or idea.
Attitude can be indicated by choice of word or by intonation. For example, if someone feels negatively about something, they can use a negative adjective, and they might say that with strong intonation. If someone is not sure about something, they can use an adverb such as 'maybe', and they might also use rising, questioning intonation.
In general, rising intonation indicates less certainty, and falling intonation indicates greater certainty.

 Listen to the lecture again. **CD 1** (10)

[a] Match the words points the lecturer talks about with her attitude about them.
[b] Then compare your answers with another student's.
[c] Did the lecturer use words, intonation or both to convey attitude?

Attitude: *certain, sad, humorous, tentative/unsure.*

Points from the lecture

- *HM's situation* _____
- *Teaching HM another language* _____
- *The size of the working memory* _____
- *The importance of sleep* _____
- *Having to motivate oneself while studying* _____
- *Whether the three-box model is accurate* _____

LANGUAGE SPOTLIGHT 2 ....

Task A | Verb forms for hypothesising and speculating

❶ Look at the following examples from the lecture in this unit. With a partner, answer the questions.

[i] *'I wonder what would have happened if someone had tried to teach him another language. It probably wouldn't have been very successful, I'd guess.'*
[ii] *'That's why when you're driving, talking on a mobile phone at the same time, even if it's a hands-free set, this can cause some pretty big problems.'*

[a] From your experience of English, which example – (i) or (ii) – feels the most hypothetical? Which feels more real?
[b] Which describes a 'timeless' situation (that is, something that applies to any time, past, present or future)? Which refers to the past?
[c] Why do you think the lecturer made this choice? What effect does it have on the audience? Hint: think about how important it is for the idea in the sentence to feel real.
[d] Which verb forms (or tenses) express the realness or otherwise, and time reference, of these examples? Complete the main clause columns of the table below.

	REAL/LIKELY		HYPOTHETICAL/SPECULATIVE	
	'IF' CLAUSE	**MAIN CLAUSE**	**'IF' CLAUSE**	**MAIN CLAUSE**
past time reference	N/A	various past tenses	**past perfect**	would have + **past participle**
'timeless' time reference			**past simple**	would + **bare infinitive**
present or future time reference	**present simple**	various future tenses		

*Note: 'Would' can be replaced by could, may, might, should etc. 'Bare infinitive' is an infinitive without 'to', eg 'eat', 'study'. Traditionally, 'was' isn't used with conditionals. Instead, 'were' is used for all subjects.

❷ How are the weak forms of the hypothetical/speculative verb groups pronounced?

> **Conversational patterns with hypothetical 'would'**
> A useful conversation pattern is as follows: The full form of 'would' is used to introduce the concept of unreality, but after that, it is contracted to ''d' (as shown above in the first example in question 1).

Task B | Verb forms in conditionals

❶ Look at examples (i) and (ii) in question 1. Notice that the 'if' clauses use different tenses from the main clauses. With another student, complete the 'if' clause columns of the table.

Task C | Practice

❶ Choose the correct verb form for the gaps in the conversation below (between two students from the same country, studying in the UK). Main verbs are given in brackets, if necessary, and some have been done for you as examples.

A: Imagine if by some chance our language ^(be) <u>were</u> more

popular in the world than English, and if people from

many countries ^(come) _____

to our country to study our language. That ^(be)

_____ interesting, <u>wouldn't</u> it!

B: Yeah! It ^(be) _____

great! We ^(come) <u>wouldn't have come</u> here,

_____ we! I guess

we _____ already ^(be)

_____ at university, without

spending all that time it takes to learn English.

A: But the great thing is that it ^(be)

_____ easy to travel

for fun if everyone in tourist resorts ^(speak)

_____ our language ... no

problems! Or, for a career, we ^(teach) <u>could teach</u> our

language to international students coming to our country

to study ... so we _____ still

^(can, meet) _____ people from other

countries!

B: Good idea! That ^(be) _____ an

interesting job ... though we ^(need) _____

to study another course!

❷ Discuss how your lives would be different if:

[a] Tertiary education were free for everyone of sufficient ability;

[b] We could live to 120 years old;

[c] You were rich enough that you didn't have to think about money;

[d] You could choose to live in any country in the world.

Try to say as much as possible about each situation.

❸ Choose three issues of interest to you. Discuss them by speculating about what would happen if each side of the issue was true. For example,

Issue: *English should be studied from the early years in primary school in your country.*

Discussion: *What would be/is the effect of this policy happening? What would be/is the effect of English not being studied until much later (or not at all) in your country?* (Choose the tense according to the situation in your country.)

Hypothetical future space station

Task A | Critical thinking – What is the purpose of higher education?

❶ Discuss these questions in pairs or small groups:

[a] For what reasons did you choose the subject of your future course?

[b] In what way will your course be useful for you?

[c] In what ways might other people choose to study in higher education?

[d] How does higher education benefit society?

❷ The points in the cloud below are sometimes said to be the benefits of tertiary education.

- broaden general knowledge
- having time for thinking and personal development without the pressures of work
- follow an interest in a particular subject
- gain exposure to a wide range of ideas
- develop social skills – meeting people from different backgrounds and origins
- gain in-depth knowledge of a particular subject
- learn and develop high-level problem-solving skills
- learn how to learn independently
- learn to use initiative and think independently
- learn to live independently – often students are living away from home for the first time
- get a high-paying job later
- develop critical thinking and analytical skills
- develop contacts who may be useful later in life.

Talk about these points in the same groups/pairs as question 1.

[a] Can you add more ideas to these?

[b] In your opinion, which ones are most important? Of medium importance? Of little or no importance? Why?

[c] Generally, in your culture, which ones are regarded as most important?

[d] Which ones benefit the whole of society, and which ones only benefit the individuals who go to university? Give reasons.

[e] What for you is the most important benefit of education? Give as many reasons as you can for your answer.

[f] Do you think that some subjects teach this benefit better than others?

[g] Do you think any of these might be bad for society? In what way? In what circumstances?

Vocabulary

exposure (n)	if you *gain exposure* to many things, you experience them; *be exposed to* (collocation)
in-depth (adj)	detailed
initiative (n)	an ability to take action and do things by yourself without waiting for someone to tell you; *take the initiative* (collocation)
regard (v)	have the opinion that, consider; eg *regard education as important* (collocation)

Task B | Academic requests and replies

Academic requests

There are many situations in which you may need to make requests to your lecturer or an administrator. Here are some things to remember:

- Use the student handbook to check whether there is a proper procedure for your request. For example, you might have to fill in a form and get it signed by your lecturer. Also, there may be set times when students can talk to certain people, or you may need to make an appointment.
- Make your request early, preferably as soon as you realise it's necessary. The more time people have to deal with the situation, the better the result is likely to be.
- Don't be afraid to speak with lecturers and administrators. They are there to help you!

❶ In groups, list as many reasons as you can think of that you might want to make a request to a lecturer at university or college.

❷ In pairs, read the three conversations below and over the page. What is being requested in each case?

Conversation 1

(Telephone conversation)

Dr Peters: Hello, Dr Peters speaking.

Student: Hello, Dr Peters. It's Daniel Stevens from your third year child psychology course. I've got a problem I'm afraid.

Dr Peters: What is it?

Student: Well, the problem is that I broke my arm in a soccer game and I can't write properly … so I just don't know how I'm going to write the essays in the exam!

Dr Peters: Mmmm, OK, I'm sure there's a way around that! I think we should be able to get someone to do the writing for you – they'll just write exactly what you say, and of course that'll be done in a special room. I'll contact the course coordinator for you and I'm sure we'll be able to sort something out.

Student: Thanks very much. That's very helpful!

Dr Peters: No problem. Just doing my job!

Conversation 2

(Student knocks on lecturer's office door)

Lecturer: Come in.

Student: Errr, excuse me. Er, am I interrupting you?

Lecturer: Oh, no, not at all. How can I help you?

Student: Yeah, oh, well, it's quite complicated, I'm afraid.

Lecturer: Would you like to have a seat?

Student: Ah, yes, thanks very much. Well, it's like this, you see, my mother has been ill for some time and er …

Lecturer: I see …

Student: … Well it was my mother who was supporting me financially. But that's the problem – she just isn't able to run the family business by herself now that she's in hospital … so I need to go back to look after her for a while.

Lecturer: Oh, I see now. I'm sorry to hear it.

Student: So what should I do about my course? I don't want to drop out and then have to apply again, and organise the visa, all this stuff, and I certainly don't want to have to restart the course again, and then repeat the first few units!

Lecturer: Oh, don't worry, there's no need for all of that. All you need to do is to complete a Leave of Absence form, and put all your reasons on that, and get it to me to sign, and, er, then we'll send it off to the admin section. I hope your mother gets better soon!

Student: Thank you very much. I hope so too!

(Continued on the next page)

(In a lecture theatre, after the end of a lecture; student walks up to the lecturer)

Student: Professor, umm, I wonder if you can help me.

Professor: Mmmm?

Student: Well, I've been getting good marks on my assignments so far, and my tutor seems quite happy with my progress, but you know the exam we did recently?

Professor: Yes.

Student: Well, I've just got the result back, and I'm really disappointed with it. I was sure I'd done much better than that. Could I ask another lecturer to mark it again?

Professor: Well, sometimes it works – there's no harm trying, I guess. Just go to the admin office and ask for a Reassessment Request Form, fill it in and then take it back to the office.

Student: And what happens after that?

Professor: Well, what'll happen is that two more lecturers will look at it and, umm, they won't see the original mark, but if their marks are very different from what you got first, then you'll get the average of the two new marks.

Student: Oh, I see. Thanks very much.

Professor: Good luck!

---

❸   With the same partner:

[a]   Mark these stages from the box to the right on the conversations. Not all stages appear in every conversation.

[b]   A stage is missed out in one of these examples. Why do you think that is?

[c]   Decide which stage each useful expression in the box is appropriate for.

[d]   Think of more useful expressions and add them to the box. Which stages is each appropriate for?

> **Stages in a request**
> These are:
> - **Preamble:** saying 'hello', etc
> - **Orientation:** quick explanation of the background to the problem
> - **Statement of problem:** explanation of the problem
> - **Question:** could request permission, advice, an explanation or something else
> - **Response:** the reply to the question
> - **Signing off:** saying 'goodbye', etc.
> Not all of these stages appear in every spoken request.

Useful expressions

_____ I've got a bit of a problem, I'm afraid …

_____ So, I was wondering whether I could …

_____ Thanks very much. Much appreciated.

_____ Sorry to bother you, but could I just ask you something?

_____ I'd really appreciate that.

_____ Excuse me, do you have a moment?

_____ Well, the issue is that …

_____ I was wondering whether you could help with a problem I have.

_____ Thanks for letting me know how the system works.

_____ Well, yesterday, there was a bit of a problem.

_____ Would it be possible to …

_____ I'm very sorry if this has caused any problems.

_____ I won't let it happen again, I promise.

_____ I know how important it is to [attend every lecture], but …

_____ Well, it works like this …

---

❹   [a]   Divide into two groups: **A** and **B**.

[b]   **A:** You will play the role of lecturer to begin with. Listen to the 'student'. Use the information in item 7.1 on page 260 (Appendix B) to reply, but don't give all the information at once – wait for further questions! When you've finished, another 'student' will ask you about situation 7.2 on page 260.

B: You will play the role of student to begin with. Use the information in item 7.1 on page 260 (Appendix B) to make a request to a 'lecturer'. Follow the request stages from question 3 above. Listen to the reply and ask further questions as necessary. You may have to use some imagination! After finishing, move to a different lecturer and use item 7.2 on the page.

[c]   When finished with 7.1 and 7.2, 'students' become 'lecturers' and vice versa. Repeat, using items 7.3 and 7.4 on page 260 (A students) and page 261 (B students).

Task C | Speaking outside class

1 In small groups, list as many ideas as you can for speaking practice outside class, such as speaking with other overseas students in English, or working with native English speakers.

2 In the same groups, discuss these questions about the list you made at question 1.

[a] Which do you find easier to find the time for? More difficult? Why?

[b] In which do you find it easier to get your message across? More difficult? Why?

3 Read the following, then rank the items you listed in question 1 according to how accurate you need to be in English.

You may find that some speaking tasks are better for your English than others. For example, when you tell your friends what you did at the weekend, you don't need to use complex language, and you've probably described similar things many times before. However, if you explain to a friend how to cook some food from your country, you have to express yourself more accurately because your friend has to understand you very clearly in order to follow the instructions.

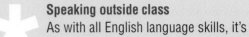

Speaking outside class
As with all English language skills, it's important that you practise speaking as much as possible, and that means outside class as well as in class. It also means practising after your course finishes.

It will help your speaking practice outside class if you choose situations in which:
* you express complex ideas or abstract ideas
* someone else has to follow your instructions or explanations.

4 Make a list of how you will practise English:

[a] outside your English lessons while your course is in progress; and

[b] after you finish your course.

Discuss your list with another student. Suggest other ideas to your partner. Refine your list in light of your discussion.

FURTHER CONNECTIONS

Task A | Education connections

1 Discuss and/or write about one or more of the following topics:

* *Should entry requirements to university be lowered for students who can pay higher fees?*
* *Should all tertiary level students be required to take part in sport?*
* *The benefits of a university experience should go beyond academic study; for example, involvement in clubs, political activities and social activities are also important. To what extent do you agree with this point of view?*

Task B | Business connections

1 Discuss and/or write about one or more of the following topics:

* *Increasingly, university departments and research projects are being sponsored by business. What are the advantages and disadvantages of this? Could it become a source of bias?*
* *Extra money from business sponsorship will enable universities to provide a greater range of subjects and increase the breadth of their research. To what extent do you agree with this point of view?*

GET READY FOR UNIT 8: WORLD BUSINESS AND ECONOMICS

Examine and read from the following website:

* <http://en.wikipedia.org/wiki/Economics>

Scroll down the reading and find the title *History of Economic Thought* and consider Sumer and early trade there using barley as money. While reading, think about:

* What characteristics of economics are the same today as they were back then?

8

'How gravely the glutton counsels the famished to bear the pangs of hunger.'

Kahlil Gibran

WORLD BUSINESS AND ECONOMICS

This chapter will familiarise you with important issues around the subjects of business and economics as well as ask you to question global inequalities amongst nations and peoples. You will greatly increase vocabulary around the topic and build your reading, writing, speaking and listening skills. You will assume new strategies and revisit previously studied ones, while critically considering important issues, such as population growth, that impact upon world business and economics.

BY THE END OF THIS UNIT, YOU SHOULD:

SKILL	TASK	PAGE
be conversant with issues around trade and global economics	Entire unit	190–211
have increased vocabulary about world trade, economics and population growth	**Speaking 1** *Task B* **Reading & Critical Thinking** Reading 1 *Task A* Reading 3 *Task A* **Further Connections**	190 191 193–197 210
have a greater understanding of, and critically consider global inequality	**Reading & Critical Thinking** Reading 2 *Task A*	 192
know how to globally examine a text and understand juxtaposition of ideas	**Reading & Critical Thinking** Reading 2 *Task B*	 193
review the skill of locating key words within reading, writing and listening	**Reading & Critical Thinking** Reading 3 *Task A Part 3*	 196
increase understanding and abilities around the application of language concerned with cause and effect; result and reason in reading and writing	**Language Spotlight 1** *Tasks A–E* **Writing** Writing 1 *Task A*	 197–199 200
use modal verbs appropriately in a spoken presentation	**Language Spotlight 1** *Task E* **Speaking 2** *Task A*	 208 210
revisit paragraph development methods	**Writing** Writing 1 *Task B*	 200
convert descriptions into comparisons using appropriate contrasting language, including metaphor and simile	**Writing** Writing 2 *Tasks A, B, C*	 202–203
be able to read, understand and write using exposition schema	**Writing** Writing 3 *Tasks A–D*	 203–205
have practised in-text referencing from an essay	**Writing** Writing 3 *Task E*	 205
listen and note-take for main ideas	**Listening and Note-taking** *Tasks A, B*	 206
gained further understanding of nominalisation and apply it in reading and writing and 'unpack' nominalised forms	**Language Spotlight 2** *Tasks A–F*	 206–210

World Business – Trade

Trade is as old as people are, as old as recorded history. In 3000 BC (**B**efore **C**hrist) the island of Minoan Crete was trading their fine pottery with those living in the Aegean islands as well as Egypt. Minoan pottery has been found in the tomb of the ancient King Djet (c 3000 BC). Meanwhile, far away from them, the early traders of the South Pacific were sailing in little pao paos (canoes) using the winds now named 'trade winds' to propel them from island to island. One wonders what sort of tariffs there were then, and if there were tariffs on imported goods and exported goods. A tariff is a tax imposed by a government of the day. Were the exchanges 'equal' in nature? Did an enormous jug of olive oil equal an enormous jug of nutmeg, spices or a beautiful, hand beaten copper ingot worn on the shoulder? Early on, there was no currency (coinage had not yet been invented), so we know they bartered or 'swapped' goods. How did the early traders assess the worth of their goods in their world market? How do countries do this today?

Perhaps the rule of 'supply and demand' has always existed. If something is rare, it is valued more highly than the thing that is not rare, the common thing.

Preliminary definition

economics (n)   the study of the way in which money and goods are produced and used. (*Longman Dictionary of Contemporary English* (2003) p409)

Task A | Orientation discussion to the unit's themes

❶ In pairs, discuss with your partner anything you understand concerning economics.

❷ What do you each know about world economics and global trade practices?

❸ Tell anything you know about your own country's trade.

❹ What do you buy that is not made or grown in your own country?

❺ Does the meat you eat come from your own country or is it imported?

❻ Are you carrying a bag that was made in another country?

❼ Check the label on your partner's shirt or blouse. Is it made by someone who lives far away from you? From your own country?

❽ If you answered 'yes', to question 7, why do you think that is so?

❾ If you drink soft drinks, are they produced in your country? Are they owned by someone in your own country?

❿ If you drink wine, are the grapes grown there, in your own country? Discuss what you buy with your partner and find out what is locally produced and what is imported.

Task B | Vocabulary concerned with world economics and world trade

Work out the following vocabulary with your teacher:

squander	disposable income
inequality	debt servicing
economic analysts	national autonomy
deforestation	

Your teacher has cards with the correct definitions. Find the person who has the card that matches your word. It should fit into the sentence on the card which is below the definition.

> **Key words**
> Key words or vocabulary (lexis) signal to the reader the main themes and topics of their writing. If a title is *Population growth*, then the two key words there are: 'population' and 'growth'. Automatically, you know what the writer must cover in the upcoming writing.

READING 1

Task A | Key words as vocabulary

❶ Look for and underline the key words in the reading text *Population growth*.

❷ Match words in the first column to the definition and write the number of the word in front of the definition in the table. You should be able to determine their meaning from the context within the text.

KEY WORDS/VOCABULARY	DEFINITIONS
i. carrying capacity (noun group)	A _____ a great deal of influence; a large amount of force
ii. growth rate (noun group)	B _____ out of proportion; too large or too small
iii. technological prowess (noun group)	C _____ the speed at which something grows
iv. disproportionately (adv)	D _____ everything around us
v. high impact (noun group)	E _____ a lot of skill, knowledge and ability around modern science and technical things
vi. environment (n)	F _____ the study of how organisms interact with each other and their environment
vii. ecology (n)	G _____ the number of people that a country can carry or hold or provide resources for
viii. resources (n)	H _____ everything available from natural to produced.

Population growth

The global economy is affected by population growth as is the environment and the ecology of our countries. Each country can only 'carry' or 'hold' a certain number of people. Resources must be provided for each individual.

Did you know that every four years, the world's population increases by about 220 million people? Earth's human population has more than doubled by 3 billion in just 40 years. The present growth rate is around 74 million additional people per year. We humans are by far the most abundant large animals, and given our technological prowess, we have a disproportionately high impact on the earth's environment.

❸ Answer the questions that follow.

[a] From the introductory paragraph, can you say approximately how many people are on earth at present? _____

_____

[b] What large animal is the most abundant on earth? _____

_____

[c] There are two or three important ideas introduced in the paragraph. What is the main or central topic of the entire paragraph? _____

_____

[d] If you answered 'population' or 'number of people on earth' you were correct. What then is another other important idea?

_____

[e] If humans have 'a disproportionately high impact on the environment', what noun group/reason does the sentence give you for this fact? _____

_____

Preliminary definition

The IMF   IMF is the International Monetary Fund, an international organisation set up by the United Nations and the International Bank for Reconstruction and Development, to stabilise relations between currencies of the subscribing countries. The world bank loans money to developing countries.
    The World Bank is an international bank set up by the United Nations in 1944 to economically assist developing countries, especially by loans. Its official name is International Bank for Reconstruction and Development. (*Macquarie Dictionary*, 1991)

Task A | Reading an extract

Sometimes, writers feel passionate about a subject. In the extract below, the writer expresses and presents a thought-provoking text concerning the inequality that exists in the world and some possible causes for that inequality. Note that the writer addresses the reader personally.

1 Students read the text that follows.

Economics and governments: Who calls the shots?

1 Why do you think it is that a small, privileged group of people who live in developed countries squander food, drive enormous cars that consume huge quantities of petrol (gasoline), take 45-minute hot showers and buy consumer goods daily, while the majority of people in the world go to bed hungry, don't own a car, have little or no access to hot water and no disposable income? Why, too, do the people of many countries walk miles to collect drinking water that other countries would not even consider fit to wash their dogs in? Why in many countries do children as young as five or six years old have to work like adults do instead of going to school and playing games in their spare time?

2 If one acknowledges the inequality that exists in the world, the next logical step is to question the reasons behind it. There needs to be an exploration of cause and effect and a questioning of the powers that control the circumstances of people in all countries. Usually, governments are expected to find solutions to economic problems which may give rise to poverty, child labour, poor working conditions and low pay. Governments are meant to consider and address problems concerning environment and progress.

3 But do governments actually control their countries? Do governments have real power on the global stage? What forces lie behind governments? According to some historians, researchers and economic theorists, it is not individual governments that hold power, it is actually the world banks and/or international monetary funds. Debt servicing in terms of interest payments on money lent to entire countries is the largest single controlling factor on the planet.

4 According to some economic analysts, servicing debt to the so-called First World countries has meant the demise of those countries in the form of eroding social, economic and environmental conditions. These claims are supported by the following argument: the banks charge interest rates which cannot ever be paid. Some countries have been paying back loans for 30 years and have paid the initial debt back many times over. It is the interest that can never be met. Further, many countries are actually re-borrowing money from the same banks in order to pay that bank their interest payments. In other words, the World Bank and the IMF lend money to pay their own selves back. In these

instances, so the arguments go, the lenders make decisions which affect the government policies of the countries in debt. Thus, it may be argued that national autonomy is seriously affected by debt servicing.

5 A few examples follow:

• Tanzania, 1983: Farmers required imported sprays for their oxen against deadly ticks and tsetse flies and pumps to administer the sprays. 'To conserve funds needed to pay its foreign debt, the government has had to impose restrictions on these and other desperately needed imports' (George, 1990, p101).

• Brazil, 1984/2002: 'The country has been shedding jobs by the hundreds of thousands' (due to the government having to pay back debt). A parallel economy of crime is the result and it may oblige shops and business premises to maintain armed guards … (Ibid, p128).

• Indonesia, Zaire, Peru and Colombia: Deforestation is increasing due to loans from the World Bank and other sources. 'Environmental issues become totally marginal' when governments face huge debts (Christine Bagdanowicz-Bindert, an economist who used to work with the IMF, Ibid, p167).

• In Bolivia in the 1980s 'the government froze salaries for school teachers under pressure from the IMF' (statement from a Bolivian teacher to Susan George, Ibid, p151).

6 On the other hand, there are those who argue that the IMF and World Bank lending policies have brought enormous benefits to countries that were barely developed. Their economies were lagging far behind the First World nations and their populations had little opportunity for any sort of industrial development. Without the aid, assistance and funds from these lenders, many countries could never have enjoyed the economic profitability that industrialisation and investment can bring.

7 There is evidence to support both positions. Solutions for difficult conundrums like those described are neither simple nor easy to discover. However, programs that concentrate on a shift to self-reliance, community action and production of local goods, less debt to governments by allowing longer times to pay back or by cancelling interest payments altogether could be, and presently are, a starting point.

Task B | Global examination of text

Analyse the **first paragraph** of the text in the following ways:

❶ What is the theme in the first sentence?

_____

_____

❷ Where might it be written?

_____

_____

❸ Who might have written it?

_____

_____

❹ Who is it written for?

_____

_____

❺ What is the author's bias or opinion?

_____

_____

❻ What is the effect of a question to the reader in the form of 'Why' at the beginning of each sentence?

_____

_____

_____

Task C | Contrast and comparison words – Juxtaposition of ideas

❶ Find all the question words and the contrast words in the first paragraph of the *Economics and governments: Who calls the shots?* and list or highlight them.

❷ Write the things being done by people which are contrasted in each example from para 1.

People in rich countries	*People in poor countries*
[a] _____ / _____
[b] _____ / _____
[c] _____ / _____
[d] _____ / _____
[e] _____ / _____
[f] _____ / _____

READING 3

Task A | Three-part task

There are three parts to this task.

Part 1 – Words and word groups list

❶ First, you are to scan the written version of the recorded lecture *Trade and more trade – What's all the fuss about?* on the next page for the following nouns, noun phrases/groups and nominalisations contained in the text. They are underlined for you within the text. Once you locate the words, write the number of the paragraph where you located the words next to the word in the list below.

❷ With a partner, match the underlined word groups to their definitions. These definitions are found within the recording script titled *Trade and more trade – What's all the fuss about?*. The first one has been done for you. To check your answers the definitions are in Part 2 on page 196.

Words and word groups list

a. _Paragraph 22_ degradation of developing countries' environments

b. _____ a commodity

c. _____ globalisation

d. _____ consumerism

e. _____ global economic integration

f. _____ very good track record

g. _____ conspicuous consumption practices

h. _____ a cursory glance

i. _____ the maxim

j. _____ excessive higher dependence on foreign capital inflows

k. _____ the trade deficit

l. _____ liberalised trade

m. _____ advocates

n. _____ integration of the international economy

o. _____ the continuing advocacy

p. _____ the assumption

q. _____ prudent master

r. _____ emerging nations' economies

s. _____ deregulated global trade

t. _____ consumption poverty

Listening: Trade and more trade – What's all the fuss about?
(16 minutes, 48 seconds)

Lecturer: *Good afternoon* to students, visitors and guests…

1   In my talk today, I hope to clarify some of the issues that surround the topic of <u>globalisation</u>. A great deal of the world's focus over the past decades, has been concerned with developed and <u>emerging nations' economies</u> and the links between *them* and the more developed, *established* economies or countries which are capable of huge <u>consumerism</u>. So, what's meant by 'economy' and what do we mean when we mention 'globalisation'?

2   Well, let's start – according to the *Macquarie Dictionary*, a discussion of economics will be a discussion, and I quote, 'pertaining to the production, distribution and use of income and wealth'. Globalisation has not made its way into the dictionary as yet as it appears to be a term (a nominal or noun term – a nominalisation) based upon the noun, 'global' which pertains to the whole world. Now, according to an article at the Center for Trade Policy Study's website entitled, 'The Benefits of Globalisation', 'Globalisation describes the ongoing global trend toward the freer flow of trade and investment across borders and the resulting <u>integration of the international economy</u>'. So, let me repeat that definition for you….'Globalisation describes the ongoing global trend toward the freer flow of trade and investment across borders and the resulting integration of the international economy'.

3   Now, <u>global economic integration</u> is a goal of the policy makers who advocate liberalised or free trade around the world. Another common term for free trade or <u>liberalised trade</u> is <u>deregulated global trade.</u>

4   <u>Advocates</u> of free trade try to explain that the reason globalisation is so good for countries is that it expands their economic freedom and spurs competition thereby raising both the productivity and the living standards of the people in countries who participate.

5   Hmmm, and that's where the debate really begins. Because, if that's true, then the countries involved in globalisation over the past 10 or 20 years will surely be able to demonstrate those promises – that is that their productivity and living standards are raised or improved. And that there are fewer poor people and those who are poor have a better standard of life. Now, before we examine that aspect of the claims for a particular economic policy, I'd like to outline briefly what I intend to cover in the talk.

6   Now, there are three main points –
   • First, I'd like to offer a brief overview of some positions concerning free trade.
   • Secondly, I'd like to point out some examples of countries who are seen to benefit by advocates of globalisation policies.
   • And, thirdly, I would like to point out some of the examples of countries who are seen not to benefit by reformers and critics of globalisation policies
   • And then to wrap up, I would like to test the truthfulness or otherwise of the statement that globalisation raises both productivity and the living standards of the people in the countries who participate.

7   Now it's beyond the scope of this lecture to discuss in depth some of the economic policies which comprise globalisation, well, for example, open or closed capital accounts, capital controls, inflation targeting, reserves and supplementary reserves and so forth. So, I'll limit my talk to issues around trade and whether or not this most important aspect of globalisation is, in fact, delivering its promise.

8   Now, by whatever term you call free trade and the push to increase it, it either has a <u>very good track record</u> or a very poor track record, and that depends entirely upon which side of the fence you sit upon, be that politically, financially or academically.

9   So, let me explain this a bit further. The main drivers for free trade are the richer, industrialised countries led by the IMF, you know, the International Monetary Fund and the World Bank. Now these advisors meet at the World Economic Forum where changes have recently taken place. Interestingly, all of these organisations state that they are committed to reducing world poverty and to increasing the wealth and wellbeing of the poorer, less industrialised or, let's call them, developing nations (as countries without the <u>conspicuous consumption practices</u> of the other nations are referred to).

10   Now, even <u>a cursory glance</u> at the World Bank's homepage on the World Wide Web reveals that its position statement or motto, if you like, is 'Our dream is a world free of poverty'. Well, regardless of the side if I may call it that, that you are on, this is the stated aim of both the opposing sides. Now, the method for the achievement of that aim is the thing that seems to be in dispute.

11   Now, deregulated, liberalised free trade in order to integrate economies is the goal of both the World Bank and the IMF. For example, the World Bank in September 2001, argued that, and again, I quote 'globalisation reduces poverty because integrated economies tend to grow faster and this growth is usually widely diffused'. (World Bank, 2001a, p1)

12   Now, the IMF's First Deputy Managing Director, Mr Stanley Fischer, states that he believes that 'Asia needs the Fund if it is to continue to benefit as it has so spectacularly over the years from its integration into the global economy'. Well, his position is clear enough. The IMF has benefited Asia in a spectacular way. Korea, for example, was one country that may have agreed, but only for a short while. They appeared to be benefiting until the Asian crisis in the late 1990s.

13   Another point of view, James Glassman, a columnist for the *Washington Post*, and a fellow at the, what is it, the … American Enterprise Institute in Washington stated that free trade creates wealth, which he says … get this … is 'more important than jobs'. So, here he is entering a debate with fellow Americans in the United States who oppose free

trade because many of their own industries and there are many (such as textiles) – are being destroyed. Now, in this theory, imports are why people trade and they are in fact the important factor. He uses Adam Smith's argument of 200 years ago that, and I quote Smith, 'It is the maxim of every prudent master of a family never to make at home what it will cost him more to make than to buy … If a foreign country can supply us with a commodity cheaper than we ourselves can make it, better buy it off them.' So, in his view, exports are only traded in order to gain the benefit of imports.

14 So, just returning for a minute to claims that global economic integration has great potential to combat poverty and economic inequality … and as I stated earlier in this lecture if this claim were true, then that could be demonstrated. But, it isn't. Listen a moment to these statistics which are provided in a research paper by Weller, Scott and Hersh in 2002. It goes like this …'In 1980 median income in the richest 10% of countries was 77 times greater, 77 times greater, than in the poorest 10%; and by 1999, that gap had grown to 122 times. The number of poor people actually rose from 1987 to 1999. The world's poorest 10%, and that's 400 million people, lived on 72 cents a day or less. In 1998, that figure had increased … to 79 cents and in 1999 had dropped again to 78 cents.' This represents no improvement for a decade of trade.

15 Now, while many other 'social, political and economic factors contribute to poverty, the evidence shows that unregulated capital and trade flows actually contribute to rising inequality and in fact impede progress in reducing poverty.' How? I hear you asking. Well, it goes like this … when trade is liberalised there is more import competition – which in turn leads to lower wages for locals. Deregulated international capital flows can lead to rising short-term capital inflows certainly and increased financial speculation. But this causes instability which causes more frequent economic crises. We only have to think of the so-called Asian crisis back in the late 90s. Governments cannot cope with crises as they do not have the reserves. Now, as we all should know, any economic problems within any country harm the poor to a greater extent than others. Poor people are not being helped by free trade, even though that could be the desire and is, indeed, the stated claim of the IMF and the World Bank.

16 Hang on a minute, I hear you say …. What about somewhere like India and the IT industry there? Surely, this unrestricted globalisation there has proved to be a boon in India. Many business opportunities for India would be the result. And they now have lots of technology. Yes, but firstly, it does not belong to them and, secondly, there is no infrastructure to provide it to people outside of a very small area of the country and, thirdly, only a very few workers benefit from it and even they work for far lower wages than they should.

17 In a detailed analysis of the IT revolution and the opening up of India to globalisation in South Asian Voice, it appears that FDI (that's Foreign Direct Investment) benefits the multinationals far in excess of the benefits to India and its own people. For example, the MNCs receive huge tax breaks that are not available to competing local companies. So

not happy with tax breaks, the MNCs also evade tax. The Minister of State for Finance in India named a number of very large and very well known companies as having been charged for serious income tax violations so, obviously, this means that the government has lost money to these huge companies.

18 And, privatisation has meant that in areas such as power supply – companies like Enron charge double to the State Electricity Board than a local supplier. And also, Enron uses imported fuels, making India even more dependent on the international market. Now, it also means again that the Indian government has lost capital. This results in a lack of funding to important infrastructures within the country, the obvious ones like education and healthcare. So once again, the poor get poorer and the rich get even richer.

19 Now, in the same article from the South Asian Voice, we have Dr DM Nanjundappa in the Deccan Herald in 1998, now he's a noted economist and also happens to be the Deputy Chairman of the State Planning Board in India, and he stated the following, and I quote from Dr Nanjundappa: 'Excessive higher dependence on foreign capital inflows and a rise in exports is likely to be dangerous. Unless there is a sustained growth in exports arising from improvement in the competitive strength of the Indian industry, our hope to recover will be the will o' the wisp'.

20 And to support that, the trade deficit in India widened to a record four billion dollars in the last quarter of 2002. It grew by a staggering 27% and this was in spite of an increase in exports. And at the same time the rupee shrank in value as well. Africa has many similar tales to tell to the Asian situation.

21 Now, the point of all of these criticisms is that economists themselves are actually questioning the value to their countries of unrestricted and deregulated trade. Certain geographical areas may benefit and certain individuals will most certainly benefit from those policies. But in terms of the overall nations who are supposed to be assisted by having markets for trading – that is a place for their exports and the development of technology within their own countries – there's not really much concrete evidence to support that that is in fact happening. So, the benefits go to the rich countries and it is on the rich country's terms that the whole concept of globalisation is constructed.

22 Now, to the second point, as for combatting poverty, the World Bank has this to say in its own report published in 2001. And this is straight from the report, 'In the aggregate, and for some large regions, all…measures suggest that the 1990s did not see much progress against consumption poverty in the developing world' (Chen & Ravallion, 2001, p18) and also the IMF, in its 2000 report, '… Part IV reports that progress in raising real incomes and alleviating poverty has been so disappointingly slow in many developing countries.' It also states that 'the relative gap between the richest and the poorest countries has continued to widen' (IMF 2000, Part IV, p 1). What is not mentioned in all of that is that not only has poverty increased, but the degradation of developing countries' environments has also increased

dramatically. To put that another way, there is greater poverty of lifestyle conditions as well. Note the air, water and land pollution as a result of demand for exports produced cheaply and with great cost to the local environment.

23 So, and I'll close here, despite the <u>continuing advocacy</u> of rich nations that poor countries must trade and trade on the terms of the more powerful nations and that in turn this trade will and must lead to greater wealth, prosperity and more equality, it appears that the number of poor people has actually risen. So, the promises of poverty reduction and more equal income distribution have actually failed to occur. Now I'd like you to consider whether or not the economic policies need to be a little newer than 200 years old and could, in fact, incorporate the economies they deal with, rather than making <u>the assumption</u> that there is but one way to create wealth and reduce poverty. It is not working. The evidence is there. Now, the theory may work, but the practice doesn't. It seems that the ideas for globalisation must take into account the infrastructures which currently exist in developing countries and work respectfully with them to create meaningful solutions to and for the ever increasing poor around the globe rather than exploiting them in an opportunistic way to create ever more poor.
Thank you.

Part 2 – Definitions for words and word groups list

a. To degrade or lower the environment of a country which is emerging.

b. Anything of value which may be bought or sold.

c. Describes the ongoing global trend toward the freer flow of trade and investment across borders and the resulting integration of the international economy.

d. To buy – the power to obtain goods and to do so.

e. Where economies join or become integrated into the world's economic policies.

f. A positive result of actions.

g. To consume a great deal, to purchase new things constantly and to have the buying power to do so.

h. A quick look at something.

i. The saying or belief.

j. For a country to rely too heavily on other countries in terms of cash/money coming into the country.

k. Money owed to other countries as a result of trade.

l. Free trade or trade which is unrestricted, trade without controls.

m. People who believe in something and ask that it be accepted – to put up an argument in favour of something.

n. For economies around the world to become integrated, to work together.

o. For people to continue to advise and argue a case.

p. A belief.

q. Wise person.

r. The economy or money base of nations which are developing along an industrial line.

s. Trade around the world which is not regulated by governments.

t. When people do not have buying power and are poorer than others who consume a lot.

Part 3 – Using the words in context

❸ Last, place the underlined word groups from part 1 (page 193) into the correct sentences which contain blanks. You will need to skim the text of the lecture, ie reread it for meaning, in order to complete the task.

CD 2

Sentences from the text *Trade and more trade – What's all the fuss about?*

1. So, in conclusion, despite _____ of rich nations that poor countries must trade and trade on the terms of the more powerful nations and that this trade will and must lead to greater wealth, prosperity and more equality, it appears that the number of poor people has actually risen.

2. '_____ on _____ and rise in exports is likely to be dangerous. Unless there is a sustained growth in exports arising from improvement in the competitive strength of the Indian industry, our hope to recover will be the will o' the wisp.'

3. _____ in India widened to a record of $4 billion dollars in the last quarter of 2002.

4. Interestingly, all these organisations state that they are committed to reducing world poverty and to increasing the wealth and wellbeing of the poorer, less industrialised or developing nations (as countries without the _____ of the other nations are referred to).

5. What is not mentioned is that not only has poverty increased, but the _____ of _____ has also increased dramatically.

6. A _____ at the World Bank's home page on the World Wide Web reveals that its position statement or motto, if you like, is 'Our Dream is a World Free of Poverty'.

7. According to an article at the Center for Trade Policy Study's website titled 'The Benefits of Globalisation', 'Globalisation describes the ongoing global trend toward the freer flow of trade and investment across borders and the resulting… _____'

8. In my talk today, I hope to clarify some of the issues that surround the topic of _____

9. A great deal of the world's focus over the past decades and coming decade, is aimed at and concerned with developed and _____ and the links between them and the more developed, established economies or countries which are capable of huge _____

_____ is a goal of the policy makers who advocate liberalised or free trade around the world. Another common term for free trade or _____ is

_____ .

_____ of free trade explain that the reason globalisation is so good for countries is that it expands economic freedom and promotes competition thereby raising both productivity and living standards of the people in countries who participate.

10. 'In the aggregate, and for some large regions, all … measures suggest that the 1990s did not see much progress against _____ in the developing world' (Chen & Ravallion, 2001, p18).

Now, by whatever term you call free trade and the push to increase it, it either has a

_____ or a very poor track record, depending upon which side of the fence you sit upon politically, financially and academically.

11. He uses Adam Smith's argument of 200 years ago that 'It is _____ of every _____ of a family never to make at home what it will cost him more to make than to buy … If a foreign country can supply us with a _____ cheaper than we ourselves can make it, better buy it off them.' In his view, exports are only traded in order to gain the benefits of imports.

LANGUAGE SPOTLIGHT 1 ....

Cause and effect – Result and reason

When a writer is writing about events that result in other events, there are language signals that are used. The following work will assist you to understand how to express and recognise cause and effect. It will show you how to see reasons and results when reading texts.

Cause and effect; result and reason

Cause and effect are based upon result and the reason for that result. For example:

> *I'm rich (result) because (reason) – I have a lot of money.*
> *OR*
> *I have a lot of money and that's why (reason) I'm rich (result).*

The opposite would be:

> *I'm poor (result) because (reason), I spent all my money.*
> *OR*
> *I spent all my money (reason) and that's why I'm poor (result).*

Preliminary definition

inflation (n) 1. a swelling up, distension. *inflationary gap* – A *gap* between purchasing power and purchasable goods; as the gap widens, it tends to initiate an inflationary spiral or vicious circle. *Webster Universal Dictionary*, Unabridged International Edition 1975; Henry Cecil Wyld, Eric H. Partridge (eds), Harver Educational Services Inc. New York, NY.

Task A | Reading to understand cause and effect/ result and reason

❶ Read the short text titled *Economic inflation – Causes and effects* and complete the work that follows. The bolded words are markers or language cues to assist you to understand cause and effect when reading and writing.

Economic inflation – Causes and effects

① Inflation involves the measurement of price increases of goods and services and is over a certain period of time. ② **If** there is inflation, **then** people will pay more for the same goods and buy less with the same dollar ③ **The cause** of inflation is price changes, prices going up. ④ **This leads to** the fact that you can buy less with the same money. ⑤ In other words, the value of your money decreases and it is more expensive to buy goods and services **as a result of** inflation.

⑥ Some parts of the population are more affected than others by inflation. ⑦ For example, people on fixed incomes. ⑧ **If** there are shortages in supply which enable sellers to raise prices, **then** it can be very hard on the elderly who

(then is ellipsed)

are living on a fixed income. ⑨ **When** prices increase and people only have the same amount of money, ^ they are unable to obtain the same amount of things they could purchase previously. ⑩ Also, **as/when/or if** inflation

(then is ellipsed)

goes higher, ^ money becomes worth less and less as time goes by.

---

❷ Write the bolded words from each sentence that relate to one another using '…' to divide them. *For example*, in sentence 2 you would write **If…then.**

[a] **The cause…** $\underline{\quad 3 \quad}$

[b] _____…_____ $\underline{\quad 4 \quad}$

[c] _____…_____ $\underline{\quad 5 \quad}$

[d] _____…_____ $\underline{\quad 8 \quad}$

[e] _____…_____ $\underline{\quad 9 \quad}$

$\underline{\quad 10 \quad}$

You have written the discourse cues/signals/signposts which tell the reader of this text that there is a reason and a result or cause and effect being explained. These are the language cues you must use to express cause and effect.

Examine sentence 1 from the text above:

The cause (the reason) is inflation **and the effect (the result)** is people are paying more.

If there is inflation, ***then*** *people will pay more for the same goods and buy less with the same dollar.*

If and ***then*** tell you, (signal) that there is a cause and an effect.

Task B | Clarifying effect/result and cause/reason

Use the models you have examined to assist you to write the effects and causes in the blanks for each sentence.

❶ **The cause** of inflation is price changes, prices going up. **This leads to** the fact that you can buy less with the same money.

Effect – (result) _____

Cause – (reason) _____

❷ In other words, the value of your money decreases and it is more expensive to buy goods and services **as a result of** inflation.

Effect – (result) _____

Cause – (reason) _____

❸ **If** there are shortages in supply which enable sellers to raise prices, **then** it can be very hard on the elderly who are living on a fixed income.

Effect – (result) _____

Cause – (reason) _____

❹ **When** prices increase and people only have the same amount of money, they are unable to obtain the same number of things they could purchase previously.

Effect – (result) _____

Cause – (reason) _____

❺ Also, **as/when/or if** inflation goes higher, money becomes worth less and less as time goes by.

Effect – (result) _____

Cause – (reason) _____

Task C | Further work on cause and effect; result and reason

To support the claim in the essay *Economics and governments: Who calls the shots?* you read previously on page 192 '… that national autonomy is seriously affected by debt servicing …', the following examples show cause and effect. The contrast is with what *should* be happening as opposed to what *is* happening. Look at example 1 and then complete the exercise using the other examples:

❶ Tanzania, 1983: Farmers required imported sprays for their oxen against deadly ticks and tsetse flies and pumps to administer the sprays. 'To conserve funds needed to pay its foreign debt, the government has had to impose restrictions on these and other desperately needed imports' (George, 1990, p 101).

Effect – (result) the farmers could not obtain the sprays they needed.

Cause – (reason) the government had to impose restrictions on imports.

❷ Brazil, 1984/2002: 'The country has been shedding jobs by the hundreds of thousands.' (due to the government having to pay back debt). A parallel economy of crime is the result … (Ibid, p128).

Effect – (result) _____

Cause – (reason) _____

❸ Indonesia, Zaire, Peru and Colombia: Deforestation is increasing due to loans from the World Bank and other sources. 'Environmental issues become totally marginal' when governments face huge debts (Christine Bagdanowicz-Bindert, an economist who used to work with the IMF, Ibid, p167).

Effect – (result) _____

Cause – (reason) _____

❹ In Bolivia in the 1980s 'the government froze salaries for school teachers under pressure from the IMF' (statement from a Bolivian teacher to Susan George, p151).

Effect – (result) _____

Cause – (reason) _____

Task D | Establishing result or reason

Write each discourse cue which serves to establish cause and effect and which illustrates reason or result.

❶ In sentence 1, there are no cues. The cause and effect is gained from the content or ideas of the sentences. 'In order to' is implied where 'To' is stated.

❷ **Effect** – (result) _____

  Cause – (reason) _____

❸ **Effect** – (result) _____

  Cause – (reason) _____

❹ **Effect** – (result) _____

  Cause – (reason) _____

Modal verbs in business language

Modal verbs
Modals serve the purpose of telling the reader how certain or uncertain an event or situation is. Is the situation possible? Is it absolutely certain? Or is it only probable? Modals are all about what will or will not happen; about what may or may not happen; and about the degree of likelihood or possibility and probability of events.

Task E | Using modal verbs

Use the following modals in the blanks in the sentences 1 – 5: *will certainly; will definitely; will probably; shouldn't; may; could; must.*

❶ Carbon trading schemes are now a reality around the world. They have a direct effect on business within countries, thus, these trading schemes _____ affect economies as well as affecting which countries increase or reduce their green house gas emissions.

❷ X company is taking a huge market share away from y company. Therefore, y company _____ work harder and create strategies that _____ win back their market.

❸ Ethics in business are important. Both small and large businesses must not lie or deceive shareholders. If they behave in an honourable manner, then their profits _____ be a problem, since their reputation will create better business for them.

❹ Things are getting better for y company. Whether they continue to improve is anyone's guess. Profits _____ be up this quarter, but no one can quite predict it yet.

❺ X company learned its lesson in 2010. It manufactured a car with a known fault but allowed the car to be released on the market anyway. People died as a result of that fault and the company was prosecuted and sued. It paid an enormous amount of money to the families. It _____ not (or won't) do that again.

WRITING 1

Task A | Applying cause and effect to your own experience

❶ Write a paragraph outlining the causes and effects of saving money in an account that you are determined not to touch.

Here are cause and effect signals to use to describe results and reasons:

if…then	when…then
as a result of	because
this leads to	so
due to	since

_____

_____

_____

_____

_____

_____

_____

_____

_____

_____

Further methods of development in paragraph writing

You have studied paragraph writing in each chapter of *EAP Now!* 2e. In this unit, you will practise writing paragraphs using a variety of methods in order to develop your thinking and make your main idea clear to the reader. Methods of development may combine in one paragraph some times.

> **✱ Methods of development revisited**
> There are several ways to develop a paragraph. In an extended paragraph you must **list details** to support the main idea and the details should be factual. Here are other methods you studied previously in Unit 4: **description; providing reasons; giving definitions and examples; showing cause and effect; analogy; compare and contrast.**

Task B | Revisit paragraph development

❶ Before you begin match the following cues (by filling in the table below) to the correct method of development.

- As….as/like
- The facts are as follows:/this; this; this; and this.
- Therefore, it follows that
- Adjectives that describe
- It is …….../It means/It is defined as/for example
- If… then/….is due to/as a result …
- Whereas x is like this…..y is like that/but/not x….but y

METHOD OF DEVELOPMENT IN YOUR WRITING	DISCOURSE CUES/SIGNALS
[a] Listing details	
[b] Describing something	
[c] Providing reasons	
[d] Giving definitions and examples	
[e] Showing cause and effect	
[f] Making an analogy/s	
[g] Comparing and contrasting	

Task C | Which method?

Add the necessary writing to the existing paragraphs where some text has been provided for you using the correct method of development. The italicised words tell you which method you are to use. For example, in the concluding sentence of paragraph 1, you read **As a result**. These words signal or tell you there must be a **cause and effect**. Complete paragraph 1 using *cause and effect* as your written method of development. Then, complete the other paragraphs, choosing the correct method from the cues provided.

❶ Economic inflation is a reality that may affect any country in the world. Recently, in many Western countries, there was an extreme acceleration of inflation in the prices of homes… *This acceleration*

_____

_____

_____

_____

As a result of the downturn in buying power of ordinary people, fewer homes were purchased and the real estate market fell severely.

❷ Mountains and the scenery around mountains are quite stunning.

_____

_____

_____

_____

_____

_____

Thus, I would like to continue to travel and **view** such beauty all my life.

❸ Ever heard the saying 'that's like **comparing** apples and oranges'? It's true that they are both fruit, **but** they are definitely two different things. An apple…

_____

whereas an orange…

_____

_____

_____

_____

Therefore,…

_____

❹ One could imagine that falling in love **is as** exciting **as** winning a million dollars. It's **like**…

_____

_____

It's **as** wonderful **as** …

_____

I think you know you're in love when all their words seem like _____ and their appearance is **as** beautiful to you **as** _____

_____.

(This paragraph combines more than one method of development as often happens).

❺ Back in 1998 and 2000, there was huge and rapid investment in the internet. Unfortunately, this resulted in an acceleration of stock prices. This can be a good thing for awhile, **but**, unfortunately, **when** _____ happens, **then**,

_____

The **reasons for this**, **as outlined above**, are solid economic principles. Once people over invest, the market heats up too much. Ultimately, this disastrous fall was bound to occur.

❻ Many people today use a mobile phone, sometimes **called** a cell phone for communication. **Then** there's the ipod! A mobile is basically a _____ _____ and is used **for** **the purpose of** _____. But, a cell phone these days, **may be defined as** a tool for everything from _____ to _____ _____. **For** **example**, _____ and _____ do all of these things.

❼ Most students carry a school bag **and/or** a handbag of some sort. These bags are useful and contain many items. Some common items are _____, _____, _____, **and**

_____

Presently, my own bag contains **the following**;

_____

Some of these items were produced in other countries. **For example**, _____, _____, _____, _____. Items in my own bag could be said to reflect world business and world trade.

WRITING 2

Task A | Converting description into comparison

1 Describe the characteristics of a large city. Mention shopping, buildings, businesses, banks, employment (jobs), housing, restaurants, entertainment.

_____

_____

_____

_____

_____

_____

_____

_____

_____

_____

_____

2 Describe the characteristics of rural (country or village) areas. Mention farming, buildings (or lack of them), businesses, banks, housing, landscape, fields, crops, restaurants, entertainment. Describe it as you would see it.

_____

_____

_____

_____

_____

_____

_____

_____

_____

_____

3 Next, turn the description you wrote in questions 1 and 2 into a comparison. Use comparison and contrast connectives such as: _but, whereas, although, on the other hand, similarly, likewise, correspondingly, in the same way, on the contrary, however, conversely, in comparison, while, instead._

Large cities and rural or isolated areas are very different...

_____

_____

_____

_____

_____

_____

_____

Task B | Writing a contrast – Free writing and thinking

1 Write a text using your own knowledge (or speculate) to contrast a typical morning of a young adult from a country with an 'approved' emerging or established economy (perhaps your own country) with that of a poorer neighbour or foreign country. An observation might be that while one adult walks from their bed to their bathroom and shower, another walks half an hour or to the village pump or faucet. Continue to compare and contrast their morning meal, the day's possible schooling or employment. Think of at least five differences.

_____

_____

_____

_____

_____

_____

_____

Task C | Metaphor and simile

> **More ways to compare and contrast**
> Another way to **compare or contrast** is through metaphor and simile:
> - a metaphor calls one thing, another thing – x = y
> - a simile compares two things using the words *like* or *as* – x is like y | x is as ….as y.

Examine the following phrases, note whether they are a metaphor or a simile and then make up some of your own!

1 That woman is an angel (*metaphor*).

2 Mark my words, that man's a dog!

_____

3 His eyes were like diamonds.

_____

4 A butterfly is like a small, lightweight bird.

_____

5 Her head felt as heavy as lead.

_____

6 His speech was as rapid as a machine gun.

_____

7 The moon was a pale pumpkin glowing over the celebrations.

_____

8 You are a flower seen today.

_____

9 You are a sparkling rose in the bud.

_____

10 My soul is a patient onlooker.

_____

11 The queen was a she-wolf of France.

_____

12 Thy bright mane for ever shall shine like the gold …

_____

13 *The moon, like a flower*
In heaven's high bower,
With silent delight
Sits and smiles on the night

(Extract from William Blake 1757–1827, 'Night')

_____

14 *From thy bright eyes love took his fires,*
Which round about in sport he hurl'd;
But 'twas from mine he took desires
Enough t' undo the amorous world.

(Extract from Aphra Behn, 1640–1689, 'Song')

_____

WRITING 3

Exposition schema: discussion and argument

> **Point of view**
> When undertaking tertiary study in an English medium, you will be expected to compose essays using researched information which argues a case for something. When you argue, you must persuade. This happens in both speaking and writing. You must persuade your listener or reader that your point of view is correct. You must have a point of view and you must convince the listener or the reader of it. In argument, people are said to 'take sides'.

Task A | Identifying an issue

With a partner:

1 Think of something that you believe in very strongly. It could be about food, religion, family, politics.

2 State that belief to each other.

3 Write the belief here.

_____

_____

_____

4 Is there a different belief about the same thing? In other words, is there any other possible position/belief that could be held?   Yes ☐   No ☐

5 If you answered 'Yes' to question 4, then you have identified an 'issue'.

Task B | Defining an issue

❶ From the definitions below, choose what you think is an 'issue'.

[a] A point in question or dispute –It has to have two or more viewpoints.

[b] A personal belief that is challenged.

[c] A factual report that has been researched.

[d] A solution to opposing viewpoints.

❷ Make a list of three things that you believe are current issues both in your own country and in your host country, if you know any here. Remember that an issue needs to be a belief or a point that is arguable. In other words, different people hold different opinions about an issue.

[a] _____

[b] _____

[c] _____

Now that you have considered the idea of an issue, read on in order to discover how to write or speak your argument to express your belief, your claim, your contention, your side or your own case! You will use exposition.

Task C | Exposition: an argument that will express your belief, claim, contention, side or case

Exposition is one of the most common essay forms that you will be required to produce. An exposition is a factual text which carries forward an argument or puts forward a point of view. You will write essays and give oral presentations based upon reading and the research of others.

An essay must be logical and the staging within its structure follows the pattern:

[a] Introduction
- Introductory general statement
- Position (thesis)
- Scope or Preview

[b] Arguments
- Individual points
- Elaborated with support

[c] Conclusion
- Restate the initial position

Notice that expositions include argument and discussion:
- Expositions often use simple present tense and logical sequencers rather than temporal (time) sequencers.

Task D | Staging in exposition and predicting text content from a title

❶ Read the text on the next page and highlight the stages of the writing to the exposition schema provided above.

❷ Before you begin reading, paraphrase the title in order to predict what the writing will be about.

_____

_____

Causes of Aqua Blue Surf and Snow Gear International's success in 2011

① Whenever a business is enormously successful, other companies and the general public want to know why. Aqua Blue Surf and Snow Gear is an international success story for the second decade of the 21st century. For a business to be successful, it is necessary to have strong consumer sales, leading to big profits which in turn inspire investor confidence. Many success stories are also based around international expansion. These elements of strong sales and profits, plus investor confidence are really key components. A business example of these principles in action is Aqua Blue Surf and Snow Gear International (ABSSI).

② Initially, ABSI was a Spanish company driven by local sales. They expanded offshore, and it was this expansion that really launched the group. Companies require continuing investor confidence and with ABSI, this confidence had waned. Now there is certainly renewed confidence in Aqua Blue Surf and Snow Gear International's earnings. The causes for this confidence are strong sales and a possible profit upgrade. Reports of strong sales in the company's major offshore markets of the US, Australia and Europe bolstered faith in market forecasts that the surf and snow wear apparel company will earn $110 million in the year to 30 June 2011.

③ If this figure is reached, or is even close to it, it will be a large profit upgrade for ABSSI due to the fact that investors believed in a target of only $85 million. Floating on the stock exchange is a sure-fire way to be successful in business. But, naturally, it takes a certain amount of success to float in the first place. Aqua Blue joined the stock market only two years after forming. The measure of success once on the stock market is the rising value of the shares. Investors are thrilled because Aqua Blue company shares have risen this quarter more than 9% to $8.90 surging clear of long-term lows. When Aqua initially floated, there was interest, and then it died down.

④ So, what caused renewed interest in their product lines? One reason Paul Minnow, company director, believes is that presently there is a resurgence of interest in his company because surfing movies have hit the US again, and young people are buying up big in a wave of enthusiasm and rekindled interest in the surf scene. Consumers have to enjoy the brand and repeat buy for a company to be successful and with ABSSI, their consumers are girls, and girls wear is the primary driver in their remarkable recovery. The rally is predicted to continue for two to three years.

⑤ The company offices will expand to Los Angeles in July of this year providing evidence that success in retail business, and ABSSI in particular is primarily based around consumer and investor confidence plus international expansion.

Review – Cited text references in an essay
You will recall from previous units analysing cited text references within student essays and other writing. A text reference is a referral to the source material where the writer located his/her information. Remember – All information must be referenced. Otherwise, you are guilty of plagiarism.

Task E | Locate and analyse in-text references

❶ Read the following text 'Extract from an essay' and circle every reference.

Extract from an essay
Bassey (1986, p18) looks at 'change' and improvement' as the search for 'right decision', while Burns (1994, p32) looks for 'a process of improvement and reform'. Both have valuable insights to assist a new student of research.

Note the last sentence: *Both have valuable insights to assist a new student of research*. This is a critical comment, ie it displays critical thinking by the <u>writer</u> of the essay – this will be YOU. First you quote, then you draw some conclusion about what you have just quoted. Reference the quote and you have not plagiarised!

❷ You should have circled Bassey (1986, p18) and Burns (1994, p32). Now answer the following:

[a] How many authors are there in the reference?

_____

[b] What year was the text from which the quote came published?

_____

[c] What page number did the quote from Burns come from?

_____

[d] What year did Burns publish the text from which the quote came?

_____

Task A | Listen and note-take for main ideas

Use the following headings for your note-taking.

- Issues
- Arguments
- Counter arguments
- Conclusions
- Recommendations.

Task B | Note-taking – Writing down the concepts

 ❶ Listen to the lecture *Trade and more trade – What's all the fuss about?*

❷ While listening try to hear the signal words such as *first, secondly*. These words will help you hear what the lecturer will present and are in an introduction stage. After that, an issue will be introduced and then discussed.

❸ Listen for cue words like *however, now, let me explain, but.* These words will help you to prepare to note-take an argument or a counter argument.

CD 2

❹ Listen for the *conclusions and recommendations* that come at the end of arguments and in the final minutes of the lecture.

Your teacher will provide you with some of the main ideas and headings as well as the key words after you assemble your notes.

LANGUAGE SPOTLIGHT 2

Nominalisation: moving towards more academic writing

Nominalisation is where:
- *Main ideas* are condensed, packed smaller, put into a suitcase where meaning needs to be 'un packed'.
- **Main ideas** are distilled and packed with meaning.
- *Verbs* are **changed** into **nouns** and **noun phrases.**
- *Agency* is removed – This means the people are taken out of the words.
- *Tense* is often moved to passive.
- **Higher lexis** (better vocabulary) is added
- *Cause and effect are not obvious*. Sometimes the cause seems to have disappeared. It is invisible without looking carefully to find the 'who' or the agent.

Task A | Forming nouns from verbs

❶ Change the following verbs to nouns. Endings in these examples are 'tion', 'ment', 'dant', 'th'.

Verb form	Noun form
to populate	population
to grow	
to exploit	
to conserve	
to preserve	
to degrade	
to develop	
to depend	
to regulate	

Did you write population/growth/exploitation/conservation/preservation/degradation/development/dependant/ and regulation?

Task B | Removing personals from writing – Creating a more academic text

❶ First read the following text and highlight or circle personals such as 'people', 'my', 'they', 'I', 'we', 'you'.

Business

If you want to be really good in business, then there are rules to follow. You have to know that there is more to it than just making money. A good business practices certain things that make it a good business. One thing is giving the people attention and really caring about what you are selling, or what you are offering if it is a service to them. I think another very important thing about a good business is that you must behave well and not cheat nor lie.

② Then remove all the personal pronouns you can find.

③ Finally, rewrite the text now, removing all the personal pronouns you highlighted. Also try to write using better vocabulary and nouns, not verbs. Change the tense of some verb groups to the passive form.

_____

_____

_____

_____

Task C | How does it all work? How to move from spoken language to the passive and then to nominalisations

① Your teacher will help you change the active form of the verb to the passive form in column 2 of the table.

Spoken language:	How people create a dictionary
Passive form:	How a dictionary is created
Nominalisation:	The process of dictionary creation

② Then work in pairs and complete column 3 of the table.

ACTIVE _How people create a dictionary_	PASSIVE _How a dictionary is created_	NOUN GROUPS/NOMINALISATION _The process of dictionary creation_
The first thing is, people think about the style they will use to show on each page.	First, style is considered and what will be shown on each page.	Consideration of page style is the initial stage.
Next, the writers have to spell all the words correctly.	Next, the words are spelled correctly.	Correct spelling is considered next.
The third thing is to make people understand how to pronounce the words		
And indicate how to say the words for the reader.		
They do this by showing phonemes.		
Then, the writers put in (or include) the words that are new in the language to finish the dictionary.		

Task D | Changing processes from active to passive/rewriting using multiple drafts

Read the following paragraph about the computer revolution.

The computer revolution

Many people are talking about the computer revolution. This is happening ten times faster than the Industrial Revolution did. They say that computers are taking jobs. However, other people say that computers are also making jobs. These jobs are different and therefore people will need to change. Some jobs will handle the information. Others will install, upgrade and maintain the equipment. Presently people even shop, date and get jobs by computer, among other things.

❶ Work together with your teacher and highlight the personals in the text. Next, underline the verbs that are in the active form and then underline future tense.

❷ Rewrite the entire text changing the verbs/processes to the passive form.

_____

_____

_____

_____

_____

❸ Rewrite again and reach for higher lexis (sophisticated vocabulary) by nominalising the passive verbs you have changed from the active form above.

_____

_____

_____

_____

_____

_____

Task E | Using multiple drafts – 'Unpacking' the meaning of noun groups and nominalisations

The next text is a paragraph from the essay titled: *Economics and governments: Who calls the shots?* from page 192, but it is the first draft before nominal groups and nominalisation were introduced.

❶ Examine the table on page 209 and continue to 'unpack' the meaning in the nominalised sentences. You are working from the academic back to the non-academic to discover the writer's original thinking. This is the opposite of moving from the active to the passive to the nominalised forms that you did in the creating a dictionary exercise.

[a] Here you will put the personals back into the text, eg *people*.

[b] You will change nouns back to their verb forms, eg *solution = to solve*.

[c] You will change the higher language back down to lower language, more spoken, eg *acknowledges = admits to knowing*.

Here is the extract academic text *Economics and governments: Who calls the shots?* para 2:

Extract from para 2

If one acknowledges the inequality that exists in the world, the next logical step is to question the reasons behind it. There needs to be an exploration of cause and effect and a questioning of the powers that control the circumstances of people in all countries. Usually, governments are expected to find solutions to economic problems which may give rise to poverty, child labour, poor working conditions and low pay. Governments are meant to consider and address problems concerning environment and progress.

ACADEMIC AND NOMINALISED	NON-ACADEMIC WITH PERSONALS
If one acknowledges the inequality that exists in the world	If a person admits to knowing that in the world, people are not equal
the next logical step is to question the reasons behind it.	people need to ask why other people are not equal. What are the reasons?
There needs to be an exploration	People need to explore
of cause and effect	what causes things to happen
and a questioning of the powers	and people need to question the powers [powers are people who make decisions and who have power]
that control the circumstances of people in all countries.	People have circumstances, circumstances are their living conditions, their employment etc. These circumstances are controlled by someone in every country.
Usually, governments are expected to find solutions	_____ _____
to economic problems which	_____ _____
may give rise to poverty, child labour, poor working conditions and low pay.	_____ _____
Governments are meant to consider and address problems	_____ _____
concerning environment and progress.	_____ _____

Task F | 'Unpacking' individual nominalised words

Work jointly with your teacher to unpack the meaning of the following nominalisations. You must use complete sentences. The first one is done for you.

❶ **Debt servicing** – This means that someone or some country borrows money and is obligated to pay it back. To service a debt means that you must do whatever it takes to 'make the debt good'. In other words, whoever borrowed money must pay the money back.

❷ **National autonomy** – _____
_____
_____
_____

❸ **A country's self-determination** – _____
_____
_____
_____

4 **Economic sanctions –** _____

5 **Dissuasive taxes –** _____

Task A | Preparing and presenting a talk

Title: *Success in business is a mind game*

1 Prepare a talk, using the 10 point procedure below which is a preparation plan.

Procedure
1. Think.
2. Decide what aspects (things, areas) of your topic you will cover. You cannot talk about every, single thing there is to do with it.
3. Define your terms. Even a term like 'business' needs a definition for there are many different ways to consider what the word 'business' means.
4. Research the topic and take notes from your researched material.
5. Begin to structure the talk by treating it like a mini essay.

It requires an introduction with staging; paragraphs in the middle section that support what your topic is; and a summary conclusion.
6. Make notes for the talk, do not write out every word and read it. That is boring.
7. Put these notes on cards or, if you are presenting with a PowerPoint or other type of audio visual, put the notes into the template in the software.
8. Practise giving the talk outloud as many times as you can.
9. Present! Smile! Be interested in what you're saying.
10. Speak with conviction.

Task A | Vocabulary enlargement – Vocabulary in context

1 Can you determine the meanings of the following underlined vocabulary from the surrounding words and sentences? Note the signals that let you know a

definition is offered… eg *or, parenthesis ( ), means that, is, in other words…*

2 Write the meaning of each numbered word within the text in the blank spaces following the text.

The IMF (or International Monetary Fund) [i] was the original architect of loans to emerging nations [ii] and countries. It was thought that these countries (which had fewer consumer products but were rich in either natural resources or inexpensive labour), would benefit both themselves and the richer Western nations by participating in trade.

Trade can be either [iii] regulated or [iv] deregulated. Regulated trade means that the act of trading is controlled or directed by rules, principles, methods and is directed by an authority.

In the case of emerging nations, that authority was government and the banks in conjunction with the IMF. Deregulated trade means that trade is open and without the same rules and controls. Decisions are made on the basis of [v] capital inflows and [vi] outflows. In other words, how much money comes into a country and how much goes out.

In countries where [vii] commodities (articles of trade or commerce) are consumed far beyond peoples' actual needs, there is a great deal of [viii] conspicuous consumption.

[i] _____   [v] _____

[ii] _____   [vi] _____

[iii] _____   [vii] _____

[iv] _____   [viii] _____

GET READY FOR UNIT 9: LANGUAGE AND COMMUNICATION

Read the following article to help you get ready for Unit 9:

* http://en.wikipedia.org/wiki/Language_death

While you are reading this article, think about:

* Why do languages die?

* Which languages have been revived?

You don't need to read every part of this article – use the headings to guide your reading.

Also, make notes of some vocabulary from these readings about language death.

Be prepared to share your answers next time you meet.

'Woe to the nation whose sage is voiceless, whose champion is blind, whose advocate is a prattler.'

Kahlil Gibran

LANGUAGE AND COMMUNICATION

In this unit, you will examine issues around communication, an area that will be relevant no matter which discipline you study in your tertiary education. You will read for implied meaning, and engage with a further authentic student essay. You will analyse and learn how to respond to complex assignment questions, and add a further note-taking method to your repertoire while listening to lecture about how people try to persuade others. Following that, you will learn how to detect fallacies in people's arguments. Near the end of the unit, you will learn how to prepare for an additional type of assessment: the poster session.

BY THE END OF THIS UNIT, YOU SHOULD:

SKILL	TASK	PAGE
have gained confidence in discussing topics around language and communication	Entire unit	214–237
have gained further practice of a range of reading skills	**Reading & Critical Thinking** Reading 1 *Tasks A, B* Reading 2 *Task A*	215–218 218–222
have developed further skills in reading for implied meaning	**Reading & Critical Thinking** Reading 1 *Task B*	218
have practised reading for main ideas with an authentic student essay	**Reading & Critical Thinking** Reading 2 *Task A*	218–221
have learned further features of referencing and citation	**Reading & Critical Thinking** Reading 2 *Task B*	221–222
have further developed accuracy in the use of articles	**Language Spotlight 1** *Tasks A, B*	222–223
be able to analyse multi-stage assignment questions	**Writing** Writing 1 *Task A*	223–225
understand that each part of a student essay contributes towards addressing the essay question	**Reading & Critical Thinking** Reading 1 *Task A* **Writing** Writing 1 *Task B*	215–218 225–226
understand how genres can be combined within an essay in order to effectively address the essay question	**Writing** Writing 1 *Tasks A, B, D*	223–227
be able to smoothly and effectively transition between different ideas and stages within essays	**Writing** Writing 1 *Tasks B, C, D*	225–227
understand how to approach short answer questions	**Writing** Writing 2 *Task A*	227
be able to take notes from lectures and review lecture content using the Cornell Method	**Listening & Note-taking** Listening 1 *Task A*	228–230
have practised selecting different information from your notes to address different assignments	**Listening & Note-taking** Listening 1 *Task B*	231
have developed a plan to practise listening outside class	**Listening & Note-taking** Listening 2 *Task A*	231
understand when a variety of strategies are being used in an attempt to persuade you	**Listening & Note-taking** Listening 1 *Tasks A, B* **Language Spotlight 2** *Task A*	228–231 231–234
be able to detect certain fallacies in others' arguments	**Language Spotlight 2** *Task A*	231–234
be able to use a variety of strategies and language features to aid in persuading people	**Speaking 2** *Tasks A, B*	234–235
understand and have practised meeting the requirements of a poster session, as an assessment requirement or otherwise	**Speaking 2** *Task C*	235
be able to effectively use internet directories in your research	**Further Connections** *Task A*	235
have practised short oral presentations	**Further Connections** *Task B*	237

Task A | Discussing language

❶ In small groups, discuss these questions. Use vocabulary from the box in your answers.

[a] How many languages do you speak?

[b] How *proficient* are you at each?

[c] In your country, are people generally *monolingual, bilingual* or *multilingual*? If not monolingual, are different languages used for different purposes (eg at work and at home)? Does one have more prestige than the others?

[d] Which languages would you like to learn?

[e] How much do you enjoy learning languages?

Vocabulary

proficient (adj)	being very good at something that involves skill; *proficiency* (n)
multilingual (adj)	being able to speak three or more languages
bi-	a prefix used to indicate two of something
mono-	a prefix used to indicate one of something
prestige (n)	well respected; *prestigious* (adj)

❷ In small groups, discuss and choose the answers to questions in the following languages trivia quiz. Speculate about any answers you're not sure about: Which answers do you find the most realistic or likely?

1. *How many languages are there in the world?*
   [a] around 23 000 ☐
   [b] around 16 000 ☐
   [c] around 7 000 ☐
   [d] around 2 000 ☐

2. *Which country has the greatest number of native languages?*
   [a] India ☐
   [b] Indonesia ☐
   [c] Papua New Guinea ☐
   [d] Kenya ☐

3. How many countries have, between them, half the world's languages?
   [a] 95 ☐
   [b] 50 ☐
   [c] 20 ☐
   [d] 8 ☐

4. Which languages have the greatest number of native speakers?
   [a] Mandarin Chinese (Pŭtōnghùa), Spanish, Portuguese ☐
   [b] Spanish, English, Hindi ☐
   [c] Mandarin Chinese (Pŭtōnghùa), Arabic, English ☐
   [d] Mandarin Chinese (Pŭtōnghùa), Spanish, English ☐

5. Vanuatu, in the South Pacific, has a population of only around 250 000 – the size of a small city in many other countries. About how many native languages do you think exist there?
   [a] 100 ☐
   [b] 50 ☐
   [c] 20 ☐
   [d] 8 ☐

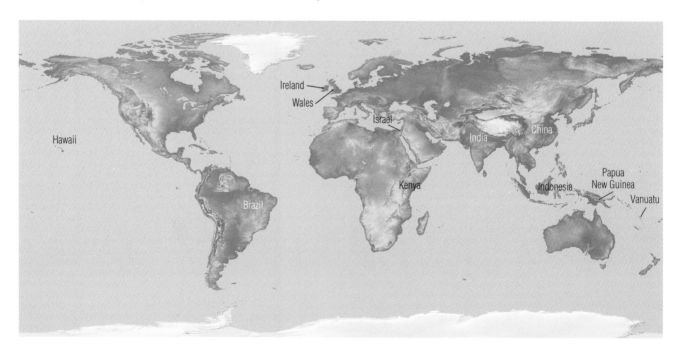

*Multilingual men
from Vanuatu wearing
traditional dance costume*

7. Approximately how often does a language 'die' (that is, have no native speakers left)?

[a] once every six months ☐
[b] once every month ☐
[c] once every two weeks ☐
[d] once a week ☐

8. Which of the following languages have been, or are being, 'raised from the dead', that is, have increasing numbers of speakers when once they were expected to die? (You may give more than one answer for this question.)

[a] Hebrew (the language of Israel and the traditional language of Jewish people) ☐
[b] Welsh (the native language of Wales, part of Britain) ☐
[c] Hawaiian ☐
[d] Irish Gaelic ☐

9. What proportion of the world's population is raised bilingually or multilingually, that is, they learn more than one language in early childhood from their family and the people around them, not through formal education?

[a] 3% ☐
[b] 20% ☐
[c] 45% ☐
[d] 66% ☐

6. The island of New Guinea, which comprises most of Papua New Guinea and also the province of Papua in Indonesia, has 0.1% of the world's population, but about how many languages?

[a] 3000 ☐
[b] 860 ☐
[c] 125 ☐
[d] 75 ☐

10. Approximately how many languages have been recorded as influencing the vocabulary of English?

[a] 350 ☐
[b] 100 ☐
[c] 35 ☐
[d] 10 ☐

READING
& CRITICAL
THINKING

READING 1

Task A | Following essay structure

❶ Orientation discussion. In small groups, discuss:

[a] At what age did you begin to learn English, or another foreign language?
[b] Is this the usual age to start learning a second language in your country?
[c] Did you wish you had started earlier or later?
[d] What do you think is the best age to begin to learn another language? Why?
[e] Thinking about your high school, which school subjects had greater prestige? Was a language regarded as a 'prestige' subject?

Looking at business now,

[f] If you worked for an organisation in your country, in which language would you conduct negotiations with organisations from other countries?

[g] If you had two potential suppliers, one of whom was happy to negotiate in your language, while the other insisted on using English, which would you prefer to deal with (all other things being equal)?
[h] What other benefits can employees with high level language skills bring to organisations?

[a] Read the essay question below. Then read the introduction to the essay response, written by an undergraduate student. Box the stages in the introduction (General statement, Thesis and Preview/Scope).

[b] With a partner, compare your boxing; discuss any differences.

[c] Are each of the three parts of the question addressed in the introduction?

[d] What is the relationship between the question and the Preview/Scope?

[e] Predict the ideas that will be given in the body: write a list.

_____

_____

_____

_____

[f] If you were about to read the essay and wanted to find a suggestion for a long-term improvement to language education, where in the body would you start to look in detail? What reading technique would you use?

Essay question

Evaluate the usefulness to business of having employees who are proficient in a variety of languages. Is language teaching in the nation's education system adequate to cope with the need for businesses to have speakers of other languages? If necessary, suggest methods of improvement.

The road to diversity: The economic benefits of universal second language education from primary school

1 Due to the increasingly globalised business environment, companies are more than ever before finding it necessary to communicate with people and organisations from other countries. Traditionally, people in English-speaking countries have relied on English as a language of communication, but the advantages of knowing other languages are rapidly becoming better known. It is now extremely important that companies employ people with high level language skills, and that improvements are made in the education system of the country to supply people with the right skills for this. This essay will elaborate some ways in which language ability is directly and indirectly useful to business, and then put forward a long-term and a short-term suggestion for how the education system can be improved in order to provide the skills needed.

❸ [a] Read the body of the essay on the next page (paras 2–7). Underline the topic sentences. How well do the main ideas in the body fit your predictions?

[b] Write your own conclusion for this essay, incorporating the usual two stages.

[c] Compare your conclusion with the one given in Appendix B, page 260. Which conclusion has the most concise and clear summary stage? How similar are the recommendations?

Linguistic diversity: Greetings in four languages

The road to diversity: The economic benefits of universal second language education from primary school

1 Due to the increasingly globalised business environment, companies are more than ever before finding it necessary to communicate with people and organisations from other countries. Traditionally, people in English-speaking countries have relied on English as a language of communication, but the advantages of knowing other languages are rapidly becoming better known. It is now extremely important that companies employ people with high level language skills, and that improvements are made in the education system of the country to supply people with the right skills for this. This essay will elaborate some ways in which language ability is directly and indirectly useful to business, and then put forward a long-term and a short-term suggestion for how the education system can be improved in order to provide the skills needed.

2 International trade depends on an ability to negotiate deals, and clearly this is much easier if a company's negotiators speak the language of the people they are doing business with – after all, this motivation is one of the reasons for the enormous size of the English language teaching industry around the world. It is true that English is a very common international language, but a company can gain an advantage over its competitors by speaking its customers' own languages. This would not only impress the customers and provide an extra tool for developing rapport, but would also enable companies to take opportunities that would otherwise be closed to them, for example dealing with organisations which have little or no English language skill. However, this is something that seems to have passed businesses in English-speaking countries by, to their disadvantage. Research by the Centre for Information on Language Teaching found that 'a third of British exporters miss opportunities because of poor language skills' (Crystal, 1997). Even in English-speaking countries, therefore, there would be considerable benefit from greater knowledge of other languages.

3 Language learning also leads to greater understanding of other cultures, that is, the cultures of a company's suppliers and customers, thus providing further competitive advantage. 'Language is part of culture' (Kramsch, 1998, p3), and therefore learning a language automatically means increased cultural knowledge, understanding and insight. This is clearly a valid educational objective in itself, but is also of great importance to business. A deeper understanding of motivations and thinking in customers' and suppliers' own countries will clearly give an advantage over other companies not only in trade negotiations, but also in dealing with all levels of government for purposes such as getting permission to build new factories. Such knowledge is also important in the public relations sphere, which can greatly assist in companies to gain acceptance in a foreign country.

4 Linked to the argument above is the idea of flexibility of thinking and being open to ideas which are different from one's own or from those of the people and culture around you. In many cultures, flexibility and originality of thought have long been considered an asset in business, and the ability to think in different languages strongly helps this. To take an ideal example, bilingual children have, given the right circumstances, been shown to have greater abilities in flexible and creative thinking than monolingual children (Saunders, 1988, p 19). Therefore, bilingualism, or at least the learning of a second language during the early years of a child's life, should be encouraged systematically across the country, and an efficient way to do this would be through the public education system.

5 Now that it has been shown how important language ability is to business, ways in which the language ability of the nation can be improved will be suggested. Native speakers of English traditionally complain that they are not good at learning languages. But perhaps the reason for this is that languages are often not taught seriously until very late: that is, after finishing primary school. It is common knowledge that language learning is most effectively done from a much earlier age – young children, if given sufficient need to learn a language, pick it up much more easily than adults. Therefore, it is imperative that language learning not only begins in primary school but also becomes an important part of the primary school curriculum.

6 However, for this to be successful, primary schools need to be sufficiently resourced. This includes the training of teachers. Presently, most primary school teachers are generalists, trained to teach a wide variety of subjects. But language education requires teachers who are fluent in the language, and the best way to provide this is to train primary school language specialists who have lived in the country where the language is spoken. While this would entail considerable investment, it is essential in order to successfully achieve a higher level of linguistic competence across the nation.

7 This is, however, a long-term solution. What is needed in the short-term is an increase in the prestige and perceived benefits of learning languages. This would increase the number and quality of students in language courses. One way forward with this is through large-scale in-school promotion campaigns which pick up on the current fashion of being interested in business and emphasise the relevance of languages to business success. Another is to emphasise the cultural and communicative aspects of language learning – which are often perceived as fun and motivating – and to get away from the image of learning language as memorising vocabulary lists and tricky grammar rules full of annoying exceptions.

(This essay's conclusion is in Appendix B, page 260: see question 3 [c] on the previous page.)

④ Discussion and critical thinking. Discuss these questions with another student.

[a] Find one claim that is
- strongly held
- weakly supported.

Which words or expressions gave you clues about your answers?

[b] List the proposals that the writer makes. Which proposals would be expensive? Why would they be expensive? In your opinion, would the expense be justifiable? Why/Why not?

_____

_____

_____

_____

[c] Do you agree with the last statement: that looking at the cultural and communicative aspects of language learning is more fun than looking and grammar rules and vocabulary?

Task B | Finding implied meaning

Implied meaning
Look at the Preview/Scope of the essay in the previous section again. Think about whether it answers the second part of the question:

'Is language teaching in the nation's education system adequate to cope with the need for businesses to have speakers of other languages?'

This is an example of *implied meaning* (sometimes called ***implicit meaning***), that is, a meaning contained in the writing, but which isn't stated directly.

A further example: 'He's not very English – he's a good cook'. This *implies* that English people generally aren't good cooks, even though this isn't stated directly.

❶ Using the essay in the previous section, answer the following questions, giving evidence. Then, compare and discuss your answers with another student.

In the author's opinion:

[a] Do skills developed in childhood continue into adulthood?

_____

_____

[b] Do native speakers of English have little ability to learn other languages?

_____

_____

[c] Currently are languages taught at primary schools at all?

_____

_____

[d] If languages are taught, is teaching done to a high standard?

_____

_____

[e] Should individual students studying languages at university pay for their own education?

_____

_____

[f] Do languages currently have high status as subjects among school children?

_____

_____

READING 2

Task A | Reading for main ideas – An authentic student essay

❶ Pre-reading orientation. Discuss these questions in small groups.

[a] List as many countries as you can where English is widely spoken.

[b] Divide them into categories according to how English is used. Example categories could be:
- As a first language by most people
- Mostly for business but not as a first language
- Only with tourists

[c] Which category, if any, does your country fit into?

[d] Which other languages are used in your country? What purposes are they used for?

[e] Why do you think English is so popular around the world?

[f] Is it a good thing or a bad thing that English is popular? Why might it be good? Why might it not be good?

❷ Read the essay titled *English around the world*. It is adapted from a genuine essay written by a student. While reading, think about the answers to these questions, but don't write anything. Do not worry about details in this text.

[a] *What is an example of an 'inner circle' country?*

[b] *What is an example of an 'outer circle' country?*

[c] *What questions will the body of the essay answer?*

[d] *What has influenced the spread of English?*

[e] *What are the positive effects of the spread of English?*

[f] *What is one problem with these positive effects?*

[g] *How are languages like species of animal?*

[h] *What can be the consequences of the spread of high-status languages?*

[i] *What three suggestions are given for improving the situation?*

3 With another student:

[a] Compare and discuss your thoughts about the questions above.

[b] Do you think the disadvantages of the spread of English outweigh the advantages?

[c] Of the suggestions given to improve the situation, which do you think is/are best? Are any unworkable?

4 Find three examples of nominalisation in the essay. Write them as complete sentences. Then compare them with a partner's.

Example:

language spread   *a language spreads around the world*

[a] _____

_____

[b] _____

_____

[c] _____

_____

Question: *In recent decades, the way in which English is used around the world has changed significantly. What are some of the issues that this has generated? Describe and evaluate a selection of them. (1500 words)*

English around the world

1. English is nowadays popularly perceived as *the* global language (Graddol, 1997, p2). It has spread extremely rapidly, the number of speakers rising from 4 million in 1500 to around 120 million in 1900 (Jespersen, 1938/1968 in Pennycook, 1995, p36) and between 700 million and 1 billion in the mid 1990s (Pennycook, 1995, p36). These speakers can usefully, though roughly, be categorised as belonging to three groups: native speakers in an 'inner circle' of countries where English has traditionally been the main first language, an 'outer circle' where it is used for much official business but where other languages are more commonly used for everyday purposes, and an expanding circle of countries where it is learnt as a foreign language and used mostly when communicating with other cultures (Kachru, 1985 in Graddol, 1997, p10). So, how has this spread occurred? Is it largely beneficial or disadvantageous? Does the answer to this question depend on the individual concerned? And what can be done to reduce or overcome any disadvantages?

2. The spread of English has been assisted by various factors. For example, David Graddol (1997, Ch.1) mentions two. Firstly, British colonialism brought the English language to many parts of the globe. Then, in the 20th century, the rise of international institutions such as the United Nations and the IMF, and the shift to English by international academic publications, continued this trend. In addition, the influence of the well-funded US and UK media and popular culture (Crystal, 1997, Ch.4; Tollefson, 2000, p10) and the rise of transnational corporations (Pennycook, 2000, p97) are also highly significant. Transnational corporations are mostly based in inner circle countries, and even when they aren't, their internal language is often English. As Naysmith (1987, p3 in Pennycook, 1995, p 43) claims, English has become '*the* language of international capitalism'. A further factor is claimed by Phillipson (eg 1992, 1994): that there is a deliberate policy by the UK and the USA to promote the use of English in other countries for their own neo-colonial benefit.

3. Is the global spread of English beneficial? There are many claims that it is, mostly based on advantages of using a single language for communication. Tollefson (2000: 9) mentions claims that the use of English as an International language can facilitate communication between countries, with positive effects including a 'reduction in chances of political conflict'. He also mentions this as a benefit of the use of English for communication across language barriers inside multilingual countries (ibid, p14). To elaborate, in some contexts where groups of people speaking particular local languages would otherwise compete for the status that goes with being the language of official communication, English can be viewed as a 'neutral' language, used to avoid this conflict (Kachru, 1986 in Pennycook, 1995, p37). In addition, considering the current trend

towards globalisation, knowledge of English is thought to lead to greater ease in doing business in other countries. From the point of view of individuals in outer and expanding circle countries, knowledge of English would appear to allow greater 'access to science, technology, education, employment and mass culture' (Tollefson, 2000, p9).

4. This all sounds very simple and clear, but if, as Pennycook (1995, 2000) advocates, we look more deeply into the social context of English use, several problems emerge. For example, many of the benefits mentioned above are only available to individuals lucky enough to have the financial or social advantages that give them access to English language education – in many countries, this is simply not available to the majority (Pennycook, 1995, p40; Rogers, 1982; Tollefson, 2000, p9). Therefore, there is discrimination against those who aren't able to use English. This linguistic discrimination is known as linguicism, a word derived in a similar way to 'racism' and 'sexism' (Skutnabb-Kangas, 1988, p13; Phillipson & Skutnabb-Kangas, 1996).

5. Linguicism is related to English linguistic imperialism, according to Phillipson (1992, p47), who defines it as policies in which '*the dominance of English is asserted and maintained by the establishment and continuous reconstruction of structural and cultural inequalities between English and other languages*'. All the reasons given above for the spread of English are interpretable as linguistic imperialism, and inequalities are caused. For example, the success of the promotion of popular culture in English means that actors and musicians from non-English speaking countries are often at a something of a disadvantage in their own country. Also the economic dominance of the world by the US and US-based corporations is frequently seen as economic imperialism, and the language spread that comes with it is therefore a linguistic manifestation of imperialism.

6. Carrying out education in English can also reduce the availability and status of knowledge that had previously been recorded or transmitted in other languages. Similarly, academic materials written and promoted by publishers based in inner circle countries may not be appropriate for outer and expanding circle countries, but are often the main ones available there, and maintain a flow of information and money that is more advantageous to the inner circle country than the other (Pennycook, 1995, pp42, 45–6).

7. A further model of language spread involves the idea of languages interacting together as different species do in an ecosystem (Tsuda, eg 1997). In

this, languages influence each other, and over time develop ways of co-existing. If a new language enters the ecosystem, and especially if it the status issues discussed above apply, the change in the ecosystem could be just as catastrophic as the introduction of a new species into the natural ecosystem. Consequences could include language death (Tollefson, 2000, p9) and changes, usually for the worse, in the ways languages are used (Mühlhäusler, 1996). For example, in Australia, it is estimated there were 250 Aboriginal languages before European colonisation, around 160 in use in the early 1990s but only 20 or so likely to survive on a long term basis (Walsh, 1993 in Malcolm, 1994, p289). In fact, the period of the growth of English has coincided with a rate of language death that is unprecedented in history (Crystal, 2000). However, this model also suggests that, just as evolution means that new species appear, so new languages also appear. For example, varieties of English in the outer circle may be considered as languages in their own right, and are evolving separately from British or American English.

8. So, these are just some of the issues associated with the spread of English, but what can be done to improve the situation? John Rogers (1982) suggests restricting the teaching of English in order to try to encourage education in other languages, but in the current global reality, to deny access to English would cause even more problems and would be even more heavy-handed than linguistic imperialism.

9. Linguistic localism was an idea suggested by Tsuda (1997). In this, the language of choice would also be a local language. For example, if a conference is held in Peru, the language used would be Spanish. However, the high cost of interpretation would make this unrealistic. Tsuda (ibid) also advocates 'neutralingual communication', that is, when two people communicate, they would use a language other than their native languages, in order to be on an even linguistic footing with each other. This is similar to calls for the use of invented languages such as Esperanto in international communication, but again, despite sounding good in theory, there are numerous practical considerations which make it difficult – for example, the fact that anyone who learns Esperanto in order, for example, to study or do business with people from other countries, will find few other Esperanto speakers to converse with!

10. Phillipson and Skutnabb-Kangas (1996) advocate using language policy as a means of preserving language ecologies, to counteract the threat posed by the continued spread of English. More specifically, they advocate the idea of language rights, for example, 'the right to identify with,

to maintain and to fully develop one's mother tongue(s) … a self-evident, fundamental *individual* linguistic human right' (Skutnabb-Kangas, 1998, p22). Also included is the right of access to official languages and the languages of education, and these are considered moral rights (ibid; a fuller definition is given in Skutnabb-Kangas, Phillipson, & Rannut, 1994, p71). However, while being a positive ideal to aim at, there are many practical and political obstacles.

11. In conclusion, while these suggestions may go some way to illuminating paths towards more equitable language policies, there are problems or disadvantages with each which need to be considered and balanced. It may well be that, like many other systems with a large number of variables, any particular local situation requires a local solution which may incorporate a combination of these ideas.

References

Crystal, D (1997) *English as a global language*. Cambridge: Cambridge University Press.

Crystal, D (2000) *Language death*. Cambridge: Cambridge University Press.

Graddol, D (1997) *The future of English?: A guide to forecasting the popularity of the English language in the 21st century*. London: British Council.

Jespersen, O (1938/1968) *Growth and structure of the English language*. Toronto: Collier-Macmillan.

Kachru, BB (1985) 'Standards, codification and sociolinguistic realism: The English language in the outer circle'. In R Quirk & HG Widdowson (eds), *English in the word: Teaching and learning the language and literatures*. Cambridge: Cambridge University Press.

Kachru, BB (1986) *The alchemy of English: The spread, functions, and models of non-native Englishes* (1st ed). Oxford; New York: Pergamon.

Malcolm, I (1994) 'Discourse and discourse strategies in Australian Aboriginal English'. *World Englishes* Vol 13, No 3, 289-306.

Mühlhäusler, P (1996) *Linguistic ecology: Language change and linguistic imperialism in the pacific region*. London; New York: Routledge.

Naysmith, J (1987) 'English as imperialism?'. *Language Issues* Vol 1, No 2, 3–5.

Pennycook, A (1995) 'English in the world/the world in English'. In JW Tollefson (ed), *Power and inequality in language education*. Cambridge: Cambridge University Press.

Pennycook, A (2000) 'The social politics and the cultural politics of language classrooms'. In JK Hall & WG Eggington (eds), *The sociopolitics of English language teaching*. Clevedon [England]: Multilingual Matters.

Phillipson, RHL (1992) *Linguistic imperialism*. Oxford: Oxford University Press.

Phillipson, RHL (1994) 'English language spread policy' *International Journal of the Sociology of Language* Vol 107, 7–24.

Phillipson, RHL & T Skutnabb-Kangas (1996) 'English only world-wide or language ecology?'. *TESOL Quarterly* Vol 30, No 3, 429–452.

Rogers, J (1982) 'The world for sick proper'. *ELT Journal* Vol 36, No 3, 144–151.

Skutnabb-Kangas, T (1988) 'Multilingualism and the education of minority children'. In T Skutnabb-Kangas & J Cummins (eds), *Minority education*. Clevedon [England]: Multilingual Matters.

Skutnabb-Kangas, T (1998) 'Human rights and language wrongs – a future for diversity?'. *Language Sciences* Vol 30, No 1, 5–28.

Skutnabb-Kangas, T, Phillipson RHL & Rannut M (eds). (1994). *Linguistic human rights: Overcoming linguistic discrimination*. Berlin; New York: Mouton de Gruyter.

Tollefson, JW (2000) 'Policy and ideology in the spread of English'. In JK Hall & WG Eggington (eds.), *The sociopolitics of English language teaching*. Clevedon [England]: Multilingual Matters.

Tsuda, Y (1997) *Pluralism: Proposing the ecology of language paradigm*, [WWW]. Available <http://www.toda.org/conferences/hugg_hon/hugg_hon_ papers/y_ tsuda.html> (19 April 2003).

Walsh, M (1993) 'Languages and their status in Aboriginal Australia'. In M Walsh & C Yallop (eds), *Language and culture in Aboriginal Australia*. Canberra: Aboriginal Studies Press.

Task B | Further referencing

❶ With a partner, try to find examples of in-text citations in the *English around the world* text in which the writer:

[a] referenced a text written by more than one author.

[b] referenced two sources that made the same point.

[c] hadn't seen the original source (perhaps because it's out of print or hard to obtain) so, instead, referenced where s/he had seen mention of the original source.

[d] used an abbreviation to avoid repeating references.

_____

[e] referenced a particular page.

_____

[f] referenced a particular chapter in a book.

_____

[g] referenced a whole article rather than a particular page (perhaps because the idea was one of the main ideas in the article).

_____

[h] referenced a work that was originally published in one year, then re-published much later.

_____

[i] referenced by giving two examples an idea that an author wrote about repeatedly.

_____

❷ With the same partner, look at the bibliography (list of references) and find:

[a] a whole book
[b] a journal article
[c] an article published in a book alongside other articles
[d] something published on a website.

How did you distinguish them?

❸ Look at the reference lists in a selection of academic articles. Discuss these questions with a partner:

[a] Do they differ from the ones in the essay here? If so, in what way?
[b] Do they differ from each other? If so, in what way?
[c] How important are small features such as commas, colons, quotation marks and italics?

 LANGUAGE SPOTLIGHT 1  ....

Task A | Review of articles, including indefinite articles

> **Indefinite articles**
> Look at the following example. Some noun groups are bolded.
>
> > When **a language** dies, it's clearly **an unfortunate event**, but it may at first glance be difficult to understand why some people consider it so catastrophic. However, when we examine carefully what has been lost with **the passing of the language, a different picture** emerges ...
>
> With 'a language', you probably already understand that 'a' was chosen because this particular language is introduced here for the first time. The audience doesn't know which language at this point. However, when the same language is mentioned again ('the passing of **the language**'), the writer shows the audience that he or she means the same language by using 'the'.
>
> However, why was 'an' chosen in 'an unfortunate event'? It appears that we know which unfortunate event because the writer just said which one – 'a language dies', so 'the' seems the clear choice. However, 'an unfortunate event' is a wider category than 'when a language dies', that is, it's less specific. That's why 'an' is chosen. If the author had chosen 'the unfortunate event', it would appear to be an event mentioned in a previous sentence, but there is no previous sentence!
>
> A common pattern is that:
>
> 'a' or 'an' follow it/this... + 'be' verb.
>
> Another way of looking at it is that:
>
> 'a/an ...X...' means 'one ...X...', but the focus isn't on which ...X....

❶ Now, apply the rule at the end of the 'Indefinite articles' box to the description of an English course on the next page:

- Choose the most likely article for each gap
- Think about how the meaning would change with a different article.

English for business course

The English for Business course is aimed primarily at students intending to enter business courses running at the college, though [1] _____ course is also open to those intending to work in business or corporate jobs. It is basically [2] _____ ten-week course, with one topic-based unit of work lasting one week. It fulfils [3] _____ standard accreditation requirements for [4] _____ full time course, consisting of 20 hours classroom study and 5 hours self access study per week, making [5] _____ 250 hour course.

Students either enter [6] _____ course from Pre-Intermediate General English classes at [7] _____ college, or students new to [8] _____ college, if demonstrating an intermediate level of English in the college placement test, may start in this class if they express [9] _____ preference for Business English as opposed to General English. Enrolment, as determined by college policy, is continuous: students can begin any Monday. After completing this course and passing a proficiency test within [10] _____ college, students can progress to the Upper Intermediate English for Business class.

Task B | Improving accuracy in speaking

❶ Work in pairs.

[a] Choose a topic for discussion, for example, the questions at the end of this Unit.
[b] In pairs, record a short conversation on this topic.
[c] Listen to the recording, focusing on noun groups containing articles.
[d] Decide where articles were and weren't used appropriately. Ask your teacher if necessary.

WRITING

WRITING 1

Task A | Analysing essay questions

❶ Look at the essay assignment question below. With a partner, put the explanations in the correct box.

Evaluate the usefulness to business of having employees with ability in a variety of languages. Is language training in the nation's education system adequate to cope with the need for businesses to have speakers of other languages? If necessary, suggest methods of improvement.

Explanations
- You would **discuss** or **argue** this point, ie you would give reasons for and/or against language ability being useful to business.
- This is a yes/no question, so you would choose to agree or disagree with this, with reasons, ie **argument.**
- You would **give ideas**, **explain** them if necessary and then **argue** for them, ie say why you think they would work.

2 In the list of *Key question words* to the right are common words used in essay questions. With a partner, write them in the *Key question words and genre* table (below) next to their common meanings. Use what you have learned earlier in this book to help you.

Key question words

account for	(critically) analyse	assess
comment on	compare	contrast
criticise	critique	describe
discuss	evaluate	explain
justify	yes/no question	to what extent do you …

Key question words and genre table

KEY QUESTION WORDS	MEANING	GENRE
describe	Give information without analysis or judgment (answers most 'what' questions).	information report
_____	Give factual information about how something works, how something is done, or why something happens (answers most 'how' or 'why' questions).	explanation
account for	Give reasons for something.	explanation
_____ _____	Show similarities (and sometimes differences) show differences.	compare and contrast
justify assess _____ _____ _____	Make an overall judgment (perhaps by looking at strengths and weaknesses and deciding which are stronger).	argument or discussion (exposition)
_____ criticise _____ _____ _____	Find strengths and weaknesses, advantages and disadvantages, etc.	discussion

3 **Analysing essay questions.** With a partner, look at the following questions and analyse them in the same way as you did in question 1. Write your comments against the arrows coming from the questions. You don't need to know the models and theories mentioned!

[a] **Critique** Porter's Five Forces Model of competitive advantage. **To what extent** can it still be applied in today's rapidly changing business environment of globalisation, deregulation and increasing use of technology?

[b] **Briefly explain** the Teaching-Learning Cycle. **Compare and contrast** this with Task-Based Learning. **Evaluate** the strengths and weaknesses of each. **How** would you adapt them to your own teaching situation? It may be useful to choose (and describe) a group of learners you have recently taught.

[c] For a listed company of your choice, use recent annual financial reports to **compare** its performance over two financial years. **Evaluate** this against its business plan. **Critically analyse** the performance of the company in terms of consistency of value to shareholders.

Analysing essay/assignment questions

Here are some tips to help you understand what to do in your university assignments:

- Use common sense with these key words! If you are asked to 'explain your opinion', 'explain' does not just mean give facts.
- While the interpretation given here for the key words is common, it is not followed by all lecturers. Sometimes, you may have to confirm the meaning with your lecturer.
- If the question says 'describe and analyse', more of the marks will be for the higher level skill (analysis) than the description, so you should use more of the word limit for that.
- One golden rule is if you give an opinion, always support it, even if the question doesn't directly ask you to!

Task B | Essay development – Further features

❶ Look again at the *Road to Diversity* essay starting on page 216, and the question which it responds to on the same page. As a reminder of what you found in the reading section of this unit, answer these questions.

[a] Which body paragraphs address the first part of the question?

[b] Which address the second and third parts of the question?

[c] Does every paragraph address a part of the question?

Keeping your essay focused on the question

Every paragraph **must** address some part of the question. Check this again and again while writing each assignment, and again before submitting – it's easy to get carried away and focus on what you find interesting rather than what the question is asking for!

Some students put the essay question on the wall next to their computer so they can check it easily and frequently.

Transition sentences between paragraphs

If your essay changes direction, tell your reader this with a special sentence (called a transition sentence) – it will make your essay flow more smoothly and be easier to follow.

② **[a]** In question 1, we noted that there are two parts to this essay, each responding to a different part of the question. Which sentence shows the transition between these parts?

_____

[b] Would the essay be as easy to read if this sentence was missed out? Why/Why not?

_____

[c] How important is this sentence?

_____

_____

[d] With another student, identify the transition sentences in the *English around the world* essay starting on page 219 of this unit. Underline them.

[e] In pairs, one person look for a transition sentence in each of these essays:
- Unit 3, *Mechanisation of Agriculture* essay, page 65
- Unit 3, *Genetically modified foods* essay, page 70.

Then, report back to your partner. Add your example transition sentences in the space below.

_____

_____

_____

_____

_____

_____

_____

The first part of the *Road to Diversity* essay (paras 2–4) is similar to a standard argument essay. However, the second part is more complex. The next two questions look at this.

③ Look at para 6 of the essay *The road to diversity*. This is similar to a mini-essay. Write the sentences which provide the following stages in this paragraph:

STAGE	WORDING
Link to previous paragraph	However,
Opinion	for this to be successful, primary schools need to be sufficiently resourced
Preview/Scope	
Problem (2nd part of question)	
Solution (3rd part of question)	
Acknowledgment that problems exist	
Conclusion	

④ Look at para 7. This is developed in yet another way. Fill in the table below, noticing how it mixes argument and explanation.

STAGE/PURPOSE	WORDING
Link to previous paragraph	
Opinion (suggestion: 3rd part of question)	
Support (argument)	
Explanation I: How?	
Explanation II: How?	

Mixing academic genres
The genres given in this book provide building blocks to be combined and adapted as necessary. Use them flexibly and intelligently!

Task C | Paragraph development – Practice of transitioning between ideas

❶ In pairs, brainstorm ideas for and against the opinions below (or other opinions that you choose).

❷ Individually, choose two of the opinions. Write:

- a paragraph for or against the opinion; followed by
- a paragraph expressing the opposite idea; with
- a smooth transition sentence between them.

Opinions

- *All university students should learn a second language as part of their degree*
- *When they visit another country for a holiday, tourists should try to communicate in the country's language, instead of relying on their own language or English*
- *Language learning is something that should continue throughout your life*
- *Companies should pay for the personal development of their staff, including language learning.*

Task D | Answering a multi-stage question

❶ **[a]** Choose from one of the essay questions below. Analyse it. Will you have to describe, explain, argue, discuss or do a combination of these?
   [b] Brainstorm ideas for responses in small groups.
   [c] Write a plan for your essay.
   [d] Compare and discuss your plan with another student who has chosen the same question.
   [e] Adjust your plan in the light of your discussion.
   [f] Write the essay.

Questions

- *It has been said that an invented language such as Esperanto is a better choice for a world language than English. What are the advantages and disadvantages of using an invented language in this way? Which language (including 'natural' ones) do you think would be a better choice for a world language? Justify your choice.*

- *Compare and contrast three grammatical features of your first language and English. Using these as evidence, state whether you agree with the opinion that speakers of different languages think in different ways. Justify your opinion.*

WRITING 2

Task A | Answering short answer questions

Short answer questions
Some tertiary level assignments require answers of a page, a paragraph or shorter. You must answer as concisely and accurately as you can, and make sure you answer fully. As with other academic writing:

- Be concise and accurate, but answer all parts of the question.
- Use full sentences and paragraphs (unless your instructions specifically allow bullet points or notes).
- Avoid personals such as 'I' and 'you' (unless specifically asked to write about personal experiences).
- Choose academic vocabulary and nominalisations to help to create an appropriate style (this also often helps you to convey lots of information while keeping your answer short).
- Write in your own words – don't plagiarise – and try to avoid accidentally using other people's words, such as using the same words as your notes, which may have been copied directly from somewhere else.

❶ Write a short answer (maximum 150 words) to one of the following questions.

   [a] Give three grammar rules that are different in your first language and English.
   [b] Give a definition of an explanation essay.
   [c] List the factors in your decision to study in another country.
   [d] What differences exist between argument and explanation essays?
   [e] Give brief reasons why this country is a good one in which to study.

❷ Check that your answer has all features of short answers listed in the box. Refine your short answer if necessary.

❸ Write short answers for two more of the questions.

LISTENING 1

Task A | Listening and note-taking – The Cornell Method

❶ In small groups, discuss these questions:

[a] In what situations (i) might someone try to persuade you, and (ii) might you try to influence another person? Think about: family, friends, politics, shopping, working in a company, academia.

[b] Are you more likely to believe someone if they speak eloquently?

[c] How easy is it to manipulate other people's thoughts and actions?

[d] Is it usually legitimate to influence or persuade people?

[e] Look at what these people are saying. What is the problem with their reasoning in each case?

> He can't be a good cook – he's from England!

> She's good looking. I think she'll work very hard – we should give her the job.

> Everyone should learn a language at university

> I can't agree –spending three or four years learning a language is too much

> I don't think he's very good at cooking – he once lied to me.

> Hmm, you know the new product we're going to introduce? Well, three of the tests on it failed and one succeeded.

> OK. We'll only tell the customer about the one that worked, and not mention the others.

Vocabulary

influence (v)	affecting how someone else thinks or acts; *influence* (n)
persuade (v)	to make another person believe or do something; *persuasive* (adj); *persuasion* (n)
eloquent (adj)	being able to talk in a very nice, fluent and clever way; *eloquent* (adj); *eloquence* (n)
manipulate (v)	to affect another person's thoughts or actions; *manipulation* (n); *manipulative* (adj)
legitimate (adj)	reasonable or fair; not breaking the rules; *illegitimate* (opposite)
reasoning (n)	logical thinking; *reason with someone* (v)

Note: *manipulate*, *persuade* and *influence* have similar meanings but *manipulate* has a more negative connotation than the other two.

Cornell Method of note-taking

This is a system of note-taking devised in the 1950s by a professor of education at Cornell University in the USA. It has become popular around the world since then.

To get ready to use this, divide each page of your notes into three sections:
- a narrow column on the left, called the 'cue column'
- a wider column on the right, called the 'note-taking column'
- about five or six lines at the bottom of the page

Also write the course name, date and any other relevant points at the top of the page.

While listening to the lecture, write main ideas and details in the note-taking column. During pauses in the lecture, or as soon as possible after the lecture, write key words, questions, people, dates etc in the cue column. You can use these later, perhaps when studying for exams, to help you find the key points.

Soon after the lecture, perhaps later the same day, write a summary in the space at the bottom of the page. The process of writing this helps you remember, and also gives you a useful reference for later study.

To use your notes for review, cover the note-taking column. Use the cue column to try to remember what you wrote about the cue, then uncover the note-taking column and check how much you remembered. Also, think about these questions:
- What is important about the information?
- How can I use the information?
- How does this information fit in with what I know already?
- How does this information influence my opinions?

Example of Cornell note-taking template

Cue column	Note-taking column

Summary

---

❷ You will listen to a lecture about rhetorical techniques (techniques people use to persuade others).

[a] Prepare two or three pages ready to take Cornell-style notes.

CD 2

[b] Listen to the lecture and take notes in the note-taking column only.

[c] After the lecture, add main points to the cue column. You may want to write questions (already answered in the note-taking column).

[d] Then, write a short summary at the bottom of each page.

[e] Compare your notes with another student's. Discuss any significant differences.

❸ Divide into two groups, A and B. Use your notes to answer the questions on the next page: students in group A should answer alternate questions [a], [c], [e] etc only. Students in group B should answer [b], [d], [f] etc only. Then, form pairs comprising a student from group A and a student from group B, and explain your answers.

According to the lecturer:

[a] *In what careers is an understanding of rhetoric useful?*

_____

[c] *Why is it useful to understand rhetoric?*

_____

[e] What is **visual rhetoric**?

_____

[g] *What are the three modes of persuasion?*

_____

[i] *Which is more important to an advertiser, feelings or facts?*

_____

[k] *Which of these is a way to apply pathos?*
- ❏ being passionate about something
- ❏ focusing on *what* is said more than *how* something is said.

[m] *How could ethos be used in visual rhetoric?*

_____

[o] *What are the two opposing arguments about guns, used as an example of the straw man argument?*

_____

_____

According to the lecturer:

[b] *Is rhetoric useful just for work?*

_____

[d] *How is rhetoric defined?*

_____

_____

[f] *Is rhetoric a Western concept, an Eastern concept, or both?*

_____

[h] *Which mode of persuasion relates best to:*

logic _____

emotion _____

character _____

[j] *Give an example of the use of pathos in visual rhetoric.*

_____

[l] *What might a politician do to implement ethos?*

_____

[n] *Which of the following is closest to inductive reasoning? Which is closest to deductive reasoning?*
- ❏ Speaking to several students who've been to university, and selecting a university based on their experiences
- ❏ Looking at the content of a university's courses, and seeing how well that can help you learn what you want to learn, eg for a future career

[p] *How important is it to understand and recognise fallacies?*

_____

❹ In the same pairs as step 3, answer this question:

- *What is the danger of:*

  Pathos: _____

  _____

  Ethos: _____

  _____

  Logos:? _____

❺ Listen again and check your answers to questions 3 and 4.

CD 2

②

❻ **Critical thinking.** With a partner, pick five points from the lecture and discuss:

- *What is important about the information?*
- *How can I use the information?*
- *How does this information fit in with what I know already?*
- *How does this information influence my opinions?*

❼ With the same partner, look back at the things people said in question 1. Which fallacy applies to each?

❽ **Critical thinking.** Still with the same partner, discuss these questions.

[a] Do you think it's morally right to 'influence the thoughts and actions of others'? Might it be morally right to do this in some situations but not others?

[b] How important do you think it is to 'protect' yourself from other people's rhetoric?

[c] Do you think the lecturer was overstating the case for 'protecting' yourself? Why (not)?

[d] What are the relative merits of each of the three modes of persuasion in the following situations:
- Explaining a scientific result to lay people
- Advertising a new mobile phone
- Advertising a new designer handbag
- Persuading people that you would be good at a particular job.

[e] How has this lecture changed your feelings about
- claims made by companies
- politicians
- the need to think critically in your everyday life.

Task B | Selecting from notes to address assignment questions

> **Identifying relevant points in your notes**
> With the notes you make from your reading as well as from lectures, you will frequently have to identify which notes are most relevant to particular assignments.

❶ Look at the two assignment questions. Mark or highlight in your notes the points relevant to the first question in one colour. Then mark or highlight the notes relevant to the second question in another colour. There may be some overlap between the two.

Assignment questions

> **Question A**
> What techniques might advertisers use to sell their wares? Identify and discuss the merits of a range of techniques.

> **Question B**
> The public is often warned to not trust politicians. Identify and discuss some rhetorical techniques that politicians commonly use.

❷ Compare and discuss what you marked with a partner.

❸ Use your notes to write a response to one of the assignment questions.

LISTENING 2

Task A | Listening outside class

❶ In small groups, discuss these questions:

[a] Where do you hear English spoken outside class?
[b] Where else could you listen to English spoken outside class?
[c] What can you do to increase your opportunities to practise listening outside class?
[d] What situations for listening outside class are difficult? Which are easier?
[e] What are some good reasons to practise listening outside class? List as many as you can between you.

❷ Write down between three and six things that you will do in the next month to increase the amount and quality of your listening practice. How will you make time for them?

> **Listening outside the class**
> • Try to find situations that are just a little bit difficult but not too difficult. Situations in which you understand everything easily are probably not pushing your listening skills to higher levels!
> • Try to find listening situations that are interesting for you. Don't watch nature documentaries if you're not interested in animals!
> • University lecturers and staff have a wide variety of accents – often they are native English speakers with strong regional accents, or non-native speakers of English. Therefore, it is important to practise listening to a wide variety of accents and varieties of English. Don't be put off just because someone has a non-native speaker accent.

LANGUAGE SPOTLIGHT 2

Task A | Language of persuasion

❶ **Orientation to the topic.** In pairs, briefly discuss the following points:

[a] What's your first language? Is it the main language of your country?
[b] What do you think will be the status of the language in a few decades?
[c] Will English be more popular?
[d] In your country, what are some minority languages?
[e] Do you have any idea how many people speak them?
[f] Do you think these languages could die?

[g] Does the government of your country give these languages support? If so, why? If not, why not?
[h] Think of as many reasons as you can why:
   • some people might think minority languages should be supported and preserved, and why;
   • some people might think it's better to support more major languages, such as the language of the country, and give no support to minority languages, or even try to suppress them.

You are going to look at a conversation between two students. At the beginning, one (Roger) doesn't see any benefit in preserving minority languages, but his friend, Kate, has a different opinion.

❷ Look at the script of the conversation and the list of reasons to preserve dying languages. Mark the four points from the list that Kate uses in her argument. Then compare your answers with another student's.

Reasons to preserve dying languages

[a] Because a person's language provides a sense of identity and a connection with previous generations.

[b] Because knowledge of languages can help the study of other subjects, such as anthropology and history.

[c] We might still learn things, for example, medical uses of some plants, if we study the knowledge that is held by native speakers of these languages.

[d] Because the more languages there are, the more culturally rich humanity is.

[e] Living languages are better than languages that appear only in books.

[f] Preserving unique cultures and preventing them from becoming influenced by other cultures is good for tourism.

[g] Different languages involve different ways of thinking, and this diversity is good for humanity.

Conversation

Roger: So, why bother to save languages? It sounds to me that when a language dies, life will be easier anyway – there'll be one less language to cause confusion.

Kate (*Surprised*): Oh!!! Do you think so?

Roger: Well, the fewer languages that're spoken, the more that people will speak just one language – probably English – and the easier people will find it to communicate.

Kate: Mmm, I don't …, I'm not sure about that. Mmm, look, I know it sounds easier that way – but don't forget it's just, it's more normal around the world to grow up speaking two languages or more, not just one like we do. You know, knowing one language is just, like, something you find in a developed country …

Roger (*Doubtful*): Uh Aahaa.

Kate: Humans are naturally good at picking up new languages, especially if they do it early enough. And you know, like the majority of children around the world, they grow up thinking, well, it's normal and natural to speak more than one language, because everyone around them does, every day, so mmm, that's exactly what, like, most kids will do – without even thinking.

Roger: Aahaa.

Kate: So it's not really a problem for people – new generations, I mean, not people who're already adult – to know at least two languages. You know, most people know their local language, and also another language for communicating with people outside the local area, or in other countries.

Roger: OK, yeah, that's all very interesting, but, still, I don't see any good reason to go to all the trouble and expense of saving endangered languages!

Kate: Oh, typical Roger! Bringing money into everything! (*laughs*). Look, one point is that languages like, they kind of like, I don't know, they kind of, like, cultural richness, they add cultural richness to human life – just like, you know, a painting, or music. Different languages have, like, different ways of expressing ideas, and different history, different folk tales, you know, anything to do with culture really.

Roger: So?

Kate: Well, look, Roger, if you lose a language, it's a bit like losing the Mona Lisa, or a Van Gogh painting – only with languages, it's, it's a bit different, because not so many people really know what they represent, because they take so much more time and effort to learn and appreciate, and so they just go away quietly without anyone paying much attention.

Roger: What do you mean, 'what the language represents'? Surely folk tales and things like that can be written down? Then we can keep them forever!

Kate: Well, you've got a good point, that's true, but don't you think there's something missing if it's just a, a story in a book? I don't know, for me, it's just like looking at a dead animal in a museum, rather than seeing the real thing, live, in it's natural environment.

Roger: Yeah, I suppose so. I guess it's just not the same, is it?

Kate: But well, for me, mmm, I think the most interesting thing really is how people express ideas. Don't you think so? Because every language has different ways of saying the same thing … Have you ever studied another language, Rog?

Roger: Mmm, French at high school.

Kate: Probably not a good example – look, look, French is reasonably close to English but just a few things are a bit different. Like, do you remember, adjectives after nouns instead of before, all that kind of thing … ?

Roger: Mmm, yeah, not so different.

Kate: But if you'd learned, say, an Asian language, you'd be thinking about a whole load of things in a different way. You know how English has all these different tenses, whereas, you know, with most Asian languages, mmm they use other ways to show time, like time words, or without so many changes in the verb as in English, or often just purely from the context.

Roger: Really?

Kate: Yeah but, if you're talking about your family, it's other languages' turn to give more information. You know how English has one word for any kind of cousin, whether they're male, female, on your mother's side of the family or your father's?

Roger: Yeah.

Kate: Well, Asian languages, they've got different words for different kinds of cousins. Isn't that amazing? And that's just a start. There are often different words for other relationships, such as, well, sometimes two or more depending on whether it's someone in your family or someone else's family, or whether you're older or they're younger than you, whatever. Like I say, it's like a totally different way of thinking.

Roger: Aaaah, I guess it is. I remember how people learning Japanese and Indonesian at school said everything was so different.

Kate: And that's just one set of languages. Just think of the richness and all those diverse ways of thinking that're being lost when languages die!

Roger: Mmm, I'm beginning to see what you mean.

Kate: Yeah, exactly. Look, I believe languages dying makes the world a less diverse place and therefore more boring. But there's an even more important reason than that – identity, or at least the part of that that's connected with people's origins. Just imagine how you'd feel if you picked up a letter from your grandfather had written, say, and you couldn't even read it at all, because it was in a different language.

Roger: Aaaah, … that must be weird. You'd feel kind of cut off, as if something was lost, I reckon.

Kate: Exactly, well, that's how people must feel when the language of their culture dies. They, they sort of lose connection with their past – you know, like their personal past as well as their cultural past. People feel lost. Just look in most countries, at mmm, who is at the bottom of society, and you'll find in most cases it's people from minority cultures –

the people you see on the streets, such as alcoholics, etc – and you know blacks and native Americans in the US, say Aborigines in Australia. They're often the people …

Roger: (*Interrupting*) But not everyone ends up like that!

Kate: No, of course not, I was just generalising … but they're proportionately far more than in the majority culture. But for many of them, one of the major factors is loss of their cultural identity, the feeling of just not really fitting in – not fitting into the dominant culture, and not having connections with their own culture. I guess it's difficult to understand unless you experience it, I suppose …

Roger: Yeah, I suppose so …

Kate: … but just try and imagine for a moment – no connections with anything, nothing about your origins that you can have pride in or have any feeling of confidence in. Imagine what that would do to your self-esteem and your sense of security!

Extracts from recording script
- … I know it sounds … er … , but …
- … it's a bit like losing the Mona Lisa, or a Van Gogh painting …
- … but don't you think there's something missing if it's just a … a story in a book?
- … it's just like looking at a dead animal in a museum …
- … the most interesting thing … is how people express ideas
- Have you ever studied another language? → answer → development of argument
- But there's an even more important reason than that.
- Just imagine how you'd feel if …
- Just look in most countries at … who …
- … not really fitting in – not fitting in to the dominant culture.

❸ **Identifying techniques for persuasion.** Look at the extracts from the recording script to the right. With another student, place them in the table below to the persuasion technique. Match the extract from the recording script to the persuasion technique. Two techniques have more than one example, and another has no clear example listed.

Persuasion techniques

PERSUASION TECHNIQUE	EXTRACTS
[a] Acknowledge another's point of view, but then refute it.	
[b] Ask questions which expect a positive answer.	
[c] Use dramatic language, to give the argument more force.	
[d] Make strong statements of opinion.	
[e] Add emphasis, for example, by repeating words, using emphatic adverbs and adjectives or using a signposting expression.	
[f] Relate the argument to the other person's experience, or to a similar idea that's more familiar to them.	
[g] Appeal to the listener to imagine a situation.	

Persuasion techniques
It's important to recognise when these techniques are being used in an attempt to persuade you. However, you don't have to use them all yourself!

④ **Persuasive intonation.** Listen while your teacher says some of the expressions from question 3. Pay attention to the intonation patterns used. Then, practise them with another student.

⑤ Work with the same partner and answer these questions.

[a] Which grammatical form is used to ask questions which expect a positive answer in reply (technique [b] in the table)? What is another grammatical form which achieves the same function?

[b] Which two linguistic devices are used for emphasis ([e] in the table)? Think of other examples of the one involving vocabulary.

[c] Write at least one extra example sentence for each function [a] to [g]. What intonation would you use with each? Be prepared to share your answers with others in the class.

Task A | Critical thinking – Reflecting on persuasion

① Discuss these questions in small groups, with reference to the persuasion techniques in Language Spotlight 2

[a] What are the equivalent techniques in your first language? Do any not translate well into your language and culture?

[b] Can you think of any techniques that are used in your own language and culture which are not listed here?

[c] Are there some that you wouldn't feel comfortable using in your own culture?

[d] To what extent do your answers depend on the situation, eg who's speaking?

② Homework: identifying attempts to persuade.

[a] Listen to the television or radio, or read some advertisements or political leaflets, and see how many of these techniques you read or hear. Take notes about the techniques used.

[b] In a later lesson, you will explain your notes to other students.

Task B | Practice in persuasion

① Follow this procedure:

• Choose four points from [a] to [f] below (or choose your own ideas)

• Prepare how you will persuade another person. You can use pathos, ethos and/or logos, and any of the language from Language Spotlight 2. Try to avoid fallacies! You are encouraged to try techniques you haven't used before, but there is no need to try anything that you feel is dishonest or rude.

• Find another student, and try to persuade each other about each other's first point. When it's your turn to listen, identify the technique that your partner uses (pathos, ethos and/or logos).

• After each turn, tell your partner which techniques you think they used.

• Repeat with a different partner.

Points

[a] Food from my country is the best food in the world.

[b] Every time someone in the class speaks their own language, they have to pay money into a chocolate fund.

[c] The class should organise a social activity after class next week.

[d] Cats are better than dogs.

[e] Everyone should learn a second language other than English.

[f] Cars should be taxed much more heavily than they are now to reduce their use and therefore the problems they create.

[g] Media such as newspapers and televisions shouldn't have any financial connection with politicians.

Task C | Poster session

> ### Poster sessions
> In your tertiary course, you may have to produce a poster session. This involves making a poster about a topic you've researched, and then displaying it with others in a room where people walk around, reading the posters and discussing it with you. Poster sessions sometimes appear at academic conferences, to provide an extra way to communicate research results in addition to normal conference sessions.
>
> To ensure your poster session is successful:
> - Prepare well: make sure you can explain your poster clearly.
> - Anticipate the questions that people might ask, and prepare questions.
> - Make sure your poster is well laid out and easy for people to understand.

A good way to learn something is to find out how people who have already learnt it achieved their success. You have achieved success in English – or you wouldn't be using this book! Therefore, you can help other students in your college or university by sharing how you did this.

❶ [a] Choose two incidents in your language-learning experience that have had a big influence on your later language learning, perhaps by motivating you or by showing you how an aspect of the language works. Here are two examples:
  - One student reported that watching a film in English for the first time was very inspirational and motivated him to want to study harder.
  - Another student found that he could understand native English speakers much better after finding out about word stress and the pronunciation of weak forms.

[b] Choose two pieces of advice from your own English language learning experience that you would give to someone who is new to English study.

[c] Explain these two incidents and two pieces of advice to another student. You will have some time to prepare your explanation.

[d] With your partner, discuss which of your incidents might be more interesting for the class to hear about. Then, do the same for the language learning advice.

❷ With the same partner as above

[a] Prepare a poster that explains the incidents and advice you have chosen.

[b] Practise explaining your poster

[c] Brainstorm questions that the audience might ask, and prepare answers

❸ Hold the poster session.

- For half of the session, visit other people's posters, listen as they explain them, and ask questions. Your teacher will tell you whether this is the first half or the second half.
- For the other half of the session, stand by your poster, explain it to visitors and answer their questions.

❹ After the session, summarise in writing in under 250 words the best advice you heard.

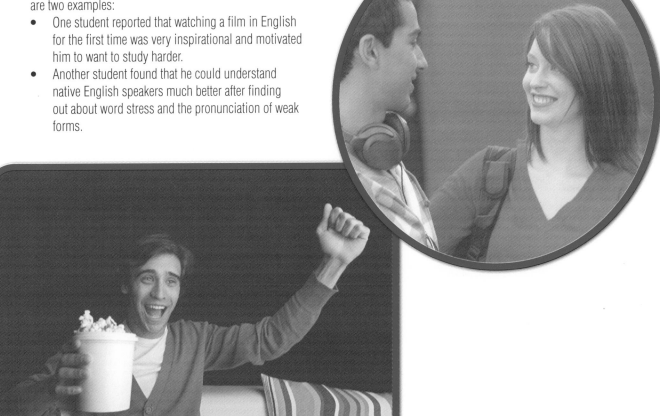

Task A | Research skills – Evaluating internet directories

Internet directories

When searching the internet, the first things people often think of using are search engines. However, most of the sites found by search engines are inappropriate for academic work. A more efficient way of finding academic information is to use academic directories or virtual libraries. All sites listed on these have been reviewed and found to be of an appropriate academic standard. Also, they are organised in a systematic way, making it relatively easy to find particular sites.

❶ Demonstration of an internet directory. Imagine you want information about sign language.

- [a] Go to <www.bubl.ac.uk>, the index page of BUBL Information Service.
- [b] Click on the main heading 400 Language.
- [c] You will see many links in alphabetical order. Choose the one for 419 Sign language.
- [d] The page you come to will give you summaries of various sites about sign language. These summaries will help you to choose useful links.

❷ Evaluating and selecting directories for your field. Work with a partner.

- [a] Look at the left hand column of the table below. Do you think that knowing these kinds of information about websites will help you to choose which ones to visit? Is there anything you would add or change?
- [b] Look for pages related to the subject of your future studies in the directories mentioned in this table, and fill in the table below with 'Yes' or 'No'.

❸ Using the information you have entered into the table, decide which the best directory(ies) for information in your field is/are. Discuss with a partner.

	BUBL (✔) www.bubl.ac.uk	INFOMINE (✔) infomine.ucr.edu	VIRTUAL LIBRARY (✔) www.vlib.org
Does it give summary information of each site listed?			
If there is summary information, is it helpful?			
Does it give the author of each site?			
Does it give the date each site was last checked?			
Does it give resource type for each site (eg journal article, list of links)?			
Is other useful information given for each site?			
Does the directory have the field you want?			

Task B | Short oral presentations – Explaining features of your language

As well as giving speaking and listening practice (explanations), this section may also help you to understand more clearly some of the grammatical features of English.

❶ Discussion. In groups of mixed nationality, if possible, briefly answer and discuss the following questions.

[a] Tell your group about a feature of English that you found difficult to learn. This could be an aspect of grammar, pronunciation or anything else. Why do you think you found it so difficult? Is there an equivalent of the feature in your own language?

[b] Which features of English did you find the easiest to learn? Is this because they are similar to your own language? Or is there another reason?

[c] Of the languages represented in your group, which sounds the most similar to English? The most different?

❷ Preparing a short presentation. Choose a feature of your language, perhaps one that you talked about in Task A. Prepare a short talk to your group in which you give a basic explanation of it. Remember to:

*   include short example expressions or sentences to illustrate your point, including translations in to English;
*   give the meaning of basic vocabulary that is necessary for your example sentences;
*   use the oral presentation skills from Appendix D;
*   think from the point of view of the listeners – are you giving enough information for them to understand what you are saying, and are you staging the ideas in a way that helps the listener?
*   predict what questions the audience may ask, and try to answer them in your talk.

❸ Giving and listening to presentations. Take it in turns to give your presentations.

While listening to other presentations, you should:

*   take notes about what you hear;
*   prepare questions to ask the presenter.

After each presentation, you should:

*   ask your questions;
*   compare your notes with other students, in pairs. How consistent are your notes with those of the other students?
*   tell the presenter the best two or three features of their talk.

❹ Discussion and critical thinking – Should English be simplified? Discuss these questions groups.

*   If you could change the English language to make it easier to learn or use, what alterations would you make? For example, would you make all verbs regular? Remove third person verb forms?
*   Do you think there should be a simplified form of English to be used for international communication? What would be the advantages of this? How about disadvantages?

Task C | Language connections

❶ Discuss and/or write about one or more of the following topics:

*   Everyone should have the right to learn and speak the language of their own culture.
*   Everyone should have the right to receive education in their first language.
*   Governments should provide legal and financial support to minority languages.
*   A second language should be part of the primary school curriculum from the earliest possible age.
*   Everyone should learn at least two languages.

GET READY FOR UNIT 10: CULTURES

Read the following articles to help you get ready for Unit 10.

*   <http://en.wikipedia.org/wiki/Culture>; Scroll down to 3 Cultural Change and follow the link. Next, scroll down in the link 'Culture' until you reach **Cultural Change**.

While reading, consider the following questions:

*   *In the first article*, consider why the images on the right side of the site are art. (Read the titles of the art works that are beneath them to assist you in your thinking.)
*   What might they indicate since they are used as examples to explain culture?
*   *The second article* concerns Australian Aboriginals. Why do you think the link to cultural change is concerned with an indigenous people? Familiarise yourself with the site and note any similarities to cultural change amongst the indigenous peoples you know about.

10

'When I wrote on my door:
"Leave your traditions outside,
Before you come in,"
Not a soul dared
To visit me or open my door.'

Kahlil Gibran

CULTURES

This unit is based upon culture. You will examine differing definitions of culture and critically consider issues around those meanings. This unit should assist you to understand more about your own, individual culture. It is also a unit that is designed to review and consolidate your learning from previous study. *EAP Now!* 2nd edition has been presented to you in increasing order of difficulty and in this unit, you will read texts and apply a combination of the skills you require for further, higher education in English.

BY THE END OF THIS UNIT, YOU SHOULD:

SKILL	TASK	PAGE
be capable of presenting ideas based around culture, in speaking and writing	**Speaking 1** *Tasks A, B*	240
apply many of the features of academic reading and writing to a reading, including tense, participant tracking, recognising there, discourse signals, vocabulary in context, staging and referencing	**Reading & Critical Thinking** Reading 1 *Task A*	240–246
be able to listen to a lecture of over 15 minutes, take notes from the lecture that will refresh your memory of it	**Reading & Critical Thinking** Reading 2 *Task A*	246–248
construct nominalisations	**Language Spotlight 1** *Task A*	249
deconstruct or 'unpack' nominalisations	**Language Spotlight 1** *Task B*	249
understand and apply the different genres of explanation, argument and discussion	**Writing** *Task A*	250
write summaries and conclusions with confidence	**Writing** *Tasks B, C*	251–252
understand and use the conventions of simile and metaphor in writing and recognise them when reading	**Language Spotlight 2** *Task A*	253
review introductory paragraphs for their linguistic features and content	**Language Spotlight 2** *Task B*	254
critically consider a major issue	**Speaking 2** *Task A* **Further Connections** *Task A*	255 255

Presenting ideas based on culture and expressed through language

Cultural awareness

In order to identify cultural differences that exist between one's home country and the country where you study, visit or carry out business, you must decide whether and to what extent the home-country practices may be adapted to the foreign environment. Some cultural differences are obvious; for example, differing dress codes and styles, language spoken, methods of greeting people, diet, and religion. These aspects can be dealt with consciously. In other words, they are obvious and notable. Other forms of cultural difference may have to be learned subconsciously; for example, how to solve a problem, when and if to make an apology, how to negotiate in business matters, how to express high regard or interest in a person.

Task A | Cultural differences in business

Case study for discussion

A US mining company went to China in 2010 to negotiate land for mining. After a series of brief talks and the signing of a document, the US representatives returned home. They began spending huge amounts of money putting everything in place for their 'deal' in China. Once ready, they contacted the business 'partners' in China and said they were on their way. The Chinese 'partners' did not consider that a deal had been made. The US mining company representatives were surprised to discover that there was no 'deal' at all, as far as the Chinese were concerned.

❶ What do you think went wrong?

❷ What do you think the US business people might have done wrong?

❸ What do you think the Chinese business people might have done wrong?

Task B | Expressing customs through language

Discussion of common beliefs and practices

Either in pairs or groups, answer the following questions. If English is your native language, answer the questions then select any country that you know something about and try to answer the same questions using your knowledge of that country and its culture.

Questions

❶ How do you greet a close relative?

❷ How do you greet a distant relative?

❸ How do you address a respected teacher?

❹ How do you introduce a friend of yours to another friend?

❺ How do you apologise to your mother for something important?

❻ How do you apologise to a friend for something minor?

❼ How do you greet a person who has a very important position?

❽ What sort of language would you use to explain a problem to a superior at work?

❾ What sort of language would you use to explain a problem to a colleague at work?

❿ From question 9, is it the same language you would use to explain a problem to a superior?

READING 1

Task A | Analysis of culture

❶ Examine the vocabulary and locate each word within the text, then read the sentences before and after the words. Next, examine the words and memorise the correct definitions that are provided.

❷ Read the entire text titled *Culture – What does it mean and what are some cultural benefits and detriments? What is cultural difference and how is it manifested?*

❸ You will then complete a series of review tasks, A–G, concerned with academic aspects of the writing.

A. Vocabulary
B. Schema or staging
C. Participant tracking
D. Discourse signals
E. Tense
F. Referencing from sources
G. Bibliography

A. Vocabulary

Vocabulary within the essay on the next page

Vocabulary

detriments (n)	loss, damage or injury
inevitable (adj)	that cannot be avoided, evaded or escaped, certain
inescapable (adj)	that cannot be escaped or ignored
Intrinsic (adj)	belonging to a thing by its very nature
embody (v)	to express or exemplify (ideas) in concrete form
ethnocentrism (n)	the belief in the inherent superiority of one's own group and culture accompanied by a feeling of contempt for other groups and cultures
reductionism (n)	the tendency to make supposedly comprehensive explanations of complex phenomena simply by analysing and describing their parts
ambiguous (adj)	open to various interpretations; having a double meaning; equivocal; *an ambiguous question*

B. Staging

❶ Analyse the essay that follows. First, locate the 'Introduction, the Body and the Conclusion'. Look back to Unit 1 page 16 if you need to.

❷ Highlight with different colours or underline, double and triple underline all the stages within the Introduction, Body and Conclusion.

Culture – What does it mean and what are some cultural benefits and detriments? What is cultural difference and how is it manifested?

1. Each country and nation has a culture. They have their own language, their customs and traditions, religions, and ways of behaving under certain circumstances. People within a culture act in ways that they don't think about. Their responses are conditioned by their upbringing and by the social fabric that makes up life around them (Hofstede, 1997, p23). Within nations and countries, culture   5

may be defined as socially transmitted values and belief systems. It involves the transmission of tradition, language, social norms and accumulated experience. It is what is supposed to distinguish one group of people or category of people from one another and it does so. It is the sum total of learned behaviour and it is transmitted from one generation to another generation (Ibid, p27). This essay will discuss both the possible benefits, (otherwise expressed as the optimistic view of culture), and the detriments of culture, (otherwise expressed as the pessimistic view of culture). It will explore the meaning of culture and explain a measurement of cultural differences and the manifestation of same.

2. Culture is inevitable and inescapable. According to Jones, Gordon and Lewis, *Culture is communication and communication is culture.* Humans are raised within a specific culture determined in part by language and geography. *The sum total of the learned behaviour of a group of people comprises their traditional ways of being* (Ibid, p58). Thus, one's 'being' is one's culture. Some theorists believe that human nature itself is formed by a person's culture. An optimistic view would be that human nature is changeable and that humans may choose any way of life they like. Within this optimistic view, there are no limits on the abilities of humans to do or to be whatever they wish. In other words, regardless of an individual's cultural conditioning, it is possible to choose a path in life outside of that conditioning. One may do what one prefers (Wesley, 2010, p67).

3. Within a negative paradigm of culture, there is the concept that humans cannot change their conditioning and they act out, carry out behaviours which are entirely shaped by their upbringing and cultural constraints. Within this view, that culture comprises most everything we are… symbols, heroes, rituals, language, and the deepest manifestation of culture, values… humans tend to believe strongly in their own way of being. (Smith, 2010, p35) This sets up the idea that one set of values is intrinsically superior to another set of values. The world view is 'my view'; the only way things may be done is 'our way', the way our culture has prescribed. Differences in viewpoint are not valid if one believes that their own cultural norms and values are the only norms and values.

4. Values are often defended as being the only values. In other words the values of a culture may be interpreted by the population within that culture as being the best values, because they belong to them. *If a different culture has different values and the two come into conflict, then the defense of those values embodied in culture may lead to serious conflict* (Jason, 2005, p148). They come into conflict as a result of one culture holding the view that they have the right to impose itself on another.

5. The problem with this view is that the imposition of one culture upon another indicates that the imposing culture considers itself superior. Dire consequences may arise between nations, countries, potential business partners and individuals as a result. Some detrimental aspects of culture are fuelled from extreme nationalism and patriotism. In the extreme, these notions give rise to war and to the idea that it is appropriate to wipe out a people who have a culture different from one's own. *The view that one's own culture is the only*

culture that is valid, is referred to as cultural ethnocentrism. It is a type of reductionism that serves no one (Smith, 2009, p208). An understanding of differing cultural view points is essential for world peace and also for international business dealings. 60

6. Cultural differences can be measured and understood more clearly through using research theories developed in the late 90s. One such theory is Hofstede's (1997). He has devised a composite-measure technique which involves using several indicators to understand 65 cultural differences among different societies:

   - Power distance index: The index measures the degree of inequality that exists in a society.
   - Uncertainty avoidance index: The index measure the extent to which a society feels threatened by uncertain or ambiguous 70 situations.
   - Individualism index: The index measures the extent to which a society is individualistic. Individualism refers to a loosely knit social framework in a society in which people are supposed to take care of themselves and their immediate families only. The 75 other end of the spectrum would be collectivism that occurs when there is a tight social framework in which people distinguish between in-groups and out-groups; they expect their in-groups (relatives, clans, organisations) to look after them in exchange for absolute loyalty. 80
   - Masculinity index: (achievement vs. relationship): This index measures the extent to which the dominant values are assertiveness, money and things (achievement). The other end of the spectrum is supposed to measure femininity based upon relationships.

7. In conclusion, there is no doubt that culture, positive and negative 85 attributes of culture and cultural differences exist. This essay has explored some positive attributes within culture, such as the belief that it is possible to entertain a world view of cultural differences and enjoy tolerance while seeking understanding. It has examined the negative view that culture controls our view and makes it impossible 90 to change. Cultural differences and a measuring index for them was presented using Hofstede's instrument from 1997. In the light of the above, the challenge for humans is to reconcile their own beliefs and attitudes, as well as their deepest values with other points of view that arise from other cultures while maintaining respect and enjoyment 95 of their own. Understanding of cultural differences is a desirable outcome for any and all cultures.

Bibliography

Hofstede, G (1997) *Cultures and Organizations: Software of the mind*. New York: 100 McGraw Hill.

Jason, L (2005) *War and Business*. New York: Harper Collins.

Jones, R, Gordon, D & Lewis, S (1999) *Masculinity and Culture*. Chicago: Oxblood University Press.

Smith, K (2009) *Cultural Relativism and Ethnocentric Environments*. UK: Wassle Longmin. 105

Smith, M (2001) 'Cultural manifestations within language paradigms'. *Journal of Difference*, Vol 54, New York: Wesley & Co, pp 35–45.

Source: Essay text created by K Cox.

1 **Track** the participants **'culture'** and **'cultural difference'** throughout each paragraph of the essay by circling each reference when you come to it.

2 Next, write the references on the lines in the order they appear within the appropriate paragraphs listed below.

Participant	*Reference*	*Participant*	*Reference*	*Participant*	*Reference*
Paragraph 1		*Paragraph 3*		*Paragraph 6*	
				Paragraph 7	
		Paragraph 4			
Paragraph 2					
		Paragraph 5			

3 In which paragraphs do the most references to the topic occur? Why?

❶ Underline or place a box around each discourse signal you find in each paragraph throughout the essay.

❷ Next, place the boxed signals/connectors in the appropriate columns and rows in the table below.

PARAGRAPHS	ADDITION Connect ideas in the same or different sentence (followed by a clause or noun group)	CONTRAST Connect ideas in the same sentence (followed by a clause or noun group)	SUMMARISE/ CONCLUDE Connect ideas in a different sentence (followed by a clause)	REASON/RESULT/ CAUSE/EFFECT Connect ideas in the same or different sentence (followed by a clause or noun group)	GIVE EXAMPLES Connect ideas in the same or different sentence (followed by a clause or noun group)
Para 1					
Para 2					
Para 3					
Para 4					
Para 5					
Para 6					
Para 7					

E. Tense

❶ Map para 1 locating the verbs and their tenses.

❷ List each verb from para 1.

_____

_____

_____

_____

❸ What tense are the verbs?
Note: *has/has got*: means a state of being, possession or relationships between things.

❹ Your teacher will instruct you as to whether or not to continue noting tenses throughout the entire text.

❺ What tense will you remember to use when writing an answer to an essay question with 'What……' in the title?

F. and G. Referencing from sources/source material

❶ Examine the reference entries to source material paragraph by paragraph. Write them beneath the paragraph numbers below.

❷ Next, match the entries from each paragraph to the Bibliography by placing paragraph numbers beside the identical entries within the Bibliography.

Paragraph 1

_____

_____

Paragraph 2

_____

_____

Paragraph 3

_____

_____

Paragraph 4

_____

_____

Paragraph 5

_____

_____

Paragraph 6

_____

_____

Paragraph 7
No new information should be introduced within a conclusion. Quotes or references may appear, for example within the recommendation stage. It is wise, however, to attempt a summary, apply critical thinking and make a recommendation based upon the research already quoted and referenced unless you have the exact quote.

Bibliography

Hofstede, G (1997) *Cultures and Organizations: Software of the mind.* New York: McGraw Hill, pp 23–156.

Para _____

Jason, L (2005) *War and Business.* New York: Harper Collins.

Para _____

Jones, R, Gordon, D & Lewis, S, (1999) *Masculinity and Culture.* Chicago: Oxblood University Press.

Para _____

Smith, K (2009) *Cultural Relativism and Ethnocentric Environments.* UK: Wassle Longmin, p 208.

Para _____

Smith, M (2010) 'Cultural manifestations within language paradigms'. *Journal of Difference*, Vol 54. New York: Wesley & Co, pp 35–45.

Para _____

READING 2

Task A | Lecture reading

❶ Read the following script from the listening lecture in this unit. Later, in this unit you will listen to the same lecture spoken and take notes in order to pass a test your teacher will give you.

Cross-cultural Communication – Creed, colour, culture. Communicative cultural competence. Critical cultural consciousness: the three Cs of life in and out of the classroom.

1 Good morning students, I'd like to begin today's lecture concerning what you will come to know as the three Cs with a story.

2 A young Australian/Lebanese man whose family own and operate the local fruit and vegetable store near my home, told me this story about travelling …

3 In Amsterdam, he enjoyed standing on bridges and viewing the water from there. He's not a drug user of any kind and could not comprehend the fact that he was approached daily several times with offers to purchase whatever he wanted. Someone would come up to him and say, 'Would you like to buy some grass, no? How about speed? Heroin then?' He finally gathered the courage to ask someone why he was constantly being approached and asked to buy these things. And they answered 'But of course, because you are standing on a bridge. This always means that you wish to make a deal. If you cross over the bridge or, if you like, continue walking slowly, then it means you are not looking.' This was a cultural norm for that part of Amsterdam and the way my friend discovered it was to gather the courage to inquire.

4 Most travellers, including yourselves, I am sure, would have a tale or two about cultural misunderstandings or miscommunications. These incidents may be humorous, entertaining or frustrating, but they can also be far worse. Misunderstanding between cultures can give rise to 'otherness' which continues the evils of prejudice, racism, and ultimately war. In today's world of mass communication, it would be wonderful to facilitate for all humans intercultural communicative competence. This goal would encompass a desire to promote understanding across continents and seas, nations and, perhaps soon, even galaxies.

5 As I said before, today's lecture concerns what I like to refer to as the three Cs. Whether we call cross-cultural communication just that, or we refer to communicative cultural competence, or we discuss the concepts of creed, colour and culture in relation to language, or we refer to critical cultural consciousness where we question and become aware of other cultures, we still come up with three Cs. Did you notice? Let me repeat those key concepts for you – cross-cultural communication; communicative cultural competence; creed, colour and culture; and critical cultural consciousness.

6 Well, what is cross-cultural communication? Mostly, research around the area defines it in terms of a process rather than as a thing in itself. Yes, a

process – the idea is that it takes effort and conscious work to really be successful at communication with anyone, and particularly when you are speaking, working or studying with people who speak different languages. They may have a different religion (or no religion at all), different values and different customs. They most probably will view certain aspects of life differently from you, and as well have more obvious things such as different food or clothing, hair styles, and perhaps skin colour.

7 Now, why should you bother gaining an understanding of people different from yourself? Why should you attempt to communicate with people different from yourself? I believe most people listening today would already know the answer to that – in that you travel and wish to make new friends, you wish to further your education, you wish to do business, you wish to speak more than one language.

8 Given that you may know why CCC is important, the next question is how to achieve it and what difficulties and further benefits may occur as a result of striving to achieve it.

9 Let's begin with some definitions of what this 'it' is before we address the other issues of difficulties and benefits. My own very short definition of CCC is to 'understand differently and to act accordingly'; yes ... to 'understand differently and to act accordingly'. I don't think it is too dramatic to state that if you become competent and expert in cross-cultural communication you will find yourself in a process which leads to transformation of yourself and to new ways of understanding. A transformation simply means a big change. You will change when you learn how to be culturally competent, when you learn about other cultures and actually understand how to engage in cross-cultural communication. It is my belief that this is a big change for the better.

10 I said before that CCC has been defined in terms of being a 'process', thus it is an evolving thing, rather than a static thing. Definitions by Paige in 1993 and also by Buttjes and Byram (in the 90s) both look at CCC in terms of the qualities and skills that people must possess in order to become competent in cross-cultural communication and intercultural understanding.

11 Here's a statement from Paige:
The process of adapting to a new culture requires the learner to be emotionally resilient in responding to the challenges and frustrations of cultural immersion. Intercultural education ... must help learners develop culture-learning skills and enable them to manage their emotional responses (1993, p1).

12 So, here we see that the learner – that is, you – is going to feel some strong emotions and be challenged and frustrated. Also, looks like you're going to need help in managing your emotions. Doesn't sound like very much fun, does it?

13 Well, the truth is, it's not very much fun for some time. I'll give you a list in a moment which gives an explanation of the process of CCC. You will note that discomfort or just plain feeling bad does seem to be a part of it. It would appear that humans are the starting point for culture and for one human to understand another is not easy.

14 Here's a short list based on Buttjes and Byram 1990's research, umm, this research is about the processes that you will go through to gain CCC: first, there's a process of reflection; second, there's a process of self-criticism and thinking; third, there is a time when your own prejudices must be thought about; fourth, you must make judgments and perhaps re-think those judgments.

15 Again, why should you bother? What real benefits may come overall?

16 In 1990, Byram and others proposed that there are human and social benefits. Here is a list of aims written by them which explains the human and social side of CCC:
   The human and social aims are:
   · to increase social competence by promoting an awareness of and sensitivity to differences in social customs and behaviour;
   · to foster positive attitudes towards other countries and those who live in them and to counter prejudice;
   · to enable learners to meet foreigners in any country and to travel abroad with confidence, enjoyment, interest and advantage;
   · to awaken, that's awaken, to awaken an interest in foreign cultures and life styles and to foster a willingness to see one's own culture in a broader context;
   · to develop a capacity for understanding and accepting the unfamiliar;
   · to encourage tolerance and a willingness to work together (Byram, Esarte-Sarries & Taylor, 1990, pp103–105).

17 Ah, yes, these are all very noble aims and perhaps you understand them and have the desire to realise them. What will you go through to get there?

18 A friend of mine who works with Indigenous peoples within her own country says this:
   · You must be prepared to not fully understand many things.
   · You have to learn to live with doubt.
   · You require perseverance. I remember she said to me one time 'I picked myself up and I went back many times'.
   · You need confidence.
   · And you must be empathetic.

19 A professor friend, this is another friend of mine, who's set up an independent research station in Cape Tribulation, Australia, tracks flying foxes, which are fruit bats and keeps a bat house. He's an active advocate for the total preservation of the world heritage areas around the world as well as particularly the Daintree Rainforest. Over the past 12 years, hundreds and hundreds of scientists and other researchers from every imaginable part of the globe have stayed as volunteer workers at the bat house in the Daintree. My friend believes that 'generosity' is a main, overriding concern within CCC. He also said to me 'The visitors to the Daintree are as diverse as the rainforest itself' (Spencer 2000 personal communication).

20 So, now you must add 'generosity' to your list.

21 I mention these personal friends' comments in order to help you understand what is meant by cross-cultural communication because they are very competent communicators in terms of CCC.

22 Let me tell you now about some students and their writing. Now, these students wrote a story based on a series of pictures. This particular series is a story about two friends from differing cultures. One girl invites her friend to her house for dinner. Upon arrival, the guest is given chopsticks which she cannot use. She pretends that she's not hungry and refuses the food, but the perceptive mother provides her with a spoon and she eats happily. Listen, now, while I read part of the differing students' comments about the story that the pictures tell. I think the answers show an awareness of cross-cultural communication, even though that isn't asked for in the task.

> Then Nancy was becoming untalkative. But she began to eat when Aki's mother gave her a spoon. Aki's mother could understand why she didn't eat, that is, Nancy just worried about her clumsy hands.
> After that, they could spend a good time. It is quite difficult for foreigners to understand the other country's customs. But we could help each other if someone wants to help.

23 Now it seems to me that this student is aware from their statement, you know it's 'difficult for foreigners to understand another country's customs' but the student says we can help each other if 'someone wants to help', in other words, if we are willing to help. Here's another student's comments:

> I mean, it is a problem about mind of challenge when we are facing a new something. So if I were Suji, I recommend her using chopstick because it is able to help understand each other and they can make a deep relationship.

24 This student recognises the difficulty and states that it is a 'problem' and it is a 'challenge' to face something new, yet she 'recommends her using chopstick(s)' in other words she thinks that 'Suji' should take a risk and try being culturally sensitive because the reward may well be a deeper understanding of each other.

25 In a different essay, a student wrote the following:

> If I could choose this, to stay here (in a country) ... because I am learning about different cultures, their thinkings, foods, idioms, and this had changed my mind. I think that this beautiful experience here will be my best experience after my university ...

26 Well this student's been going through the process where his mind has been changed or his mind has grown and expanded to understand new things about the country where he is. He considers it a 'beautiful experience'.

27 Well, in conclusion, students, I hope that your understanding of the concepts around CCC, and you will remember, cross-cultural communication; cultural communicative competence; creed, culture and colour; and critical cultural consciousness has increased today. These key concepts concerned the fact that when a person makes the decision to consciously become more culturally competent in a country and a culture and a language outside their own, they will undergo a transformation. They will change. And in the process of this change, they will experience discomfort. As well as that, their own beliefs and knowledge of the world may be challenged. They may have to change their thinking and open their minds. They will grow.

28 You may remember being a teenager or perhaps you still are one now. There's a time when you grow very rapidly and you experience aches and pains. Becoming expert in CCC is rather like that. You grow rapidly and painfully, but the result is maturity. And this maturity, I believe, has the power to change the world. I truly believe that ... gaining understanding between people and entering into harmonious communication between diverse cultures will create a world where people may work together and create their own world view. They can work together to decide how the world should be organised – socially, economically and environmentally. With cross-cultural communication, people do not believe in a world view based upon prejudice, racism and the belief that we are all too different to get along with one another. With critical cultural consciousness, you have the power to become yourself, one among a complex multiplicity woven together in interdependence and mutual respect.

Thank you.

Nominalisation

You have studied nominalisation previously in Unit 8 and since then you have been attempting to recognise and to use it as a feature in academic writing. Below is a review around constructing and deconstructing nominalisations and noun groups.

Task A | Constructing nominalisations

❶ Construct nominalisations for the concepts within 1 to 4.

Example

'A student understands something and is familiar with it'. So the nominalisation would be **student familiarity**.

'A group of people who have come to and settled in another country from different parts of the world are called migrants. They have formed a group and become associated legally.' The nominalisation would be a **migrant association**.

[a] In a forest all the trees have been cut down. This is a process that people made happen over time and where that *forest* was, now there is nothing. The nominalisation would be:

_____

[b] A government wishes to make changes in the *tax* system of a country. They consider these changes a type of *reform*. The nominalisation would be:

_____

[c] Women in many countries, but particularly in the West, believed they should have completely equal rights with men. They were labelled 'feminist' as opposed to 'masculist'. Their activities became known as a *movement*. The nominalisation would be:

_____

[d] This refers to the custom of respecting your elders, in particular, your parents. A person should not place their own values over those of their parents. They should be obedient and act piously. *Filial* refers to the children who must act in a *pious* and obedient manner. The nominalisation would be:

_____

Task B | Deconstructing nominalisations

❶ Examine the following paragraph and locate all nominalisations and noun groups which need 'deconstruction' or 'unpacking' to make their meaning clear.

Text 1

Lack of familiarity with a country's customs, especially those around showing respect, may lead to cultural misunderstanding. For example, in the case of Chinese students, 'Teachers need to remember that learners are likely to use relative age and status as a primary determinant of the level of politeness to be used and this may result in socially inappropriate speech' (Brick, 1999).

Write all the nominalisations and noun groups and explain them:

a _____

_____

_____

_____

b _____

_____

_____

_____

c _____

_____

_____

d _____

_____

_____

_____

e _____

_____

_____

_____

Task A | Essay analysis – Explanations, arguments and discussions

1 Select a text that appeals to you from any unit in this course book.

2 and **3** Analyse the selected text by using the form entitled 'Essay genre overview', which follows.

Essay genre overview

ESSAY STRUCTURE	EXPLANATION	ARGUMENT (EXPOSITION)	DISCUSSION
Introduction	Introductory statement Purpose: rewording of essay topic Definition (optional) Preview: points that will be in the body paragraphs	General statement Definition (optional) Position (thesis) Preview reasons or arguments that will be in the body paragraphs	General statement Definition (optional) Issue Statement/position Preview: points for both sides that will be in the body paragraphs
Body	Topic sentence (from points in preview) Elaboration (supporting sentences with facts and examples); optional concluding sentence (summary of paragraph)	Topic sentence (from reasons or arguments in preview) Elaboration	Point 1 – topic sentence – side 1 side 2 Point 2 – topic sentence – side 1 side 2 Point 3 – topic sentence – side 1 side 2 OR Side 1 – Point 1 Point 2 Point 3 Side 2 – Point 1 Point 2 Point 3 (points from preview)
Conclusion	Restatement of preview Summary May contain recommendation, may not (optional in explanations)	Restatement/reiteration of position Summary of body paragraphs Recommendation/prediction	Restatement of issue Summary of body paragraphs Position Recommendation
Question words	Outline How? What? Describe how/why Explain Account for Give reasons for	Should? Why? Give reasons for the statement that Do you agree? Is this realistic? Account for Explain the reasons for Evaluate Do you think?	Discuss Analyse Evaluate Do you think? NB There is an overlap between exposition, argument and discussion genres

Task B | Summary writing

❶ Previously, you have studied how to write summaries. The paragraph below is basically an explanation of memory based upon current scientific research.

Rewrite the paragraph, summarising it. You may quote the numerical information, and place it in quotes, but put the rest of the information in your own words.

Sometimes, it helps to reverse word order and substitute vocabulary in order to summarise information. You may also begin with the information found in the last two sentences: *Our physical substance changes. Indeed, it is always changing, every moment, even as we sleep* and put that idea first!

MEMORY

What is memory? The best that neuroscientists can do for the moment is this: A memory is a stored pattern of connections between neurons in the brain. There are about a hundred billion of those neurons, each of which can make perhaps 5 000 to 10000 synaptic connections with other neurons, which makes a total of about five hundred trillion to a thousand trillion synapses in the average adult brain. By comparison, there are only about 32 trillion bytes of information in the entire Library of Congress's print collection. Every sensation we remember, every thought we think, alters the connections within that vast network. Synapses are strengthened or weakened or formed anew. Our physical substance changes. Indeed, it is always changing, every moment, even as we sleep.

Memory

_____

_____

_____

_____

_____

_____

_____

Task C | Writing conclusions

❶ Choose the appropriate discourse signals that might indicate a conclusion from the list below by placing a tick next to them:

1	Next ☐	5	Finally ☐
2	After that ☐	6	However ☐
3	In conclusion ☐	7	Sometimes, it occurs that ☐
4	Thirdly ☐	8	In summary ☐

❷ Using your skills and knowledge of paraphrasing and summary writing, summarise the following information within Text 1 and 2 on the next page, as briefly as possible in order to write the conclusion stage of the essay. Make a recommendation, if required.

Text 1: Bangkok ferries

Introduction

1   The problems with the traffic in Bangkok are that the roads are crowded, the river is congested by both private and public transport, there is pollution, not enough public boats and those provided are not regular. So by closing the river between the hours of 7:30 am and 5:30 pm to private boats and only opening the river for use by ferries and express boats we will hopefully increase the number of people using public transport on the rivers and reduce traffic on the roads.

2   Our overall plan for the river is to extend a small section to increase tourism, and have fast express boats for the early morning and after work commuters into the Central Business District. We hope by doing this we can decrease road traffic problems and pollution.

Body

3   Our display is a model of where the new river has been proposed to be extended and of the bypass walkways which will connect to tourist attractions such as the new Botanical Gardens, the Zoo etc.

4   Our express boats will have a red stripe across them to indicate that they are express. Our tourist ferries will have a yellow stripe and our all-stop boats will be green.

5   The ferries will have such facilities as bathrooms, cafés and newsagents. The 'all stops' and express will also have light snack bars.

6   The tourist fares are cheap – costing $10 for a family of 4 for an all day pass; $5 single; $4 concession; and small fees for one or two stops, or return tickets.

7   The tourist ferries are to seat 100–150 people, the express 50–70 and the all-stops 80–120 people.

8   The timetable for the ferries will be posted clearly at each station. The express will come every 15 minutes, the all-stop every 20 minutes and the tourist every 30 minutes. There will be a total of 15 express boats, eight tourist ferries and 12 all-stops.

9   *Conclusion*

_____

_____

_____

_____

_____

Text 2: Capital punishment: right or wrong?

1   Capital punishment is the execution of a criminal under a death sentence imposed by a qualified public authority. But one question for those of some faiths and those who live in modern, civilised society is – Is capital punishment right or wrong?

2   Capital punishment is an ancient practice, and existed in the ancient middle eastern kingdoms. The death penalty was usually for murder, and some religious or sexual offences. In Israel it was declared that 'whoever sheds the blood of a man, by man shall his blood be shed' (Gen. 9.6). It is also said 'If injury ensures, you shall give life for life, eye for eye, tooth for tooth, hand for hand' (Ex. 21.23–24). It was understood that this principle of revenge was to stop offenders by excessive punishments. When the death penalty was given in these ancient times it was by stoning, hanging, beheading, strangling and burning.

3   In primitive times death and mutilation were frequent penalties. Capital punishment has a long history, but is it too old fashioned to be used in today's society? Are prison cells overflowing and are there too many crimes being committed? And if they are, is that reason enough to kill people? Is capital punishment the way to fix our modern day problems about murder, crime etc? These are some of the questions at stake.

4   In conclusion,

_____

_____

_____

LISTENING & NOTE-TAKING

Listen and take notes from the lecture on cross-cultural communication. Your teacher may give you a test after you have listened.

CD 2

3

LANGUAGE SPOTLIGHT 2

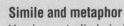

✳ Simile and metaphor
You have studied simile and metaphor previously in this book on page 203. Recall that a simile states that things are **like** or **as** something else whereas a metaphor states that something **is** something else.

Task A | Locating similes and metaphors

❶ Read the *Aircraft carrier* text below and then place (parenthesis) around each simile or metaphor you find and write S or M – for simile or metaphor – above each one.

Aircraft carrier

Each time we sailed out of the harbour, I was as free as the wind once again. In the waters of the harbour, the boat was a cradle and it rocked quietly until the huge engines purred and we were on our way. I never tired of the feeling, like a child, my excitement burst over me in waves just like the waves sending spray over the bow and sides of the now moving aircraft carrier. On our craft went, as nimble as a dolphin, picking up speed, sailing towards the horizon beyond the islands. We were islands now, each of us alone on board, companions but divided by deck, duties and thoughts. Soon, when the weather became an enemy and when the other enemy appeared, we would have to become a team. We were, after all, Navy soldiers as well as sailors.

Task B | Review of information covered in introductory paragraphs

As you will recall, introductions in English contain a great deal of information. They tell the reader about the topic to be discussed and they usually begin to define that topic.

❶ Read Texts 1 and 2 concerned with learning. Answer the questions that follow.

Text 1

When attempting to learn anything new, it is advantageous to maximise your understanding of your own learning. All individuals have learning styles and there are differences. You can discover which learning style you feel most comfortable with (concrete, reflective, abstract or active) and explore different learning opportunities for yourself. The following test was devised to analyse individual abilities.

Questions

1. Who has a learning style?

   _____

2. What is the perfect learning style?

   _____

3. What are some examples of learning styles?

   _____

4. What is going to follow this introductory paragraph?

   _____

5. What is the test that is mentioned in the introductory paragraph going to measure, discover or test?

   _____

Text 2

A great deal of research has been carried out around learning styles of individuals. All individuals have learning styles and there are differences. Four major styles which have been in the literature for a number of years are concrete, reflective, abstract and active. In this paper, in addition to a thorough examination of these categories, the concept of multiple intelligences is explored.

Questions

1. In what way is this paragraph (Text 2) different to the first paragraph (Text 1) that you read?

   _____

2. What two areas will the 'paper' cover, according to the scope in this introduction? (Do not quote the scope exactly, but think and write what the paper must actually be about.)

   _____

3. Write the sentence which orients the reader to the topic.

   _____

4. Write the sentence which is general and introduces the topic.

   _____

5. Which of these two texts would assist you to answer an essay question titled '*Individuals have learning styles and multiple intelligences. Discuss.*'

   _____

   Why?

   _____

SPEAKING 2

Critical cultural consciousness: political protest

Your teacher will lead your discussion and set up the tasks around this important concept.

Task A | Cross-cultural comparison around political protest

In this section, you will consider political protest. You need to think about what it is, where it occurs, the sorts of issues that give rise to it, what types of people carry it out and whether or not, in your culture, it is ever an appropriate response to governments and their policies.

FURTHER CONNECTIONS

Task A | Cultural understanding or misunderstanding?

❶ With a partner, decide who will read section 1 and section 2 of the following extract from the lecture earlier in this unit. When finished reading, person 1 explains their half of the text to person 2, then person 2 explains the last half to person 1.

❷ Next, discuss and answer the questions that follow.

Section 1

A young Australian/Lebanese man whose family own and operate the local fruit and vegetable store near my home, told me this story about travelling …

In Amsterdam, he enjoyed standing on bridges and viewing the water from there. He's not a drug user of any kind and could not comprehend the fact that he was approached daily several times with offers to purchase whatever he wanted. Someone would come up to him and say, 'Would you like to buy some grass, no? How about speed? Heroin then?'

Section 2

He finally gathered the courage to ask someone why he was constantly being approached and asked to buy these things. And they answered 'But of course, because you are standing on a bridge. This always means that you wish to make a deal. If you cross over the bridge, or if you like, continue walking slowly, then it means you are not looking.' This was a cultural norm for that part of Amsterdam and the way my friend discovered it was to gather the courage to enquire.

Questions

❶ What nationality is the man in the narrative?

_____

❷ What kind of drugs does he take?

_____

_____

❸ What happened to him when he was standing on a bridge and enjoying the view?

_____

_____

❹ Why does the writer mention 'courage'?

_____

_____

❺ What did the young man discover when he asked why he was being offered drugs?

_____

_____

❻ What is a cultural norm?

_____

_____

❼ Where was the young man when these events occurred?

_____

_____

APPENDIX A
CORRECTION CODES

Use of these correction codes is practised in Unit 2 on page 56.

SYMBOL	KIND OF ERROR	EXAMPLE	CORRECT SENTENCE
A	wrong or omitted article	*A* We're studying good book.	We're studying a good book.
c	capitalisation	*c* I went to england, once.	I went to England, once.
P	punctuation	*P* She said, yes, that's right.	She said, 'yes, that's right'.
PS	word form (part of speech)	*PS* She was hope.	She was hopeful.
ref	incorrect, inappropriate or omitted reference	There are 27 types of hummingbird *ref* living in the area.	There are 27 types of hummingbird living in the area (Whitehurst, 2011).
reg	inappropriate register	*reg* His research is really interesting.	His research has generated a considerable amount of interest.
S	spelling	*S* My freind is here.	My friend is here.
spec	try to be more specific	*spec* The number of hummingbirds in the area has increased.	The number of hummingbirds in the research area increased from 456 to 1201 between 2007 and 2011.
T	verb tense mistake	*T* Last week I <u>have</u> a great party.	Last week I had a great party.
W	wrong word	*W* Turn write at the corner.	Turn right at the corner.

SYMBOL	KIND OF ERROR	EXAMPLE	CORRECT SENTENCE
↑	add a word	They are my house. ↑	They are (coming to) (going to visit) my house.
[ ]	delete (erase)	I'm going [to] shopping tonight.	I'm going shopping tonight.
//	new paragraph	// (start a new paragraph)	
o	plural/singular mistake	I have three sister.o	I have three sisters.
↶○	reverse word order	That was a movie (long.)	That was a long movie.
○↱	word order mistake	I you see will.	I will see you.
~~	rewrite (meaning unclear)	I very often trying new.	I often try new things.
/	separate these words (new sentence)	They'll eat dinner/ they'll go home.	They'll eat dinner. Then they'll go home.
⌒	should be one word (combine sentences)	There was rubbish every where.	There was rubbish everywhere.
#	subject-verb agreement	# She like swimming.	She likes swimming.

UNIT 3: LISTENING & NOTE-TAKING

Task B | Vocabulary of mathematics

<u>Student A</u>

❸ Say the following to your partner. She/he will write down what you say. Don't let your partner look!

[a] $3 + 2^2 =$

[b] $\dfrac{1.308}{0.654} =$

[c] $3\frac{1}{2} \times 2\frac{3}{4} =$

[d] $\frac{3}{8} + \sqrt{16} =$

[e] $3 \times 1.62 - \frac{1}{3} =$

[f] $a = 3x^3$

[g] $y = \dfrac{3.7x}{5}$

UNIT 3: FURTHER CONNECTIONS

Task B | How to remember for longer

Unit 3: Graph I – Retention versus time without review

This is how much is remembered as time passes after a lesson if no reviewing is done. To see what happens if reviewing is carried out regularly, see Graph II on page 261.

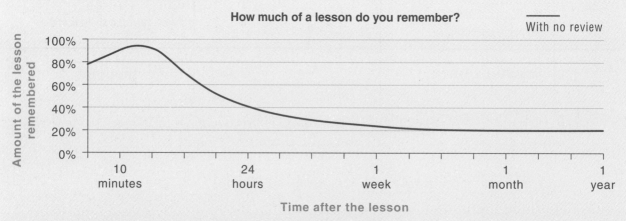

How much of a lesson do you remember?

— With no review

Source: Adapted from Tony Buzan (1995) *Use Your Head*, 4th ed, BBC Books, London, p 65. For further information: Buzan Centres Limited web site: www.buzancentres.com; e-mail: buzan@buzancentres.com; TEL: +44-1202-674676

UNIT 7: SPEAKING 1

Task C | Noticing tutorial discussion techniques

❷ [d] With a partner, mark the functions listed on the script.

Functions
- Asking a question that expects agreement in reply
- Indicating understanding, but not agreement
- Steps in a logical argument
- Illustrating a point using a hypothetical situation
- Making a new point
- Supporting a point with examples
- Showing understanding by restating the other person's point in own words
- Referring back to a previous argument

Recording Script

Tutorial discussion: Funding for education

Dr Lee: So, then, do you think it's OK that many governments are reducing funding to university arts and pure science departments?

Hamid: Well, yes, of course, it sounds like common sense to me! The money to fund them has to come from somewhere – and, ultimately, it must come from the taxpayer, mustn't it?

Dr Lee: Yes, …

Hamid: Well, you know, how many taxpayers do you think would be happy to pay for people to study literature or sociology, just for their own pleasure?

Eleanor: Mmmm (*Doubtful intonation*)

Hamid: If you are studying something that society values enough that it leads to a job with a good salary, I think you have a much stronger right to government support. When you are earning a good salary you'll automatically pay back what the government gave you because you'll be paying the higher tax. And of course you'll always provide some economic benefit for the country. But those arty people doing it just for fun – that's a luxury – and why should governments give money for people to buy luxuries?

Eleanor: (*Aggrieved*) But what about the arts and pure sciences? Where would our society be without them? We'd be in a cultural black hole! There'd be nothing in the way of art except for the mass-market stuff like Hollywood movies that simply follow the same old boring formula. Not to mention …

Hamid: (*Interrupting*) No, no, no, no, no, I don't mean those subjects shouldn't be studied at all – just that students on those degrees should be selected very carefully, and the numbers should be kept low, unless students can pay their own way. Now, that way, the resources could be moved to more productive departments.

Eleanor: But don't you think that expanding society's knowledge and experience of arts has its benefits? I mean for everyone in society, not just the elite? But I'd also like to make a point about transferable skills – things you learn in an arts or pure science course which can be later used in any situation, even business. Things like analytical skills, and the ability to argue a point of view with the support of solid evidence. All these are important for just about anything you do!

Dr Lee: Excellent point!

Hamid: Yes, yes, yes, I take your point there – these skills are all things that universities should develop and encourage – but I see no reason why that can't be done with subjects that have benefit to business. That, surely, would make it easier for the students to transfer their skills later on and they'd be killing two birds with one stone – Learning the subject and the skills at the same time!

Eleanor: Ah, I have to disagree with that – for the reasons I gave before – society as a whole benefits from diversity and people who've had a variety of experience, and who haven't just studied and worked in the same thing, are not just more rounded but also more interesting to be with …

UNIT 7: READING & CRITICAL THINKING

Task C | Reading from different points of view

Student A's assignment question

Your assignment question is:

What is indirect discrimination? How can it be identified? What policies do organisations implement to help deal with it? Critically evaluate each policy you choose.

UNIT 7: SPEAKING 2

Task C | Academic requests

Student A's parts (Lecturer roles)

The following are the prompts for the student–lecturer role plays:

7.1 (Lecturer role) **How to apply for a further degree?**
- Must obtain a distinction or high distinction in current studies.
- Must have reference from your tutor to say your work is of sufficient academic standard – I'll be happy to give you one!
- Fill in Further Studies Application Form.
- Submit to department office. Deadline: 23 December.

7.2 (Lecturer role) **Advice – problems at home, worried about assignment deadlines**
- Fill in 'Genuine Reason for Extension of Deadline' form.
- Explain problem to counselling service – someone will sign the form for you.
- Give a copy to each of your lecturers.

Student A's parts (Student roles)

7.3 (Student role) You feel you are falling behind in your studies. Other students have finished their first assignment of the term, but you've hardly started. Ask for advice from your lecturer.

7.4 (Student role) You need a particular piece of equipment to carry out your research. You have heard that if you get your lecturer's permission, you can buy it and the university will pay. Ask for permission from your lecturer.

UNIT 9: READING & CRITICAL THINKING

Conclusion to essay

8   In conclusion, it is clear that there would be great economic benefit for English speaking countries if they improved the ability of their population to speak other languages. It is also clear that this has to be done from the earliest levels of primary school, and that this requires significant investment. Investment is also needed in campaigns to promote and increase the prestige and intrinsic interest of language learning. It would be beneficial therefore if these changes were set into motion as soon as possible.

References

Crystal, D (1997) *English as a Global Language.* Cambridge: Cambridge University Press.

Kramsch, C (1998) *Language and Culture.* Oxford: Oxford University Press.

Saunders, G (1988) *Bilingual Children: Guidance for the Family.* Clevedon: Multilingual Matters.

UNIT 3: LISTENING & NOTE-TAKING

Task B | Vocabulary of mathematics

Student B

❸ Say the following to your partner. She/he will write down what you say. Don't let your partner look!

[a] $2 - 3^3 =$

[b] $\dfrac{0.008}{1.609} =$

[c] $3\frac{1}{3} \times 2.6 =$

[d] $\sqrt{25} - \sqrt{16} =$

[e] $7 \times \frac{1}{4} - 2\frac{1}{2} =$

[f] $y = 2ab + \dfrac{x^3}{2}$

[g] $z = \dfrac{\sqrt{y}}{3x}$

UNIT 3: FURTHER CONNECTIONS

Task B | How to remember for longer

Unit 3: Graph II – Retention versus time when reviewing
This graph shows what happens when review is carried out at regular intervals.

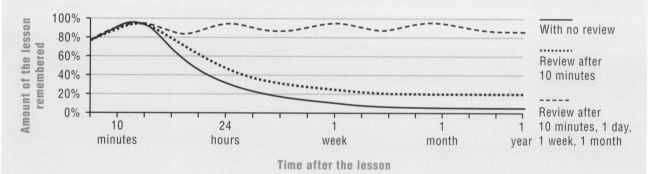

How much of a lesson do you remember?

Source: Adapted from Tony Buzan (1995) *Use Your Head*, 4th ed, BBC Books, London, p. 65. For further information: Buzan Centres Limited web site: www.buzancentres.com; e-mail: buzan@buzancentres.com; TEL: +44-1202-674676

UNIT 7: READING & CRITICAL THINKING

Task C | Reading from different points of view

Student B's assignment question
Your assignment question is:

Compare and contrast policies affecting the employment of women in a multinational organisation, a medium-sized business, an academic institution, and a branch of government. Look also at the implementation of these policies. Which would you expect to be most effective at recruiting and retaining women?

UNIT 7: SPEAKING 2

Task C | Academic requests

Student B's parts (Student roles)

The following are prompts for the student–lecturer role play.

> **7.1** (Student role) You want to apply for a further degree in the department you're studying in now. Find out from your lecturer how to do this.

> **7.2** (Student role) You have urgent family problems in your own country and dealing with them will make your assignments very late. Find out from your lecturer what you can do.

Student B's parts (Lecturer roles)

> **7.3** (Lecturer role) **Advice – study problems**
> - I understand the problem – it affects many first year students.
> - Thank you for letting me know before it's too late.
> - The academic advice service can provide excellent advice and help.
> - It's on the third floor of the Collingwood building, which is on South Road, on the left about ten minutes' walk past the university library.
> - There's also an English language support service available if you want to make use of that.

> **7.4** (Lecturer role) **Permission for equipment purchase**
> - Yes, that's within the department's budget.
> - I need to give you a letter which explains why it is necessary.
> - I'll prepare that by the end of the week.
> - Take it to the requisitions section – they will order it for you.

APPENDIX C
EXTENDED ESSAY PROJECT

Task A | Project information

> **Gathering information about your assignments and assessment**
> Whenever you are set an assignment, it's important to gather certain information about it. In many cases, your lecturer will give you written information, either on a handout or in a course handbook. This information should include how the assignment will be assessed – by considering this all the way through your project from the beginning, you can give yourself the best chance of getting good marks.
>   In addition, it is useful to set yourself a schedule for such things as when you should complete your first draft. This will help you with the all-important skill: time management.

1 Your teacher will explain your extended essay project. Complete this table with information you receive. Then, discuss a possible schedule for the stages of the project with a partner.

Extended essay project

Length: _____ words

Due date: _____

General topic: _____

_____

Assessment criteria: _____

_____

Project stages and dates:

Preliminary list of sources: _____

Thesis chosen by: _____

Plan to be completed by: _____

First draft to be completed by: _____

Other requirements:
- Your essay must give an opinion and this must be supported with evidence from your reading, and with logical argument. In other words, it is most likely to include argument or discussion genre.
- You should go to a library to carry out your research.
- Your essay should show that you have read information from several sources.
- It should show that you have critically analysed the information you read.

Task B | Narrowing down your topic

1 Follow this procedure to narrow down an essay question and a thesis:

[a] Choose an area within your discipline that you think might be interesting.
[b] Brainstorm ideas and opinions within that area. Reading general information such as that in encyclopaedias, including online encyclopaedias) will help with this.
[c] Try to find resources in two or three of those areas (see Task C below).

[d] Look at those resources and decide whether they:
- are easy enough to understand
- provide enough information in the area you're looking at

Choose the area that looks as though it fits these two criteria best.

[e] Think of possible thesis statements in this area

[f] Continue your research with these thesis statements in mind; eventually you will discard and/or modify ideas, according to what you find in your research, until you have a single thesis statement!

Task C | Using library catalogues

Library research

Even in the internet age, libraries are still excellent places to do research for academic essays. Before you go to the library though, there are two things you should do.

1. Have a very clear idea about what you want to find out, even if your essay topic is open. Writing your thoughts in note form, and perhaps writing a draft thesis statement, will help you with this.
2. Most university libraries have on-line access to their catalogues. This means that you can find out what books and journals they have on your topic before you go. This may save you time.

❶ Go to a university web page (eg <www.uts.edu.au> for University of Technology, Sydney), and find the link for the library and then the catalogue (at some universities, this might be labelled OPAC = On-line Public Access Catalogue). Search for this book.

[a] How would you find it on the shelf?

[b] Does the site tell you whether it's available for borrowing?

[c] How can you find out about more books on the same subject?

[d] How can you find out if it's the latest edition?

❷ Search for some resources (including journals) on the topic of your essay. To help you find them in the library, fill in the following table.

AUTHOR (Family name first)	TITLE	EDITION NUMBER	CALL NUMBER	FOR LOAN? DATE DUE BACK?	OTHER (eg reserve collection)

❸ What further information, if any, is required to write references?

❹ Make a list of books, with their CALL numbers, that you will look for when you visit the library.

Task D | Choosing books, and finding information in books

> **Finding information in books**
> Here are several techniques for finding information within books.
> - The information on the back cover of the book usually tells you who the book is intended for; put back books that are likely to be too complex or too basic. For example, if you haven't studied the field before, a book with 'advanced' in the title or one that says it's for postgraduate students probably won't be appropriate.
> - Let the Table of Contents be the first place you look inside the book; look for titles that are relevant to the areas you have chosen for your essay.
> - Go straight to the parts of the book that are most likely to be useful for your essay.
> - Above all, remember that reading a factual book is very different from reading a novel: it is rarely a good idea to start at the beginning and read the whole book, especially when researching an assignment.

❶ Go to the library and:

[a] Find the books that you chose in Task C.

[b] Read the backs of the books and the tables of contents; put back any books which are not likely to be useful.

[c] Skim and scan the relevant sections of the books you have chosen to decide where to read in detail.

[d] Take notes from the books. Make sure that your notes have full details of where the information came from, so that you can easily write your references and bibliography later.

You may have to go through this process a few times as you refine the thesis of your essay.

Task E | Planning, drafting and refining the essay

❶ When your have chosen your thesis and have found some information in the library, follow these steps:

[a] Plan your essay; this plan will be a guide for your further research as well as for writing your essay.

[b] Begin writing: some people find that the body paragraphs are best developed first, with the introduction and conclusion left until last.

[c] While writing, you will most likely be continuously refining your plan, your writing and the direction of your library research.

[d] When you have a reasonable first draft (enough for another person to follow), swap it with another student. Read your partner's draft essay while your partner reads yours.

[e] Discuss with your partner where the draft essay is clear, unclear, relevant to the thesis, etc.

[f] Refine your first draft in light of your discussion at step 5.

[g] Make sure your essay is in the required format (eg double-spaced, with page number, your name and assignment number on each page and with the correct cover sheet attached). Then, submit!

[h] Then submit in accordance with your institution's procedure.

EXTENDED ESSAY ASSIGNMENT COVER SHEET

Student's name	Family	Given ....

Assignment title

Class/Course ....

Date due ....   Date submitted ....

I hereby declare that:

[i]   this work is entirely my own.

[ii]   all sources used in the preparation of this assignment are fully referenced.

[iii]   no part of this work has been submitted for assessment in any other course of study.

Date: _____   Signature: _____

ASSESSMENT:

AREA	GRADE
Clear argument	
Strong support	
Appropriate staging throughout	
Key concepts and terms defined	
Evidence of extensive library research	
Critical analysis	
Full and appropriate in-text referencing	
Full reference list	
Vocabulary (use, register and variety)	
Sentence structure (accuracy and variety)	

General comments (continue on other side if necessary):

_____

_____

_____

_____

Final grade	**Teacher's signature:** _____

APPENDIX D
ORAL PRESENTATION PROJECT

Task A | Project information

> **Gathering information about your assignments and assessment**
> Oral presentations are set as assessed assignments on many university courses. The mark you are given for it usually contributes to your final mark, and might be quite a high proportion of it.
>
> As with the extended essay assignment in Appendix C, whenever you are set an assignment, it's important to gather certain information about the requirements. In many cases, your lecturer will give you written information, either in a handout or in a course handbook. This information should include how the assignment will be assessed – by considering this all the way through your project from the beginning, you can give yourself the best chance of getting good marks.
>
> In addition, it is useful to set yourself a schedule for such things as when you should complete your first draft. This will help you with the all-important skill: time management.

❶ Your teacher will explain your oral presentation project. Complete this table with information you receive. Then, discuss a possible schedule for the stages of the project with a partner.

ORAL PRESENTATION PROJECT

Length: _____ minutes + _____ minutes for questions

Due date: _____

General topic: _____

_____

_____

_____

Assessment criteria: _____

_____

_____

_____

Project stages and dates:

Preliminary list of sources: _____

Thesis chosen by: _____

Plan to be completed by: _____

Handouts and/or visual aids _____

Other requirements:
- Your presentation must give an opinion and this must be supported with evidence from your reading, and with logical argument. In other words, it is most likely to include argument or discussion genre.
- You should go to a library to carry out your research.
- Your presentation should show that you have read information from several sources.
- It should show that you have critically analysed the information you read.

Task B | Using discourse signals and signposting expressions to mark stages of a presentation

❶ Work in pairs. Place the discourse signals and signposting from the box in the most appropriate column of the table.

INTRODUCTION	BODY	CONCLUSION

Discourse signals and signposting expressions

Today, I would like to …; In conclusion; There are three main points …; In 2002, Barker and Johnston …; To summarise …; In order to define 'cactus', it is important to consider …; This talk will cover two current theories around the topic of …; Thus, it is obvious that the government should provide …; It is beyond the scope of this presentation to include everything around the topic of forestry, so …; It would appear that one solution might be to …; Actually, there is not a great deal of research that has been carried out around this subject …; Let me begin by …; A great deal of research has been carried out around this aspect of the subject since 1922 …; Next; However; It is worth considering …

Task C | Using visual aids in presentations

❶ Sharing knowledge about visual aids. In small groups, discuss the following questions.

[a] What visual aids can you think of, in addition to overhead transparencies (OHTs) and computer presentations such as PowerPoint and Keynote?

[b] Why are visual aids useful?

[c] Tell your group any useful advice you already know about using visual aids. Discuss this advice as a group.

② **Useful techniques for using OHTs and computer presentations**. With another student, match the comments below with the advice in Tables 1 and 2.

Comments

- It's very embarrassing to interrupt your talk to look for the right OHT!
- This is common graphic designers' advice for good layout.
- This helps the audience to focus on the point you're making, and creates a sense of anticipation about what's coming next.
- It's very difficult for an audience to read and listen at the same time, so too much writing on the OHT will take attention away from what you're saying. Therefore it's important for the OHT to be concise, clear and focused. It's not necessary to write in complete sentences.
- 'A picture is worth a thousand words', as long as it's clear and well captioned!
- Making sure that your audience can see comfortably is important.
- A simple trick that will make things much easier when setting up for the presentation!

Table 1: Making your slides

ADVICE	COMMENTS
1 Design your slide with plenty of 'white space' – that is, don't fill it completely with text.	
2 If possible, use pictures, flowcharts, organisation charts, tree diagrams, tables or other visual representations, depending on the topic.	
3 Write only important ideas. Note form, with bullet points, is fine. Indenting is a useful way to show which ideas are the main ideas.	
4 If using OHTs when you have finished making your slides, number them in sequence in a corner of the transparency.	

Table 2: Setting up and giving your presentation

ADVICE	COMMENTS
5 Make sure your slides are in a pile, in order, on your desk, before you start your presentation.	
6 Before you start make sure your projector is positioned so that everyone in the audience can see the screen, and that it's focused.	
7 At the beginning of your talk, hide everything except the title. During the talk, reveal one point, speak about it, then reveal the next point, explain that, and so on.	

❸ [a] Prepare a short presentation of around five minutes about a familiar topic. Some suggestions for topics are:

- your country
- your home town or city
- places for tourists to visit in your country
- the best ways to travel around your country
- natural attractions or national parks in your country
- your opinion about particular environmental problems.

[b] Prepare your presentation, remembering the advice, stages and oral discourse markers you learned in Unit 5.

[c] Prepare slides to accompany your presentation.

[d] Give your presentation to a small group of students.

[e] Comment on each other's presentations.

Task D | Advice for presentations

❶ In groups, discuss what is the same and what is different about presentations in your country. Think about:

- any presentations you have given, for example, at school
- presentations you have heard in your own country
- any general advice you have heard in your own country about giving presentations.

❷ Work with another student. From each pair of instructions below, choose the best advice.

[a] i Impress your audience by using long, complicated sentences.
    ii Help your audience understand your talk by taking into account how much they already know about the topic.

[b] i Hold your notes in front of your face so that you don't miss anything written on them.
    ii Hold your notes in one hand, to leave one hand free for gestures.

[c] i Use small notes, the size of your palm ('palm cards'). On these, write only main points and any details that are difficult to remember, such as statistics and references. These are called palm cards.
    ii Write everything you're going to say on your notes so that you don't forget anything.

[d] i Speak as quickly as you can to fit as much as possible into your presentation.
    ii Speak a little slower than your normal speed, but not too slowly.

[e] i Use gestures and move around.
    ii Stand in the same place so that everyone focuses on you, and wave your hands as much as possible to make it look exciting.

[f] i Ask your audience questions during your talk to involve them, and respond to their answers.
    ii Use plenty of questions but don't wait for answers.

[g] i Make eye contact with everyone in the room, without lingering for too long on each person.
    ii Look just below the level of people's eyes to show respect.

[h] i Make a special effort to make eye contact with people on the edge of the room as well as those in the middle, because people on the edge can easily be missed out.
    ii Look especially at the people in the audience who appear to be the most interested.

[i] i Try to talk for as long as possible so that you can give as much information as possible – if you use up the time for questions with your talk, that's OK.
    ii Leave time at the end for questions – it gives your audience chance to check their understanding and find out more about the topic.

[j] i Give out your handouts at the beginning of the talk, so that people can read them while you're talking
    ii Give out handouts only when the information in them comes up, or even wait until the end of the talk

[k] i Don't spend any time rehearsing before the day of the presentation – it's better to use your time to do as much research as possible.
    ii Rehearse several days before you present, ideally with a friend. That way, if you find that there's something missing, you'll have time to do more research and to improve your presentation.

[l] **i** If you are nervous about the presentation, practise beforehand – the more you rehearse, the more confident you are likely to feel.

ii If you are nervous about the presentation, try not to think about it before the day of the presentation; that will only make you more nervous.

Task E | Dealing with questions

Questions during presentations

Questions after a talk are an important part of the presentation – tutors often give marks for asking as well as answering questions.

The best way to deal with difficult questions is to make sure you know your topic well. It's also a good idea to try to predict the questions that might come up, and think about the answers.

Work with a partner for questions 1 to 3.

❶ If you asked a question, and the presenter didn't know the answer, which of the following would you prefer the presenter to do?

[a] Guess the answer.

[b] Admit honestly to not knowing, or not being sure about, the answer.

[c] Explain why he or she doesn't know, eg no one knows.

[d] Suggest where to look for the answer.

[e] Explain that the talk doesn't address the issue.

❷ Match the expressions below with the functions in Question 1. Each expression may match more than one function.

[i] I'm afraid that's beyond the scope of this presentation.

[ii] That's a very interesting question – but not sure, I'm afraid, though I think the answer might be in Richards and Rogers.

[iii] That would be an interesting research topic! I'm not sure anyone has done that yet.

[iv] I'm not sure, but I'll try to find out for you.

[v] I think it might be around 80, but I'm not sure. I'll check for you.

❸ Predict at least three questions that you might be asked at the end of your presentation. Make sure you can answer them!

❹ Work in small groups.

[a] Prepare a short talk (two or three minutes) on one of the topics below.
- Differences between English lessons in your own country and here or between your current course and a previous course.
- Your expectations about education in this country before you came here, and any differences you've found since arriving here.
- Educational experiences in your own country that help you to learn about your traditional culture, eg school trips, dance classes.
- How do you apply to university in your country?

[b] During each talk, the audience should mark the features in Task D that the speaker includes.

[c] At the end of each talk the audience asks questions.

[d] After all presentations are finished, work in pairs. Tell your partner which features from Task D they used. Does your partner agree?

Task F | Giving constructive criticism

1 Imagine you have just given a presentation, and students are giving you feedback about it. Which of the expressions below would you prefer to hear?

- *You should have made clearer slides.*
- *Your talk was generally very good, especially the way it was structured, but perhaps making the slides clearer would help.*
- *I didn't understand your slides.*
- *Your slides weren't so clear.*
- *It might be useful next time to make the slides clearer.*

2 With another student, place the useful expressions on the next page in the appropriate place in the table.

Positive feedback	Suggesting alternatives

Replacing negative words with positives	De-personalising

Mitigating the not so good by also mentioning the better

- *There were very few references → There weren't so many references.*
- *(Your slides) really helped me to understand your presentation because ...*
- *It might be better to ...*
- *It was an interesting presentation because ...*
- *It was difficult to understand that section → It wasn't so easy to understand ...*
- *... I'll do the same in my presentation*
- *(I think) it might help to ...*
- *It was great how you (made it clear with your slides)*

- *How about ...?*
- *Your slides could have been better → The slides could have been better*
- *I liked the way you (explained the ...)*
- *What do you think about ...?*
- *I would suggest ...*
- *Your first point was easy to follow because you used plenty of discourse signals, but the next section, I think, needed a few more of them.*
- *It might be useful to ...*
- *One thing you could do is work on ...*

❸ With a partner, underline syllables that might carry sentence stress.

❹ With the same partner, practise saying these with pleasant, polite intonation. Your partner will tell you whether you sound polite!

Task G | Critical listening and peer marking of presentations

Now is the time to give the presentation you've been preparing for the last few weeks!

❶ Work in pairs while you watch the presentation. One student in each pair should use the *Oral Presentation Observation Sheet 1: Content*. The other should use the *Oral Presentation Observation Sheet 2: Technique*. Both are at the end of this appendix. Remember to ask questions at the end of the presentation.

Tip
One of the best ways to learn to do something well is to watch other people doing it, and notice their good points. Then you can use these good points yourself!

❷ After the presentation, explain to your partner what you've written. At the same time, the person who gave the talk should also fill in both Oral Presentation Observation Sheets.

Tip
Reflecting on your own performance is an excellent way to improve!

❸ Then, using techniques from Task F (*Giving constructive criticism*) and the sheets you filled in at Step 1, discuss the presentation with the presenter.

❹ [a] After your have watched the presentations, make lists to answer these questions.
- What three (or more) things did you do best in your presentation?
- What three (or more) things will you do differently next time?
- Are there any things that the class, in general, needs to improve on?
[b] With a partner, compare, explain and discuss your listens.

ORAL PRESENTATION OBSERVATION SHEET 1: CONTENT

Write notes, not sentences!

Introduction

Background

Definitions

Thesis/discussion point

Main points to be covered (preview/scope)

Body

Main point 1
Support

Main point 2
Support

More supported ideas

Continued ...

Conclusion

Summary

Recommendation

Question time

Question 1

Answer

Question 2

Answer

More questions

After the presentation:

- Were the main ideas in the Preview/Scope, body and summary the same?

_____

- Comment on the strength of support for the opinions expressed.

_____

- Were there sufficient references?

_____

- Did the talk sound well researched?

_____

- Were ideas from the literature questioned and analysed (critical analysis)?

_____

- Write down the most interesting things you learned about the topic of this presentation.

_____

_____

ORAL PRESENTATION OBSERVATION SHEET 2: TECHNIQUES

Signposting

STAGE	FUNCTION	SIGNPOSTING EXPRESSIONS USED (X = none used)
Introduction Definitions	To define	
Introduction Thesis/ discussion point	To give opinion(s)	
Introduction Preview/Scope	To introduce Preview/Scope	
Body	To move on to new main idea	
	To move on to a new supporting idea	
Conclusion	To summarise	
	To recommend	
	To give sources	

Presentation techniques

Start time: _____   Finish time: _____

TECHNIQUE	NOTES
Use of visual aids	What used? Comments
Gestures, eye contact etc	Eye contact with all sections of the audience? Other paralinguistic features used? Comments
Involvement of audience	How? Comments
Voice and clarity of expression	Comments
Timing	Comments

After the presentation:
- What techniques did the presenter use most effectively?

_____

_____

- What techniques need improvement?

_____

_____

ORAL PRESENTATION OBSERVATION SHEET 3: OUTCOMES

OUTCOME/COMPETENCY	ACHIEVED? (YES OR NO)
Can provide appropriate background and context	
Can define technical terms used	
Can clearly give thesis/discussion point	
Can give preview and scope of talk near beginning	
Can clearly state main points of the talk	
Can provide adequate support	
Can summarise the talk	
Can give recommendations based on ideas mentioned	
Can deal adequately with audience's questions	
Can ensure overall coherence to the talk	
Can argue logically	
Can sustain an argument throughout the talk	
Can critically analyse the issue	
Can research a topic using library resources	
Can provide clear signposting throughout	
Can use a visual aid effectively	
Can use appropriate paralinguistic features, such as gestures and eye contact	
Can involve the audience, eg by asking questions	
Can express ideas clearly and audibly	
Can present within a time limit	

Notes:

APPENDIX E
WATCHING, LISTENING AND NOTE-TAKING

Task A | Watching for signals or cues (body language or paralinguistic features) which signal important ideas and features of a lecture

Your teacher will guide you to observe certain features while watching and listening to the lecture *The human senses: Special senses* on DVD. Watch the film and note down whatever you can about the lecturer's:
- lips and face
- hands
- head.

Task B | Questions with regard to the lecture

1 'Olfaction' is the special word we use for what sense? _____

2 Where is the olfactory epithelium located? _____

3 How many different olfactory receptors do humans have? _____

4 Olfactory receptors have cilia. What is another name for cilia? _____

5 Another name for olfactory molecules is? _____

6 Look at the diagram of the olfactory tract. In which part of the diagram are the glands of the epithelium?

_____

7 Again, look at the diagram from the PowerPoint presentation and name the three cells listed there.

_____

8 Where are papillae found? _____

9 Name the four types of papillae. _____

10 Match the descriptions below of each papillae to its correct form in question 9:

    a. mushroom shaped elevations on the tongue.
    b. thread-like elevations.
    c. contain the most sensitive taste buds and are on the side of tongue.
    d. very raised elevations or 'bumps' found far back on the tongue.

11 Children have fewer papillae than adults. True or False? _____

12 Cilli are located on what portion of the tongue? _____

13 Taste buds are on top of the tongue. True or False? _____

14 Gustatory receptor cells react to how many tastes? _____

15 The lateral taste buds react to which of the following: sweet or savoury? _____

16 The back of the tongue has taste buds which react to which of the following: sweet or bitter?

_____

17 The tip of the tongue has taste buds which react to which of the following: sweet, salty, bitter, savoury?

_____

18 List three cranial nerves shown on the diagram within the PowerPoint presentation. _____

19 How does the thalamus function? _____

20. What flavours are the most apparent in highly processed foods? _____

21. What flavours do humans have a very high threshold for? _____

22. After the first bite of food, what happens to your perception of the taste? _____

23. List three main regions of the ear. _____

24. The auditory canal is located within which region of the ear? _____

25. The *oracle* is another name for which portion of the external ear? _____

26. Where are the three small bones or auditory ossides found? _____

27. What is the name of the portion of the ear responsible for balance? _____

28. *Snail* is another term for, or is also known by, what name? It is located within the inner ear. _____

29. What is/are inserted in children's ears as a medical procedure? _____

30. List the names of the three tiny bones that transmit vibrations to the inner ear. _____

REFERENCES

Audit Commission (1996) *Misspent Youth: Young People and Crime.* London: Audit Commission.

BBC (2001) Secondary Schools, BBC News. <http://news.bbc.co.uk/hi/english/education/uk_systems/newsid_115000/115872.stm> (6 May 2002).

Billington R & Stanford P (1988) *Child Workers Around the World.* London: Fount.

Brown, K (1999) *Developing Critical Literacy.* Sydney: Macquarie University (NCELTR).

Bryden, HL, Longworth, HR & Cunningham, SA (2005) 'Slowing of the Atlantic Meridional Overturning Circulation at 25° N'. *Nature,* Vol 438, pp 655–657.

Burns, RB (1994) *Introduction to Research Methods.* Melbourne: Longman Cheshire, p 2.

Butt, D, Fahey, R, Feez, S, Spinks S & Yallop, C (2000) *Using Functional Grammar: An Explorer's Guide* (2nd ed). Sydney: Macquarie University (NCELTR).

Buzan, T (1995) *Use Your Head* (4th ed). London: BBC Books.

Callendar, Gae (1987) *Antiquity: The Minoans.* Australia: Shakespeare Head Press, p 69.

Columbia University Press (1998) Basic CGOS Style *About the Columbia Guide to Online Style.* <http://www.columbia.edu/cu/cup/cgos/idx_basic.html>.

Commonwealth of Australia (2002) 'Australian way of studying', *Study in Australia.* http://studyinaustralia.gov.au/Contents/WhatToStudy/AustStudy.html (21 April 2002).

Comstock, Botsford A (1961) *Handbook of Nature-Study.* Cornell, Ithaca, NY: Comstock Publishing, pp 496–97.

Cox, K (1994) 'Tertiary Level Writing by Magic – Presto! Nominalisation'. *EA Journal,* Vol 12, No 1, Autumn.

Cox, K & Eyre, J (1999) 'A Question of Correction'. *English Teaching Professional,* 12.

Cox, K (2000) *Changing Cultures, Changing English.* Paper presented at the 13th EA Educational Conference, Fremantle.

Cox, K (2007) 'KVZK Educational Television in Pago Pago American Samoa from 1962–1978'. American Samoa Historic Preservation Office: AS Government Publication. p 96.

Coxhead, A (2006) *Essentials of Teaching Academic Vocabulary.* Boston: Thomson Heinle.

Crystal, D (1997) *English as a Global Language.* Cambridge: Cambridge University Press.

Crystal, D (2000) *Language Death.* Cambridge: Cambridge University Press.

Derewianka, B (1990) *Exploring How Texts Work.* Sydney: Primary English Teaching Association.

DETYA (2000) Australia Country Education Profile, 3rd ed Online. Canberra: DETYA <http://www.detya.gov.au/noosr/cep/australia/index.htm> (21 April 2002).

Fairclough, N (1992) *Discourse and Social Change.* Cambridge: Polity Press.

Feez, S (1998) *Text Based Syllabus Design.* Sydney: Macquarie University (NCELTR).

Fischer, S (2001) 'Asia and the IMF: Remarks at the Institute of Policy Studies'. *IMF News.* <http://www.imf.org/external/np/speeches/2001/060101.htm>.

Foer, J (2007) 'Remember This', *National Geographic Magazine,* Vol 212, No 5, November, pp 34–36.

Fulbright Commission (2001) *School Education in the USA.* <http://www.fullbright.com.uk/eas/school/school.htm> (12 May 2002).

Gage, D (2009) SAP to buy inventory specialist for $91 million'. In *Information Week The Business Value of Technology,* 20 July, p 48. Downloaded from <www.informationweek.com/news/windows/operatingsystems> (10 May 2009).

George, S (1990) *A Fate Worse than Debt.* London: Penguin.

Ghuma, K (2001) 'It's Not Just Watcha Say'. *IATEFL Issues,* Vol 161, pp 11–12.

Gibran, K (1990) *Spiritual Sayings of Kahlil Gibran.* A Ferris (ed and translator), New York: Carol.

Häkkinen, S & Rhines, P (2004) 'Decline of Subpolar North Atlantic Circulation During the 1990s'. *Science,* Vol 304, pp 555–559.

Halliday, MAK & Hasan, R (1989) *Language, Context and Text: Aspects of Language in a Social-Semiotic Perspective.* Melbourne: Deakin University Press.

Halliday, MAK (1985) *An Introduction to Systemic Functional Grammar.* London: Edward Arnold.

Hardi, P (1999) 'Introducing Nominalisation to Secondary Students', *ATESOL Newsletter,* Vol 25, No 1, April.

Harmer, J (1991) *The Practice of English Language Teaching* (2nd ed). Essex: Longman.

Haycraft, J (1986) *An Introduction to English Language Teaching* (revised impression ed). Harlow: Longman.

Hill, D (2010) *Academic Connections 2.* White Plains, NY: Pearson Longman.

HMIC (1998) *Beating Crime.* London: Her Majesty's Inspectorate of Constabulary, Home Office.

HMIC (2000) *Calling Time on Crime.* London: Her Majesty's Inspectorate of Constabulary, Home Office.

Hoey, M (1997) *How Can Text Analysis Help Us Teach Reading?* Paper presented at the IATEFL Conference, Brighton, England, April 1997.

Hume, C et al (2009) 'Walking and Cycling to School: Predictors of Increases Among Children and Adolescents'. *American Journal of Preventative Medicine*, Vol 36, No 3, pp 195–200.

Janks, H (1993) *Language, Identity and Power.* Johannesburg: Hodder & Stoughton.

Kaplan, RB (1966) 'Cultural Thought Patterns in Inter-Cultural Education'. *Language Learning*, Vol 16, pp 1–20.

Kaplan, RB (1993) 'TESOL and applied linguistics in North America'. In S Silberstein (ed) *State of the art TESOL essays*. Alexandria, VA: TESOL Inc.

Kenworthy, J (1987) *Teaching English Pronunciation.* Essex: Longman.

King, S (2000) *On Writing, A Memoir of the Craft.* London: Hodder and Stoughton.

Kramsch, C (1998) *Language and Culture.* Oxford: Oxford University Press.

Kress, G (1993) 'Genre as social process'. In B Cope and M Kalantzis (eds) *The powers of Literacy*. London: Falmer Press, p 36.

Lambert, T & Barreto, L (2001) *UTS Students' Association Postgraduate Handbook 2001.* Sydney: UTS Students' Association.

Larsen-Freeman, D (2000) *Techniques and Principles in Language Teaching.* Oxford: Oxford University Press.

Leake, J (2005) 'Britain Faces Big Chill as Ocean Current Slows'. *Times*, 8 May.

Lewis, M (1993) *The Lexical Approach: The State of ELT and a Way Forward.* Hove: Language Teaching Publications.

Lewis, M (1997) *Implementing the Lexical Approach: Putting Theory into Practice.* Hove: Language Teaching Publications.

Li & Karakowsky (2001). Do We See Eye-to-Eye? Implications of Cultural Differences for Cross-Cultural Management Research and Practice. *The Journal of Psychology*, Vol 135, No 5, pp 501–517. Downloaded from <http://www.tamu.edu/classes/cosc/choudhury/culture.html> (10 November 2009).

McCarthy, M (1990) *Vocabulary.* Oxford: Oxford University Press.

Macquarie Library *Macquarie Dictionary* (2nd ed) (1991). Sydney: Macquarie Library.

Malouf, D (2002) 'A great escape'. *The Age*, 31 August.

Martin, JR (1991) 'Nominalisation in science and humanities: Distilling knowledge and scaffolding text'. In *Functional and systematic linguistics: approaches and use*, E Ventola (ed). Berlin; New York: Mouton de Gruyter.

Modjeska, D (2002) 'The fictional present', *The Age*, 31 August.

Moore, M (2001) *Stupid White Men … and other sorry excuses for the state of the nation.* New York: Harper Collins, p 204.

Nunan, D (1991) 'An Empirically Based Methodology for the Nineties'. In S Arivan (ed) *Language Teaching Methodology for the Nineties*. RELC, p 78.

Nunan, D (1992) *Research Methods in Language Learning.* Cambridge: Cambridge University Press.

O'Brian, PE et al (2010) 'Laparoscopic Adjustable Gastric Banding in Severely Obese Adolescents: A Randomized Trial'. *The Journal of the American Medical Association*, Vol 303, No 6, pp 519–526.

Osborne, D & Powell, R (2010) 'Debate over gastric surgery for teens', *ABC Science Show*, 12 June.

Oshima, A & Hogue, A (1991) *Writing Academic English* (2nd ed). California: Addison-Wesley.

Oxford University Press (2000) *Oxford Advanced Learner's Dictionary* (6th ed). Oxford: Oxford University Press.

Phillipson, R (1992) Linguistic Imperialisation. Oxford: Oxford University Press.

Pilger, J (1989) *A Secret Country.* London: Vintage Press.

Rahmstorf, S (2006) 'Thermohaline Ocean Circulation'. In SA Elias (ed) *Encyclopaedia of Quaternary Sciences*. Amsterdam: Elsevier. Downloaded from <www.pik-potsdam.de/~stefan/Publications/Book_chapters/rahmstorf_eqs_2006.pdf> (16 March 2010).

Rubin, J (1994) 'Review of Second Language Listening Comprehension Research', *The Modern Language Journal*, Vol 78, pp 199–221.

Saunders, G (1988) *Bilingual Children: Guidance for the Family.* Clevedon: Multilingual Matters.

Schlosser, E (2001) *Fast Food Nation: What the All-American Meal is Doing to the World.* London: Penguin.

Skogan (2004) *Fairness and Effectiveness in Policing: The Evidence.* Washington: National Research Council/National Academic Press.

SIL International (2001) 'Languages of Vanuatu'. *Ethnologue: Languages of the World* (14th ed). <http://www.ethnologue.com/show_country.asp?name=Vanuatu> (11 August 2002).

Small, A (2008) 'Show me how you will measure me and I will show you how I will perform'. University essay, Management Course, university in Australia.

Small, A (2009) 'Strategic Intent'. University essay, Economics Course, University in Australia.

South Asian Voice (2000) Unrestricted globalisation – boon or hazard? *South Asian Voice: Views from South Asia.* <http://members.tripod.com/~India_Resource/globalization.html> (17 September 2002).

Superville, D (2001) 'Many world languages on brink of extinction, UN says'. *Global Policy*. <www.globalpolicy.org/globaliz/cultural/2001/0619language.htm> (11 August 2002).

Swan, M & Smith, B (eds) (2001) *Learner English: A Teacher's Guide to Interference and Other Problems* (2nd ed). Cambridge: Cambridge University Press.

The US-UK Fulbright Commission (1999) School Education in the US. *The US-UK Fulbright Commission* <http://www.fulbright.co.uk/eas/school/school.html> (12 May 2002).

Underhill, A (1994) *Sound Foundations*. Oxford: Heinemann.

UNEP (2000) *Global Environmental Outlook 2000: UNEP's Millennium Report on the Environment*. London: Earthscan Publications.

UTS Equity & Diversity Unit (nd) 'Preventing discrimination and harassment'. *UTS Equity & Diversity Unit*. <http://www.uts.edu.au/div/eounit/unit/discrim.html> (25 August 2002).

Våge, K et al (2009) 'Surprising Return of Deep Convection to the Subpolar North Atlantic Ocean in Winter 2007–2008'. *Nature Science*, Vol 2, pp 67–72.

Vellinga, M & Wood, RA (2002) *Global Climatic Impacts of a Collapse of the Atlantic Thermohaline Circulation*. Bracknell: UK Meteorological Office.

Wacquant, W (2009) *Punishing the Poor: The Neo-liberal Government of Social Inequality*. Trans J Ingram Durham, North Carolina; Duke University Press.

Wade, C & Tavris, C (2008) *Psychology* (9th ed). New Jersey: Pearson Education.

Weller, C, Scott, RE & Hersh, A (2001) 'The unremarkable record of liberalised trade after 20 years of global economic deregulation, poverty and inequality are as pervasive as ever'. *EPI Briefing Paper* <http://epinet.org/briefingpapers/sept01inequality.html> (October 2001).

Whitehouse, D & R (1975) *Archaeological Atlas of the World*. London: Thames and Hudson, p 13.

Wilkinson, R & Pickett, A (2009) *The Spirit Level: Why More Equal Societies Almost Always Do Better*. New York: Bloomsbury Press.

Wolpert, E (1984) *Understanding Research in Education – An introductory guide to critical reading*. USA: Kendall/Hunt, p 113.

Young, Lynne (1994) University lectures – macro-structure and micro-features. In John Flowerdew (ed), *Academic Listening, Research Perspectives*. Cambridge: Cambridge University Press, pp 159–176.

Zimbardo, PG, Johnson, RL, Weber, AL & Gruber, CW (2007) *Psychology*, AP* edition, Boston: Allyn & Bacon.

CREDITS

INDEX